The Sacrifice of Isaac is one of the most well-known stories in the Bible. It is also a shocking account of how Abraham's faith in God was demonstrated by a willingness to sacrifice his long-awaited son at God's command. This story has been a source of fascination for Jews and Christians for many centuries, and here Edward Kessler offers an enthralling account of Jewish and Christian interpretations of this biblical story. For understandable reasons, it has been assumed that Judaism influenced Christian interpretation, but relatively little attention has been given to the question of the influence of Christianity upon Judaism. Kessler provides an insight into this absorbing two-way encounter and argues that neither Jewish nor Christian interpretations can be understood properly without reference to the other. As Jews and Christians lived, and continue to live, in a biblically orientated culture, Kessler shows how both were 'bound by the Bible'.

EDWARD KESSLER is a Founding and Executive Director of the Cambridge Centre for Jewish–Christian Relations. He is the author of *An English Jew: The Life and Writings of Claude Montefiore* (1989, new edition 2002) and co-editor of *Jews and Christians in Conversation: Crossing Cultures and Generations* (2002).

BOUND BY THE BIBLE

Jews, Christians and the sacrifice of Isaac

EDWARD KESSLER

CAMBRIDGE
UNIVERSITY PRESS

CAMBRIDGE UNIVERSITY PRESS
Cambridge, New York, Melbourne, Madrid, Cape Town, Singapore, São Paulo

Cambridge University Press
The Edinburgh Building, Cambridge CB2 2RU, UK

Published in the United States of America by Cambridge University Press, New York

www.cambridge.org
Information on this title: www.cambridge.org/9780521835428

First published 2004
This digitally printed first paperback version 2005

A catalogue record for this publication is available from the British Library

Library of Congress Cataloguing in Publication data
Kessler, Edward
Bound by the Bible : Jews, Christians and the sacrifice of Isaac / Edward Kessler.
p. cm.
Includes bibliographical references and index.
ISBN 0 521 83542 9 – ISBN 0 521 54313 4 (pbk.)
1. Isaac (Biblical patriarch) – Sacrifice. 2. Bible. O.T. Genesis XXII, 1–19 – Criticism, interpretation,
etc. – History – Early church, ca. 30–600. 3. Bible. O.T. Genesis XXII, 1–19 – Criticism,
interpretation, etc., Jewish – History – To 1500. 4. Christianity and other religions – Judaism –
History – To 1500. 5. Judaism – Relations – Christianity – History – To 1500. I. Title.
BS1238.S24K47 2004
222.´11092 – dc22 2003069571

ISBN-13 978-0-521-83542-8 hardback
ISBN-10 0-521-83542-9 hardback

ISBN-13 978-0-521-54313-2 paperback
ISBN-10 0-521-54313-4 paperback

To Trish, Shoshana, Asher and Eliana
who exemplify George Santayana's saying that
the family is one of nature's masterpieces.

Contents

Illustrations

Preface

This book has been in and on my mind for seven years. During that time I have felt as if I had accompanied Abraham and Isaac on their journey to and from Moriah.

I would like to thank my colleagues at the Centre for Jewish–Christian Relations (CJCR), especially Deborah Patterson-Jones, Melanie Wright, Lucia Faltin, Maty Matychak and Tunde Formadi. CJCR provides a wonderful forum to engage in the study and teaching of Jewish–Christian relations. I also acknowledge with gratitude the students at CJCR, especially those who elected to study my course on Jewish and Christian Biblical Interpretation. They have helped me think through the ideas discussed in this book.

I would like to acknowledge the support of other colleagues who have been kind enough to offer constructive comments. They include James Carleton Paget, William Horbury and Robert Hayward. During my PhD research I was guided by Nicholas de Lange, to whom I am most grateful, and was taught patristic Greek by Liz Irwin, whose patience was beyond measure.

The support of my fellow Trustees at the CJCR has also been a great help in the writing of this book, especially Martin Forward and Julius Lipner who cajoled me into completing the manuscript, as well as Barry Fenton, Bob Glatter, Leslie Griffiths, Peter Halban, David Leibowitz and Clemens Nathan.

Thanks also to Kevin Taylor and Kate Brett of Cambridge University Press who have been most encouraging. I also appreciated the positive comments offered by the anonymous CUP readers in their reviews of the original manuscript.

A number of scholars from overseas have also taken the time to respond to queries, especially Jo Milgrom, John Pawlikowski, Peter Ochs and Gunter Stemberger.

Finally, this book would not have been written without the support of my family, my parents, my wife Trisha, and my children Shoshana, Asher and Eliana. Together they remind me daily of the priorities in my life and I am deeply grateful for their love and affection. This book is dedicated to them.

Abbreviations

NAMES

Aq.	Aquila
Athan.	Athanasius
Basil of Sel.	Basil of Seleucia
Cyril of Alex.	Cyril of Alexandria
Chry.	John Chrysostom
Diod.	Diodore of Tarsus
Eph. Grae.	Ephrem Graecus
Euseb.	Eusebius of Caesarea
Greg. of Nys.	Gregory of Nyssa
Greg. of Naz.	Gregory of Nazianzen
Iren.	Irenaeus of Lyons
Jos.	Flavius Josephus
Onk.	Onkelos
Ps.-Chr.	Pseudo-Chrysostom
Ps.-Eph. Grae	Pseudo-Ephrem Graecus
Ps.-Greg. Nys.	Pseudo-Gregory of Nyssa
Ps.-Ph.	Pseudo-Philo
Rom.	Romanos
Sym.	Symmachus
Succen.	Succensus of Diocaesarie

WORKS

ANRW	*Aufstieg und Niedergang der römischen Welt*
Adv. Iud.	*Adversus Iudaeos*
Ant.	*Jewish Antiquities*
ARN	*Avot de Rabbi Nathan*
Barn.	*Barnabas*

BT	*Babylonian Talmud*
CSEL	Corpus Scriptorum Ecclesiasticorum Latinorum
CSCO	Corpus Scriptorum Christianorum Orientalium
Ecc. Rab.	*Ecclesiastes Rabbah*
EJ	*Encyclopedia Judaica*
Ex. Rab.	*Exodus Rabbah*
Frg. Tg.	*Fragmentary Targum*
Gen. Rab.	*Genesis Rabbah*
JT	*Jerusalem Talmud*
LAB	*Liber Antiquitatum Biblicarum*
Lam. Rab.	*Lamentations Rabbah*
LCL	Loeb Classical Library
Lev. Rab.	*Leviticus Rabbah*
LXX	Septuagint
M.	*Mishnah*
MHG	*Midrash ha-Gadol*
MdRI	*Mekhilta de Rabbi Ishmael*
MdRSbY	*Mekhilta de Rabbi Shimon ben Yochai*
Mid. Tan. on Deut.	*Midrash Tannaim on Deuteronomy*
Mid. Teh.	*Midrash Tehillim*
Paed.	*Paedagogus*
PG	J.-P. Migne (ed.), *Patrologiae cursus completus. Serie Graece.* Paris, Petit-Montrouge, 1857–83.
Pes. R.	*Pesikta Rabbati*
PP	*Peri Pascha*
PRE	*Pirkei de Rabbi Eliezer*
PRK	*Pesikta de Rab Kahana*
REJ	*Revue des études juives*
RHS	*Rosh ha-Shana*
San.	*Sanhedrin*
SC	Sources Chrétiennes
Stroma.	*Stromata*
Tan. Eli.	*Tanna debe Eliyahu*
Tan. B.	*Tanhuma* (Buber Edition)
Tan. Y.	*Tanhuma* (Yelamdenu)
Tg. Ps.-Jon	*Targum Pseudo-Jonathan*
Tos.	*Tosefta*
TU	Texte und Untersuchungen zur Geschichte der altchristlichen Literatur
WUNT	Wissenschaftliche Untersuchungen zum neuen Testament

Prologue

As a Jewish scholar who has been engaged in the study and teaching of Jewish–Christian relations for over twelve years, I have thought a great deal about the past history of Jewish–Christian relations, especially in relation to the Bible. During that time I have noticed increasing interest being shown in scholarly and religious circles to both the Jewish context of the New Testament as well as to the influence of Jewish biblical interpretation on the formation and development of Christianity.

For understandable reasons, it has generally been assumed that Judaism influenced Christianity but relatively little attention has been given to the other side of the same coin: the question of the influence of Christianity upon Judaism. Did Christian teaching and interpretation influence the Jewish commentators? The purpose of this book is to consider this relatively unexplored question, to ask whether this influence developed into a two-way encounter and to investigate to what extent Jews and Christians are bound by the Bible. On the basis of a study of the Binding of Isaac, I examine whether there was some kind of a meeting or interaction between Jewish and Christian interpreters during the first six centuries CE and what this may tell us about relations between Jews and Christians in late antiquity.

The background to this book is a reawakening among scholars to the Jewish origins of Christianity, a trend that became noticeable in the first half of the twentieth century. Figures such as Travers Herford (1860–1950) from the UK and George Foot Moore (1851–1931) from the USA produced important works, and their studies shed light on the vitality of Judaism in the first few centuries of the Common Era. This, it became more and more apparent, was essential for a proper understanding of the development of the early church. Their works challenged and overcame the misconceptions and prejudices of the majority of their contemporaries, who were influenced by the enlightening but nevertheless partial writings of scholars such as Emil Schürer and Julius Wellhausen. The latter argued coherently, but inaccurately, that rabbinic Judaism was a form of barren legalism, which was simply rejected by Jesus and replaced by Christianity. In their view, rabbinic Judaism represented a decaying religion. Thankfully, Herford and Moore pointed out the errors and preconceptions of their German colleagues and expressed a hitherto unheard-of appreciation of rabbinic Judaism. They taught their students, and a new generation of scholars, that the Judaism that was contemporaneous with Jesus and the early church not only showed vibrancy and vigour but also had a positive influence on Jesus and the development of the early church.

In more recent years, Geza Vermes and E. P. Sanders, among others, contributed to this process and, as a result, their writings increased our understanding of relations during this period. Both scholars have produced important studies on the New Testament, which highlighted the close relationship between Jesus and his fellow Jews, especially the Pharisees. They were not alone, and scholarly awareness of first-century Judaism, in all its varieties, is greater than ever before.

The ramifications are manifold. We are now taught that Jesus, his family and his followers were Jewish. The Jewish background to Christianity is now stressed. The rediscovery of the Jewishness of the origins of Christianity has not only led to a greater awareness of the Jewish context but also to the realization that too often Christians have pictured Torah as a burden rather than as a delight. It is now appreciated more than ever before that Jesus was a faithful Jew and that Jesus was born, lived and died a Jew; that the first Christians were Jews; that the New Testament is, for the most part, a Jewish work.

This development has significance for Jews as well as for Christians. In the early twentieth century European Jewish scholars, such as Franz Rosenzweig, Martin Buber and Claude Montefiore, produced important works. Like Moore and Parkes they were pioneers, ahead of their time, who strove to overcome occasional hostility but more often a lack of interest in Christianity among Jews. They began a move towards a positive reassessment of Christianity and reminded Jews that Jesus was a fellow Jew (their 'great brother' as Martin Buber described him). In the second half of the twentieth century up until the present day Jewish scholars have increased their presence in New Testament studies. The comments of Samuel Sandmel, Professor of New Testament at Hebrew Union College in Cincinnati, illustrates:

Two hundred years ago Christians and Jews and Roman Catholics and Protestants seldom read each other's books, and almost never met together to exchange views and opinions on academic matters related to religious documents. Even a hundred years ago such cross-fertilization or meeting was rare. In our ninety-seventh meeting we take it as a norm for us to read each other's writings and to meet together, debate with each other, and agree or disagree with each other in small or large matters of scholarship. The legacy from past centuries, of misunderstanding and even animosity, has all but been dissolved in the framework of our organization.[1]

Today, Jewish scholars are building on his legacy and making a significant contribution to New Testament studies and related subjects, especially in the USA.[2] For example, both Alan Segal and Daniel Boyarin have authored important studies on Paul,[3] Amy-Jill Levine and Adele Reinhartz have contributed significantly to the study of the Gospels of Matthew and John respectively.[4] Jewish scholars have also contributed to the study of early Christian liturgy such as Jacob Petuchowski's work on The Lord's Prayer[5] and Lawrence Hoffman's collaborative studies with Paul Bradshaw.[6] This list could doubtless be expanded.

The impact of these changes extends beyond university classrooms and has begun to influence the curriculum in seminaries and in other educational institutions. A number that focus on the Jewish–Christian encounter have been established in recent years in both Europe and the United States. For example, the Centre for Jewish–Christian Relations founded in Cambridge in 1998 has developed innovative multi-disciplinary curricula, which are being implemented at undergraduate and postgraduate levels.[7] It is also worth mentioning the International Council of Christians and Jews, established in 1947, which serves as an umbrella organization of thirty-eight national Jewish–Christian dialogue bodies representing thirty-two different countries. As a result, the study of Jewish–Christian relations is being transformed. Most Protestant denominations and the Roman Catholic Church now teach their seminarians that there was a close relationship between Jesus and the Pharisees. Until recently, this subject was limited to the consideration of a few, but more and more are now learning that, according

---

[1] Sandmel 1961: 13.   [2] Cf. Bowe 2002.   [3] Boyarin 1994, Segal 1990.
[4] Levine 1988, Reinhartz 2001.   [5] Petuchowski 1978.
[6] See the series entitled *Two Liturgical Traditions* published by University of Notre Dame Press.
[7] In Europe, as well as the Centre for Jewish–Christian Relations in Cambridge, these include the Institute for Jewish–Christian Research at the University of Lucerne and the Institute of the Church and Jewish People in Berlin. In the USA, the most significant educational centres are: the Joseph Cardinal Bernardin Center at the Catholic Theological Union in Chicago; the Center for Catholic–Jewish Studies at Saint Leo University in Florida; the Center for Christian–Jewish Learning at Boston College in Massachusetts; the Center for Christian–Jewish Studies and Relations at the General Theological Seminary in New York; the Center for Christian–Jewish Understanding at the Sacred Heart University, Fairfield, Connecticut; the Institute of Judaeo–Christian Studies at Seton Hall University, South Orange, New Jersey; the Jay Phillips Center for Jewish–Christian Learning at the University of St Thomas, St Paul, Minnesota. For a more detailed list see http://www.jcrelations.net.

to the Roman Catholic teaching, Jesus 'had very close relations' with the
Pharisees to whom 'he was very near'.[8]

There is also increasing awareness in theological circles of the perils of
relying on the literal text of the New Testament and that the final text of the
Gospels was edited long after the events described; that the authors were
concerned with denigrating those Jews who did not follow Jesus; that they
were concerned with vindicating the Romans, whose goodwill they were
seeking. This was acknowledged by the Vatican's 1985 document on the
teaching of Judaism, which stated that, 'some references hostile or less than
favourable to the Jews have their historical context in conflicts between the
nascent Church and the Jewish community. Certain controversies reflect
Christian–Jewish relations long after the time of Jesus.'[9]

Since 1985, there is also increasing interest being shown in the significance
of post-biblical writings, notably the rabbinic literature. In 2001, for example, the Pontifical Biblical Commission published a document entitled *The
Jewish People and their Sacred Scriptures in the Christian Bible*. It called for
greater collaboration between Jewish and Christian biblical scholars and
noted that 'the Jewish reading of the Bible is a possible one, in continuity
with the Jewish Sacred Scriptures . . . a reading analogous to the Christian reading which developed in parallel fashion'.[10] The World Lutheran
Federation issued a statement three years earlier, which stated, 'Christians
also need to learn of the rich and varied history of Judaism since New
Testament times, and of the Jewish people as a diverse, living community
of faith today. Such an encounter with living and faithful Judaism can be
profoundly enriching for Christian self-understanding.'[11]

On the Jewish side there have been stirrings of a new interest in Chris-
tianity. In September 2000 a statement entitled *Dabru Emet* ('Speak Truth')
was published. Prepared by four Jewish theologians it was signed by over 250
Jewish leaders and scholars, which gave it an unusual amount of authority.
It consists of a cross-denominational Jewish statement on relations with
Christianity and asserts that

Jews and Christians seek authority from the same book – the Bible (what Jews
call 'Tanakh' and Christians call the 'Old Testament'). Turning to it for religious
orientation, spiritual enrichment, and communal education, we each take away

---

[8] 'Notes on the Correct Way to Present the Jews and Judaism in Preaching and Catechesis in the
     Roman Catholic Church' (1985) http://www.jcrelations.net/stmnts/vatican5-85.htm.
[9] Ibid.
[10] 'The Jewish People and Their Sacred Scriptures in the Christian Bible' (2002) http://www.vatican.va/
     roman_curia/congregations/cfaith/pcb_documents/rc_con_cfaith_doc_20020212_popolo-ebraico-
     en.html.
[11] 'Guidelines for Lutheran–Jewish Relations' (1998) http://www.jcrelations.net/stmnts/elca2.htm.

similar lessons: God created and sustains the universe; God established a covenant with the people of Israel, God's revealed word guides Israel to a life of righteousness; and God will ultimately redeem Israel and the whole world.[12]

These statements, issued on behalf of Christianity and Judaism, provide a modern context to an age-old problem: are Jews and Christians bound together by the Bible? The question is not simply of academic interest, shedding light on events many hundreds of years ago. It has significance today because the Bible and its varied interpretations continue to influence the relationship between Judaism and Christianity. Modern Jewish and Christian biblical interpretation is partly based on (or perhaps it is more accurate to say, is a reaction to) interpretations developed in the formative period – in other words, the first 600 years of the Common Era. As we shall see later in this book, interpretations of Scripture, which originated long ago, still play an important role in the Christian–Jewish relationship. The uncovering of an exegetical encounter, therefore, not only tells us about historic relations between Christians and Jews but also informs us about the contemporary encounter.

The story of Abraham's attempted sacrifice of Isaac is one of the most well-known stories of the Bible. It has been an important passage for Judaism and Christianity from an early period. For Jews, from at least as early as the third century CE, the passage, known as the Akedah or Binding of Isaac, has been read on Rosh ha-Shana, the Jewish New Year. For Christians from around the same period, the story, commonly titled the Sacrifice of Isaac, is mentioned in the Eucharist prayers and read in the period leading up to Easter.

The focus of the biblical story concerns Abraham's relationship with God and how his faith in and commitment to God was demonstrated by his willingness to sacrifice his long-awaited son at God's command. Little attention was given to Isaac. Both the rabbis and the church fathers reflect a great deal on the story. Indeed, it is the central thesis of this book that neither Jewish nor Christian interpretations can be understood properly without reference to the other.

The primary purpose of this study is not to describe rabbinic or patristic interpretations. Nor is it to make moral judgements on texts of dispute and polemic. Rather, its goal is to explore Christian influence on Jewish exegesis (and vice versa) and consider whether Jewish interpreters interacted with Christian interpreters (and vice versa). In other words, I ask to what extent

---

[12] 'Dabru Emet' (2000) http://www.icjs.org/what/njsp/dabruemet.html.

it is possible to demonstrate that a two-way encounter took place between interpreters of the Bible.

Bound by the Bible assumes that Jews and Christians share a sacred text. It asks whether they also share a common exegetical tradition. One might argue against the existence of a shared sacred text because the Jewish canon consists of the twofold Torah (the Written and the Oral Torah). The rabbinic writings, alongside the Hebrew Scriptures (and especially the Pentateuch), make up this canon while the two Testaments make up the Christian canon.[13] Is it possible to study a common exegetical tradition if no shared text exists? Yet, although Jews and Christians developed distinct and separate literary traditions, a significant overlap existed and continues to exist, most notably in the area of biblical texts and common biblical stories such as Genesis 22. It is this overlap that provides an opportunity to ask whether and to what extent Jews and Christians encountered each other on the level of biblical interpretation.

Nevertheless, one must be aware of the limitations of an overlap. For instance, it is likely that a Jew would have little understanding of Christological debates, which took place at the Council of Nicea and elsewhere. On the other side of the same coin, it is also unlikely that a Christian in third-century Galilee would possess an appreciation of the halakhic sensibilities of rabbinic Judaism. However, the extent to which Jews and Christians exhibited knowledge of each other's biblical interpretations appears a fruitful area of exploration because the biblical narrative is important to and is shared by both religions. *Bound by the Bible* challenges the assumption that a rabbinic Jew might not have understood some of the biblical interpretations found in the *Catena* of the sixth-century Palestinian Christian Procopius, as well as the homilies of Origen. Similarly, it challenges the assumption that a contemporary Christian could not have understood some of the rabbinic interpretations found in the midrashim. In other words, the possibility of an exegetical encounter exists because Jews and Christians share a similar and somewhat overlapping heritage.

In the history of Jewish–Christian relations, arguments over this heritage have led to fierce dispute. Even today Jews and Christians cannot agree on a title for this heritage, although it seems that the term 'Hebrew Bible' is becoming more commonly used in scholarly and theological writings. The reason for this is clear: for Christians, the Hebrew Bible is understood with reference to the life and death of Christ, whereas for Jews it is generally read alongside traditional Jewish writings such as the rabbinic literature.

---

[13] Neusner 1987:114–45.

Even though Jewish and Christian interpretations of the Hebrew Bible are put to different uses, some interpretations may offer examples of mutual awareness, influence and even encounter. The Binding of Isaac provides us with a text that is of significance for both Judaism and Christianity. In the following chapters we will discover whether exegetical encounters took place in the first six centuries CE and consider to what extent echoes may still be heard and how they continue to influence the Jewish–Christian relationship today.

Introduction

Did an exegetical encounter take place in Jewish and Christian interpretations of Genesis 22.1–14 over many hundreds of years? By the term 'exegetical encounter' I mean that a Jewish interpretation either influenced, or was influenced by, a Christian interpretation and vice versa. The term does not imply that Jewish and Christian exegetes met to discuss their interpretations (although this might not be ruled out); rather, an exegetical encounter indicates awareness by one exegete of the exegetical tradition of another, revealed in the interpretations.

In my view, the existence (or non-existence) of an exegetical encounter sheds light on the extent of interaction between Judaism and Christianity in late antiquity. It may also have relevance for the contemporary Christian–Jewish relationship because the study of the Bible as well as Jewish and Christian biblical interpretation is becoming increasingly popular in the present dialogue between Christians and Jews.

In particular, I consider the writings of the Greek church fathers and the Palestinian rabbis before the Islamic conquest of Palestine, so chosen because writings after this period possess the additional and complicating factor of the possible influence of Islam. Although I refer to the writings of the Latin fathers as well as to the Syriac writings, and also make reference to the Babylonian Talmud, the focus is primarily on the Palestinian tradition and the works of the Greek fathers. The reason for this is that, if examples of an exegetical encounter are to be discovered, evidence will be found in these writings. This in turn is because many of the Jews who produced the Palestinian writings either inhabited the same cities as Christians or visited areas in which there was a significant Christian presence. Palestinian rabbis are often portrayed as being in discussion with the *minim* (heretics), a term that sometimes refers to Christians, and it is usual for these discussions to revolve around the interpretation of Scripture.[1]

The use of biblical interpretation in the study of Jewish–Christian relations demands careful attention to methodology. Stemberger has warned against the use of exegesis in the study of early Jewish–Christian relations because, he argues, whilst Jews and Christians shared a common Bible, a number of problems exist in demonstrating exegetical contact. These include the particular interest of Jews and Christians in different books of the Bible, such as Christian interest in the prophetical writings in contrast to Jewish interest in the Pentateuch. For example, Christian commentators more commonly cited verses from Isaiah than Jews and Jewish commentators more commonly cited verses from Leviticus than Christians.

Jews and Christians also possessed different texts of the Bible and consequently Christian interpretation depended on the Septuagint (LXX), a Greek translation from the second century BCE, while the rabbis relied on the Hebrew Masoretic Text.[2] The LXX was used originally by Jews living in the Diaspora but was taken over by the early church.

There is also a danger of an over-reliance on parallels, which can be both vague and misleading. The existence of parallels between rabbinic and patristic interpretations provides the basis for the modern study of the Jewish–Christian encounter in late antiquity, which began in the late nineteenth century. Scholarship at that time was almost wholly dependent upon uncovering parallels in the writings of the church fathers and the rabbis. As a result of their demonstration of the existence of parallels, scholars argued that interaction between Christianity and Judaism was common. The propensity to rely on parallels to a certain extent continues in contemporary scholarship and, as we shall shortly note, can be noted in recent works. However, parallels do not, in themselves, prove the existence of an exegetical encounter in the writings of the church fathers and rabbis because they might have resulted from earlier writings, such as those of Philo and Josephus, or might be found in the Apocrypha and Pseudepigrapha. Parallels might also have arisen as a result of similar methods and presuppositions in the interpretation of the same biblical text. Sandmel has warned against 'parallelomania', which he defines as an 'extravagance among scholars, which first overdoes the supposed similarity in passages

---

[1] According to Kalmin (1996:288–9) these exegetical writings are primarily Palestinian because non-Jewish awareness of Scripture in Babylonia was limited.
[2] Stemberger 1996a:571–3.

and then proceeds to describe source and derivation as if implying literary connection flowing from an inevitable or predetermined direction'.[3]

Another difficulty is the issue of dating. The historical background of a text – primarily, but not only, the rabbinic text – is often unknown, as a consequence of a complicated process of redaction as well as censorship.[4] The unreliability of dating interpretations undermines a dependency on parallels and has resulted in unsuccessful attempts at identifying the historical sequence of interpretations. Thus, for example, many of the previous studies of Genesis 22.1–14 have focused on whether certain rabbinic interpretations were in existence before or after the lifetime of Jesus in order to determine whether they might have influenced Jesus and the formation of Christianity. In fact, it is extremely difficult, if not impossible to have any certainty – one way, or the other.

In response to these problems I develop a series of criteria, based upon a study of biblical interpretation, which identify occurrences of an exegetical encounter. Although individually none of the criteria conclusively proves its existence, their occurrence, at the very least, suggests its possibility. Indeed, as the number of criteria fulfilled increases, the likelihood of an exegetical encounter likewise increases.

The criteria are not dependent on the existence of parallels in the writings of the Palestinian rabbis and the Greek church fathers, or on the dating of the interpretations. In addition, they are applied to interpretations of a text that is not only of significant interest to both Jews and Christians, but that is also very similar in the LXX translation as well as in the Masoretic Text. *Bound by the Bible*, therefore, sheds light on a question that has troubled scholars of Jewish–Christian relations in late antiquity: to what extent, if at all, did there exist an exegetical relationship between Judaism and Christianity?

PREVIOUS APPROACHES

Three approaches can be observed in previous studies of Jewish–Christian relations in late antiquity. Each tackles a different aspect of the Jewish–Christian encounter – polemic, proselytism and studies of individual church fathers – and each has failed to produce a consensus.

---

[3] Sandmel 1961:1. Although he directs these comments to studies of rabbinic literature, the New Testament, Philo and the Dead Sea Scrolls, the same lesson applies to the (mis)use of parallels in the patristic and rabbinic writings.

[4] For a summary of the complexities of dating rabbinic texts, see the articles by Schäfer (1986, 1989) and Milikowsky (1988).

The first approach, the study of polemic, is epitomized by the writings of the nineteenth-century scholar Adolf von Harnack, who dismisses the view that an encounter between Jews and Christians continued to take place after the end of the first century CE. He bases his opinion on an examination of early Christian writings and, in particular, the *Adversus Iudaeos* literature, which consists of anti-Jewish writings. In his view, their existence was either the result of internal needs and, therefore, directed at other Christians, or of external needs and directed at pagans. For Harnack, from the second century CE onwards, Christians were no longer interested in 'real' Jews and there was no ongoing encounter between Judaism and Christianity. Although he admits that there were exceptions, such as Justin Martyr and the *Dialogue with Trypho*, he argues that the *Adversus Iudaeos* literature presented Jews in a stereotypical way, which bore no relation to real Jews. The Jewish adversary did not exist in reality but only in the imagination of the Christian – in other words, it was the image of the Jew as an opponent of Christianity that counted, not the Jew as a human being.

He goes on to argue that the *Adversus Iudaeos* writings were a result of a Christian encounter not with Judaism, but with paganism, because as far as the Christian was concerned, 'the Jew simply represented the pagan'.[5] Christians consequently argued with pagans for the reasonableness of their religion and its fulfilment of the promises found in the Jewish Scriptures. In response, pagans rejected this assertion by referring to Jews who did not agree with the Christian interpretations. As a result, concludes von Harnack, pagan passages that purport to be Jewish arguments against Christianity were in reality pagan arguments against Christianity. The Christian responses to these arguments appeared in the guise of arguments against Jews, but were actually arguments against pagans. The figure of the Jew was, therefore, purely a conventional figure, a 'straw' Jew of the writer's imagination. Thus, according to von Harnack, the *Adversus Iudaeos* literature was entirely artificial and shed no light on the subject of Jewish–Christian relations.

Although von Harnack primarily examines Christian writings, his view has received some support from scholars who have examined the Jewish writings. Jacob Neusner, for example, claims that Judaism was not interested in Christianity until (at the earliest) the fourth century CE and that the two scarcely interacted.[6] Although they share some of the same Scriptures, these writings form part of a larger canon: the Old Testament and the New Testament for Christians; the Written and Oral Torah for Jews. Others

---

[5] Harnack 1883:57, 73–4.   [6] Neusner 1991:17–64.

argue that there is no evidence of Jews and Christians being involved in an encounter and point to the Bar Kochba revolt as the turning point. According to this argument, from the middle of the second century CE, Christian attention turned to pagans, and Jews were merely in the middle of a polemic between pagans and Christians.[7]

A number of studies of anti-Judaism in the early church also suggest that Christian polemical writings do not illustrate a real encounter with Judaism. In his classic work on the origins of antisemitism, James Parkes states that in the fourth century CE 'there was practically no interchange of theological discussion between Jew and Christian'.[8] Rosemary Radford Ruether also minimizes the extent of the relationship between Judaism and Christianity and states that the 'Christians' opponents are the Jews of Christian imagination'.[9] More recently Miriam Taylor suggests that the church fathers were concerned with Jews on a 'symbolic level' rather than on a 'living level'. She argues that

the Jewish oppressors portrayed in the church's literature represent an intellectual and not a literal reality. When the fathers spoke of Jewish hostility towards the church, they were neither simply referring to events of the past, nor alluding to concrete circumstances in the present, but to a theological reality whose truth transcended time.[10]

In her view, Christian anti-Judaism implies the loss of direct contact between Christians and Jews and consequently, when one comes across Christian anti-Jewish writings in the patristic literature, they refer not to contemporary Jews but to Jewish figures from an earlier period. It is interesting to point out that although the *Adversus Iudaeos* literature may have affirmed the identity of the church, there is no reason to assume it would automatically ensure that the encounter between Judaism and Christianity ceased.

Heinz Schreckenberg also suggests that Christians were more concerned with strengthening self-identity than with debating with real Jews, who were simply portrayed as literary figures. He argues that 'very rarely did open discussions take place' and that arguments found in the patristic writings were 'artificial'.[11] The early Christian community may have held little or no interest for the Jewish communities until after Constantine, and it is noticeable that there exist few, if any, references to Christianity

---

[7] Rokeah 1982:78.

[8] Parkes 1934:153. Parkes (1934:106–9) admits, however, that competition for proselytes did increase Christian knowledge of Judaism and Jewish knowledge of Christianity.

[9] Ruether 1974:120.   [10] Taylor (1995:95). See criticisms of Carleton-Paget (1997:196–227).

[11] Schreckenberg 1993:26.

in Jewish writings from this period. Some have interpreted this to mean that Jewish interest in Christianity was sparked much later, possibly as a result of the conversion of Constantine in the fourth century or even as late as the seventh century, as a result of the dramatic rise of Islam and the consequent Jewish interest in both Christianity and Islam. They also argue strongly against a view that rabbinic references to the *minim* refer to Christians, suggesting that the term might refer to any number of groups.[12]

Most recently, Gunter Stemberger has cautioned against assuming that when a church father refers to a Hebrew or Jew a real encounter takes place. This is because the reference may have been copied from an earlier text or because the person cited may not have been an actual historical figure. He suggests that it is often open to doubt whether a rabbi, who has been clearly identified in the rabbinic writings, actually uttered the words attributed to him. It is quite possible that the words were spoken by his followers who, in order to give them more authority, placed them in the mouth of the named rabbi.[13] Yet Christian influence on Judaism has not been explored fully, and it is easier to prove Christian dependence on Jewish exegesis than the other way around.[14]

Stemberger returns us neatly to the view of von Harnack – that the Jews portrayed in the patristic writings were not representative of living Judaism. These scholars represent a school of thought that argues that there was minimal contact between Jews and Christians from an early period. It asserts that the Christian writings, which mention Jews and Judaism, do not imply living contact between the communities and that the Jewish writings are too vague to be seen as evidence to support the view that Jews were interested in Christianity. Consequently, this school dismisses the possibility of an ongoing encounter.

Their view is opposed by a number of scholars who suggest that there continued to be an encounter between Jews and Christians after the end of the first century CE. Contemporaries of von Harnack reject his argument and maintain that the writings of the church fathers imply ongoing contact. They acknowledge that the existence of a large number of parallels in the writings of the church fathers betrays an artificiality and therefore admit the possibility that the *Adversus Iudaeos* writings might be a literary genre. However, descriptions of close associations and meetings between Christians and Jews, which are scattered throughout the patristic literature, indicate that the *Adversus Iudaeos* literature demonstrates real discussions

---

[12] Maier 1982:196–99.
[13] For a discussion of this problem, see Stemberger 1996b:57–62.   [14] Stemberger 1996a:573–5.

with Jews. They therefore dismiss the view that discussions reported in Jewish and Christian writings did not actually take place. They identify numerous parallels in the patristic literature that were borrowed from the rabbis. According to this view, the *Adversus Iudaeos* literature illustrates the continuation of an encounter, for 'the force of Jewish faith was not yet extinguished'.[15]

The writings of early twentieth-century scholars such as Samuel Krauss and Jean Juster provide the basis for the important work of Marcel Simon, who is perhaps the best-known opponent of von Harnack's thesis. Simon suggests that the *Adversus Iudaeos* literature would not have been generated had there not been criticisms from Jews. Indeed, there could be no Judaizing Christians without Jews. Simon concedes that the *Adversus Iudaeos* writings were connected with internal requirements, such as the fostering of Christian identity, but that this reason on its own is insufficient to explain their existence. In his view the 'proselytising spirit of the rabbis continued for centuries'.[16]

Simon is supported by scholars who suggest that, although the Bar Kochba revolt resulted in a rift between Judaism and Christianity, Judaism continued to influence the development of Christianity, and that Jews, Christians and pagans took part in an ongoing encounter until at least the reign of the emperor Julian in 361 CE. Tertullian's condemnation of those who name idols is cited as an example of rabbinic influence.[17] William Horbury takes a middle position. He accepts some aspects of von Harnack's argument and does not dismiss them outright, but comments that he 'was right in recognizing the internal importance of exegesis *Adversus Iudaeos* for Christian education, but wrong in supposing that significant contact between Jews and Christians ceased'.[18] In other words, on the one hand the *Adversus Iudaeos* writings had internal importance for the church but, on the other, probably reflected Jewish opinion.[19]

One of the by-products of the study of polemic is an examination of proselytism and its role in Jewish–Christian relations in late antiquity. If, for example, it can be shown that Jews were not involved in active mission, alongside Christians, the argument against an ongoing encounter is greatly strengthened. The extent of Jewish proselytism is an important element in this debate.

[15] Juster 1914, I:53–76; Krauss 1892:123; Krauss and Horbury 1995:13.   [16] Simon 1986:271–305.
[17] Baer 1961:91–5. Note, however, the critical comment of Barnes 1971:91.   [18] Horbury 1992:75.
[19] Krauss and Horbury 1995:14. Waegeman (1986:313) holds a similar position and states that although the *Adversus Iudaeos* writings provide examples of the fictitious and theoretical kind, 'there had been plenty of contact between Jews and Christians'. For a summary of recent discussion on the evidence of the *Adversus Iudaeos* writings, see Horbury 1998:21–5.

Von Harnack and those who support his view argue that Jews became so preoccupied with internal problems that they separated themselves from outside influences. As a result, 'intercourse with pagans was confined with the strictest of regulations and had to be given up as a whole'.[20] As a result, Jewish proselytism was non-existent.

In response, a number of scholars argue for the existence of Jewish missionary activity. Juster, for example, examines Roman and Christian legislation concerning Jewish proselytism and argues that Judaism actively continued to seek converts. He suggests that the lack of Christian reference to Jewish proselytism is due precisely to its success because the church fathers did not want to publicize the success of the Jewish mission.[21] Its existence is also a key element in Marcel Simon's argument that Jews and Christians were involved in a struggle for new adherents, and that only after Christianity won the struggle in the fourth century CE did Judaism desist from its mission to the gentiles and turn its attention inward.[22]

In recent years, a number of studies have been published that challenge this conclusion[23] and argue against the existence of a universal Jewish mission by suggesting that the universal mission of the early church was unparalleled in the history of the ancient world. Martin Goodman, for example, finds no evidence for a universal mission in first-century Judaism, although he accepts that in a later period proselytism did occur (but claims that this was a reaction to Christian mission). In his examination of early pagan comments that discussed Jewish proselytism, Goodman argues that the texts were corrupt or that references, such as the expulsion of the Jewish community from Rome, were a result of the introduction of a new cult rather than of proselytism.[24]

Goodman's opinion mirrors the view of David Rokeah, who states that 'no special inclination or effort can be discerned on the part of Judaism to absorb new ethnic elements through large-scale proselytism in the two hundred years between the Bar Kochba revolt and the establishment of the rule of Constantine. Christian literature seems to contradict this statement, but this contradiction is only an apparent one.'[25]

Both scholars reject the argument that the writings of Philo and Josephus provide evidence of a Jewish mission even though Philo states that 'those of

---

[20] Harnack 1908:18.
[21] Juster 1914, I:289 n. 2: 'It was necessary to be silent about the success of Jewish missionary activity so that the enemies of the Church would have nothing to celebrate'.
[22] Simon 1986:369–71. Cf. Georgi 1986: 83–151.
[23] McKnight 1991, Orrieux and Will 1992, Goodman 1994.
[24] Goodman 1994:60–90.   [25] Rokeah 1982:65.

other races who pay homage to them [the Jews] they welcome no less than their own countrymen'.[26] For his part, Josephus describes how 'all who desire to come and live under the same laws with us, he [Moses] gives a gracious welcome'.[27] Goodman and Rokeah argue that these writings offer no evidence of an active and universal Jewish mission. Philo and Josephus indicate that Jews may have accepted or even welcomed proselytes, but in the view of these scholars, these writings do not provide evidence that Jews actively sought converts at the time.

There are, however, three significant weaknesses to this treatment of proselytism: the scarcity of evidence, the definition of the word 'mission' and the diversity of first-century Judaism. First, the sources available are not extensive and do not provide a balanced picture, which means that arguments are sometimes constructed more on conjecture than on fact. This is of course true for both sides of the argument. Even though circumstantial evidence, notably literary references, for such activity is considerable,[28] there is no single item of conclusive evidence for an aggressive mission. Second, Goodman offers a narrow definition of proselytism and distinguishes a proselytic mission from an informative mission, an educational mission and an apologetic mission.[29] It is the assertiveness of the Christian mission, in other words its proselytic nature, that made it unique in the first centuries, and as a result Goodman dismisses a number of previous studies because they fall outside this category.[30]

Third, and perhaps most importantly, Judaism was enormously diverse during this period with little administrative or religious uniformity. Given this complexity, it is not surprising that arguments can be made for, or against, the existence of a universal Jewish mission. In sum, there is insufficient evidence upon which to make a convincing argument.

We shall now consider a number of studies of individual church fathers: Origen, Cyril of Alexandria and Tertullian. These studies illustrate the wide range of scholarly opinion rather than lead to a consensus.

Origen lived in Caesarea, capital of Palestine, in the third century CE, a city inhabited by Jews, Christians, pagans and others. It is clear that he had access to Jewish scholars, and, with the possible exception of Jerome, no other church father knew the Jews as well as Origen. An important study

---

[26] Philo, *De Legat.* 211.   [27] Jos., *Contra Ap.* 2.210.   [28] Cf. Feldman 1993:293ff.

[29] Goodman 1994:3–7. Cf. cogent criticisms of Carleton Paget 1996a:65–103.

[30] Georgi (1986:83–117), for example, suggests that the synagogue was a centre of missionary activity. However, Goodman (1994:84–7) explains that there is a difference between welcoming proselytes and actively seeking them. Georgi's understanding of mission is placed in the category of 'apologetic mission' rather than 'proselytic mission'.

by de Lange suggests that Origen was involved in debates with Jews and, like Chrysostom, addressed congregants on a Sunday when they had been to synagogue the previous day. Origen's writings, it seems, indicate that he was involved in the ongoing encounter between Judaism and Christianity in third-century Caesarea. Yet only occasionally does Origen refer to his disputations and discussions with Jews, and no full record of such dialogues has come down to us, although it may be possible to reconstruct from his surviving remarks the form and subject matter of his arguments.[31]

However, this view has been questioned by a number of scholars, who claim that Origen shows no evidence of being familiar with Hebrew. Brooks sounds the following caution:

Origen's school and the rabbinic academies may have prospered in the same city; students in each may have discussed portions of the Bible together; Origen himself may have produced parallel systems to regulate life under the Roman Empire. Nevertheless, a warning bell ought to sound. The Jewish background and culture available to Origen throughout his life seems to have been remarkably superficial. Certainly Origen had some familiarity with a few scraps of Jewish exegesis – he knew some fine details of rabbinic Sabbath law for example. Yet, on the whole, Origen simply had no understanding of the rabbinic movement gaining prominence around him.[32]

It has also been suggested that much Jewish literature would not have been of interest to Origen, and even his interpretations of the Song of Songs should not automatically be claimed as part of the Jewish–Christian encounter.[33] This view points out that Origen's writings use many arguments that are commonly found in the *Adversus Iudaeos* literature, indicating that they were part of a literary genre rather than an example of a genuine Jewish–Christian encounter. For example, Origen attacked Jewish exegesis for its literal interpretation of the Bible. Was his criticism based on genuine understanding of Jewish biblical interpretation or was it simply an effective rhetorical tool with which to oppose Judaism?[34]

The writings of Cyril of Alexandria also provide conflicting evidence. Cyril, bishop of Alexandria, was instrumental in expelling the Jews from the city in 416 CE, partly because, it seems, Christians attended Jewish services. According to Robert Wilken, Cyril was preoccupied with Judaism and 'the Jews became the natural and inevitable foil for the development

---

[31] De Lange 1976:86–9.
[32] Brooks 1988:95. McGuckin (1992:1–13) also questions the extent of the interaction between Origen and the rabbis.
[33] See the articles on this subject by Loewe (1966), Kimmelman (1980) and Hirshman (1996:83–94).
[34] Cf. de Lange 1976:82–3.

of his thought'.[35] However, like Origen, many of Cyril's comments are identical with criticisms found in the *Adversus Iudaeos* writings. Another complicating factor is that Cyril, like other church fathers, did not name the Jews from whom he claimed to have received exegetical traditions and it is, therefore, not possible to gauge whether he was involved in a real encounter with Judaism.

It is worth noting that a lack of scholarly consensus is also found in studies of the Latin fathers such as Tertullian. There seems to be evidence on the one hand to suggest that Jews and Christians, although they were rivals, regarded each other as jointly fighting the evil of idolatry. Aziza and Horbury suggest that Tertullian was influenced by rabbinic writings on idolatry and immorality.[36] On the other hand, however, Timothy Barnes rejects this view in words reminiscent of von Harnack and states that 'Tertullian's references to contemporary Jews betray a lack of contact. His *Adversus Iudaeos* was written not to convert Jews but pagans . . . Of contemporary Jewish ideas Tertullian was ignorant.' Barnes somewhat softens his view in a 1985 revision of his study but still envisages Tertullian looking at Jews 'on the streets of Carthage with a gloomy and baleful gaze . . . not as engaging them in conversation still less as seeking their company in social or intellectual gatherings'.[37] Barnes' view is supported by Rives who comments that 'while it is possible that Tertullian was familiar with some of the ideas of the local Jews . . . it is extremely unlikely that he had discussed the matter [of idolatry] with the rabbis'.[38] These portraits of Tertullian conflict so much that readers may be forgiven for believing that they are reading about two different historical characters.

A COMMON BIBLICAL CULTURE

The three most common approaches to the examination of Jewish–Christian relations in late antiquity – polemic, proselytism and studies on individual church fathers – fail to provide a scholarly consensus. *Bound by the Bible* proposes a fourth: the study of Jewish and Christian biblical interpretation. The exegetical approach is complementary to the previous three and is intended to supplement rather than replace. A study of biblical interpretation can shed light on Jewish–Christian relations because

---

[35] Wilken 1971:227, cf. Haas 1997:91.
[36] Aziza 1977:208–29 following Baer 1961:88–95. Horbury 1972 also points to evidence of Tertullian's dependence on Jewish sources in *De Spec.* 30.
[37] Barnes 1971:92; 1985:330.   [38] Rives 1995:220.

both Jews and Christians lived in a biblically orientated culture. Thus the exegetical approach is prima facie reasonable because, to a certain extent, Jews and Christians shared a common Bible. This is expressed by the early church in a number of ways, the most striking of which can be found in Justin Martyr's *Dialogue with Trypho*. After having quoted a number of biblical passages Justin states,

> For these words have neither been prepared by me, nor embellished by the art of man; but David sung them, Isaiah preached them, Zechariah proclaimed them, and Moses wrote them. Are you acquainted with them, Trypho? They are contained in your Scriptures (*graphai*), or rather not yours, but ours. For we believe them; but you, though you read them, do not catch the spirit that is in them.[39]

Justin is not satisfied by the possibility that Jews and Christians can share the same Scriptures but lays claim for Christian ownership, at the expense of Judaism. Justin's description of the transfer of the Scriptures from Jews to the new Israel, the church, illustrates a pervasive patristic supersessionist teaching, which is known as the doctrine of replacement theology.[40] This is the teaching that, since the time of Jesus, Jews have been replaced by Christians in God's favour, and that all God's promises to the Jewish people have been inherited by Christianity. This teaching (which still exists in some Christian circles today although it is rejected by the Roman Catholic Church and the majority of the Protestant denominations[41]) is a feature of the *Adversus Iudaeos* literature. It is based on a patristic interpretation of Scripture, which suggests that, because Jews had rejected Jesus, they were punished by having the Temple destroyed and by being exiled from the land of Israel. As a result, a teaching of contempt for Judaism developed, which strongly influenced the formation of Christian identity.

Hand-in-hand with the teaching of contempt, there also developed an admiration for Judaism. The history of Jewish–Christian relations is generally portrayed as a history of Christian rejection and denunciation of Judaism. A study of the exegetical encounter challenges this assumption because it allows for a positive story also to be told: the story of a two-way encounter and the existence of a more mutually beneficial relationship. For example, the willingness by Christians to order the Hebrew Bible in

---

[39] Justin, *Dia.* 29 Goodspeed.

[40] This can be seen most explicitly, perhaps, in the *Epistle of Barnabas*, which states that, just as the Scriptures belong to the Christians so does the covenant. Barnabas admonishes his readers not to 'heap up your sins and say that the covenant is both theirs and ours. It is ours.' *Barn.* 4.6–8 Lake.

[41] Replacement theology is held by many Southern Baptist Churches in the USA.

a canonical form recognized by Jews demonstrates a common biblically orientated culture, shared by Jews and Christians. In other words, the Christian canon is itself indicative of Jewish influence.[42]

It is also not surprising to learn that in some of the most brutal anti-Jewish polemic produced by the church fathers during this period – the *Adversus Iudaeos* sermons of John Chrysostom – there is strong evidence of Christian reverence for the synagogue. Chrysostom attacks his own Christian community in Antioch for their close relationship with the Jewish community. He railed against Christians who respected the synagogue and attended Jewish services partly because it was the place in which the holy Scriptures were held.[43]

Evidence of the significance of the role played by the Bible in the encounter with Christianity can also be found in Jewish statements, particularly those originating from the Palestinian rabbinic tradition. Palestinian rabbis employed biblical interpretation not only as a defence against Christian biblically based criticisms of Judaism, but they also acknowledged, as Tosefta witnesses, that Jews and Christians met around Scripture.[44]

Burton Visotzky goes further and claims that there exist a number of quotations from the New Testament in the rabbinic writings, particularly in early Palestinian literature. As an example, he points to a text in the Jerusalem Talmud (repeated in *Genesis Rabbah*) which paraphrases 1 Corinthians 1.11, 'in the Lord woman is not independent of man nor man of woman'. The rabbinic commentary reads,

The heretics asked R. Simlai, How many gods created the world? He answered them, Me you are asking? Let us ask Adam, as it is said, *for ask now of the days that are past, which were before you, since the day that God created Adam* ... (Deut. 4.32). It is not written, since gods created [pl.] Adam but *since the day that God created [sing.] Adam*. They said to him, But it is written, *In the beginning God [elohim is a plural construct] created* (Gen.1.1). He answered them, Is *created* written [as a plural]? What is written here is *created* [sing.]. R. Simlai stated, Every place that the heretics rend [a verse from context to make their point] has the appropriate [textual] response right next to it. They returned to ask him, What of this verse, *Let us make man in our image, after our likeness* (Gen. 1.26) [in which the subject, verb and objects appear in the plural]. He answered them, It is not written, So God created [pl.] man in his image [pl.] but *God created [sing.] man in his own image* (Gen. 1.27). His disciples said to him, Those you pushed off with but a straw, but what shall you answer us?[45] He told them, In the past Adam was created from dust, while Eve was created from Adam. From Adam onward, *in our image, after our*

[42] Horbury 1992:80–91.   [43] Chrysostom, *Adv. Iud.* 1.6 Migne.   [44] Hirshman 1996:9.
[45] In other words, the disciples are not convinced by the argument and ask for a better answer from their teacher.

likeness (Gen. 1.26); it is impossible for there to be a man independent of woman, nor is it possible for there to be woman independent of man, neither is it possible for both of them to be independent of the Shekhina.[46]

Visotzky rejects previous studies of this passage that suggest that the interpretation was pre-Pauline and influenced Paul. Rather, in his view, it was post-Pauline and represents a rabbinic response to Paul's teaching. In the earliest extant version in the Jerusalem Talmud, this passage is located in a section that is part of an anti-Trinitarian polemic.

These examples of a dependence on the Bible in the Jewish–Christian encounter result in a number of similarities between Jewish and Christian approaches to Scripture. These include an insistence on the harmony of Scripture and an emphasis on the unity of the text. Consequently, many Jewish and Christian interpretations were understandable to adherents of both religions. This situation explains the decision of exegetes, such as Origen and Jerome,[47] to turn to Jewish contemporaries for help in translating and understanding biblical texts. Although it goes without saying that the rabbis and the church fathers developed their own distinctive literary methods, we can be confident that their approaches would not necessarily have prevented particular interpretations from being understood in both communities.

This conclusion is reinforced by Origen's decision to produce the Hexapla and to consult translations of the Bible other than the LXX. The Hexapla consisted of six columns including the Hebrew text, a transliteration of the Hebrew into Greek, the independent Jewish translations of Aquila and Theodotion as well as the LXX and the translation of Symmachus. Origen desired to understand Jewish biblical exegesis in order to argue better with Jews who engaged him in disputations. He makes this clear in a letter to Africanus:

And we try not to be ignorant of their various readings, in case in our controversies with the Jews we should quote to them what is not found in their copies, and that we may make some use of what is found there, even though it should not be in our scriptures. For if we are so prepared for them in our discussion, they will not, as is their manner, scornfully laugh at gentile believers for their ignorance of the true readings as they have them.[48]

Origen's concern with arguing directly with Jews is repeated elsewhere in the patristic literature, as indicated by the following statement of Cyril of Jerusalem who wrote that 'the Greeks plunder you with their smooth

---

[46] *JT Ber.* 12d–13a, Visotzky 1995:61–74. Cf. *Gen. Rab.* 8.9. See comments of Kalmin (1996: 288–9).
[47] Cf. Hayward 1995:17–23; Kamesar 1993:176–91.   [48] Origen, *Epis. ad Africa.* 9.

tongues . . . while those of the circumcision lead you astray by means of the Holy Scriptures, which they pervert *if you go to them* [my italics]. They study Scripture from childhood to old age, only to end their days in gross ignorance.'[49] It is not by chance that Cyril refers to meetings between ordinary Jews and Christians, which he implies took place on the basis of Scripture and its interpretation. These meetings indicate a closer and more fruitful relationship than may previously have been assumed.

THE EXEGETICAL APPROACH

The exegetical approach is first mentioned by Raphael Loewe, who identifies the study of exegesis as a way forward in the study of Jewish–Christian relations in late antiquity, and asks whether it is possible 'to look for traces of influences and reactions that are less obvious [than parallels], and which may reflect on the whole a mutual stimulation of Jewish and Christian biblical theology'.[50] In his view, wherever a piece of rabbinic exegesis implicitly emphasizes Jewish repudiation of a belief prominently associated with Christianity, anti-Christian apologetic may be assumed as a main motivation, though not necessarily as the sole motivation.[51] Since then, a number of studies of Jewish and Christian biblical interpretation have been published, which gathered the major interpretations in the rabbinic and patristic writings on books of the Bible, individual verses as well as biblical characters. These include consideration of Genesis 1.28, a study of the book of Exodus,[52] as well as studies of Seth,[53] Enosh,[54] Noah,[55] Abraham,[56] Melchizedek,[57] Jethro, Balaam and Job.[58]

For the most part, these studies follow the same format: individual chapters devoted to pre-Christian interpretation, rabbinic interpretation, early Christian interpretation and, sometimes, the Qumran and/or Gnostic literature.[59] The division by chapter between the Jewish and Christian writings reduces the possibility of identifying an exegetical encounter because Jewish and Christian interpretations are not examined interpretation by interpretation. By separating the interpretations, the study of the relationship between them is made more complicated. As a result, these studies successfully identify parallels between the Jewish and Christian commentators but they fail to examine in any detail the existence and the significance of the interaction between the exegetical traditions.

---

[49] *Catechetical Lectures* 4.2.   [50] Loewe 1957:495.   [51] Loewe 1966:174.
[52] Cohen 1989; Larsson 1999.   [53] Klijn 1977.   [54] Fraade 1985.   [55] Lewis 1978.
[56] Siker (1991) examines interpretation until the end of the second century CE.   [57] Horton 1976.
[58] Baskin 1983.   [59] The exception is that of Larsson 1999, which follows the order of Exodus.

Bound by the Bible, however, aims to identify whether an exegetical encounter took place and to consider the consequences. It allows for the fact that, for the most part, it is not possible to demonstrate an actual point of contact between Jews and Christians. This difficulty arises out of the problems of dating Jewish texts as well as those caused by an internal and/or external censorship of the texts. Geza Vermes's solution to these problems is to adopt aspects of the historical-critical method. He argues that Jewish biblical interpretation should be studied according to the principles of historical and literary criticism. Vermes believes that the development of biblical interpretation can be traced from its birth in the post-exilic period to the rabbinic period.[60] He applies this emphasis on the historical framework to the study of the Sacrifice of Isaac in an attempt to prove that the rabbinic interpretations were pre-Christian and influenced the development of Christianity.

One of the main difficulties with a historical approach, such as that of Vermes, is its dependence upon the dating of key non-rabbinic texts, such as 4 Maccabees and *Liber Antiquitatum Biblicarum* (*LAB*, also known as Pseudo-Philo), the dating of which is subject to disagreement. Some scholars argue for a second-century CE date for 4 Maccabees and for a date around 150 CE for *LAB*. Vermes argues for a date early in the first century CE for both.[61] The historical approach is to a large extent therefore restricted to texts, which can be dated either from internal data or by referring to external texts. Those texts and interpretations that are difficult to date are excluded from consideration, and even those texts included are, as we have noted above, sometimes the subject of disagreement.

By contrast, the exegetical approach is not wholly dependent on a historical method, nor on dating interpretations before or after the rise of Christianity. It does not examine whether one interpretation was a response to another but simply considers whether an exegetical encounter occurred. For example, it is generally accepted that the rabbinic commentary *Genesis Rabbah* was redacted at least two hundred years after the lifetime of Origen, but that it incorporated interpretations that had existed before.[62] According to the historical-critical method, it would only be possible to prove that some interpretations were earlier than Origen with recourse to pre-third-century texts such as the book of *Jubilees*, in other words, with reference to dateable literary parallels. This is clearly a limiting factor because there

---

[60] Vermes, whose work is based upon the research of Bloch, concentrates on the historical development of an interpretation and is less interested in exegetical influence. Vermes 1961:7–10, Bloch 1955:202.

[61] Van Henten 1997:73–8, Jacobson 1996:209, Vermes 1961:197–8.

[62] For a summary of studies that consider the dating of *Gen. Rab.*, see Stemberger 1996b:279–80.

exist a multitude of interpretations either with no parallels, with undateable parallels or with parallels with unreliable dating.

The exegetical approach, however, concentrates on solely exegetical interaction and whether, in this example, evidence can be produced of a relationship between the interpretations of Origen and those of *Genesis Rabbah*, regardless of chronology. The results of such a study are significant because, if an exegetical encounter can be proven, some or all of the following become possible:

1. The redactors of *Genesis Rabbah* in the fifth century were aware of Origen's exegesis.
2. The redactors felt the need to respond to Origen's teaching.
3. Origen's writings must have been understandable and relevant to Jews, otherwise the redactors would not have considered them worthy of a response.
4. Origen used exegetical methods that were similar to, and sometimes the same as, the rabbinic exegesis, which implies that Origen was aware of rabbinic exegesis.

The exegetical approach therefore enables us to offer the following hypothesis: if there is evidence of an exegetical encounter, then the relationship between Judaism and Christianity was one of familiarity – this may have contributed to a teaching of contempt, but there may also have been occasions when familiarity resulted in respect and appreciation. Since the period under review is key to a proper understanding of the formation of Judaism and Christianity, as well as to Jewish–Christian relations, the existence of an exegetical encounter may have significance for today's relationship. The study of biblical interpretation sheds light on relations not only in the past, but also in the present. Indeed, it may also have implications for the future relationship, because the bond of Scripture will always underpin Jewish–Christian relations.

THE CRITERIA

The following five criteria provide the basis for this study. Although none conclusively prove the existence of an exegetical encounter, their occurrence is significant. If examples are found, not in isolation but multiply attested, the more likely it is that an exegetical encounter played a significant role in the interpretation. While each example on its own may be explained as coincidental, or as a result of exegetes separately arriving at the same conclusion, multiple attestation implies an exegetical encounter.

1. An explicit reference to a source

The clearest indication of an exegetical encounter is an explicit reference to an opposing view, although it is essential to remember that the prevalence of *Adversus Iudaeos* writings as a literary genre in the patristic literature means we have to be cautious even in cases where a church father explicitly refers to a Jewish source. Such references may have been copied from earlier Christian texts.[63] Nevertheless, patristic references to Jewish teachers and Jewish exegesis or rabbinic references to the *minim* should be taken seriously, particularly if they exist alongside other criteria.

Example

In *Dialogue with Trypho* Justin examines Genesis 1.27, and especially the phrase 'let us make man'. He claims that Jews misrepresent Scripture and complains to Trypho that

you [i.e., Jewish interpreters] may not, by changing the words already quoted, say what your teachers say, either that God said to Himself, 'Let us make . . .' as we also, when we are about to make anything, often say, 'Let us make' to ourselves; or that God said, 'Let us make . . .' to the elements, namely the earth and such like, out of which we understood that man has come into being.[64]

Justin's explicit reference to a Jewish interpretation of Genesis 1.27 seems to indicate an exegetical encounter. This is confirmed when we examine the early Palestinian rabinic commentary, *Genesis Rabbah*:

'And God said, let us make man . . .'. With whom did He take counsel? Rabbi Joshua ben Levi said, 'He took counsel with the works of heaven and earth, like a king who had two advisors without whose knowledge he did nothing whatsoever . . .' Rabbi Ammi said, 'He took counsel with His own heart.' It may be compared to a king who had a palace built by an architect . . .[65]

It should not be assumed that an exegetical encounter was one way. We also find rabbinic interpretations that represent an exegetical encounter with Christian teaching. For example, the following interpretation of Genesis 22 in *Aggadat Bereshit*, an eighth-century Palestinian text, condemns the view that God had a son:

How foolish is the heart of the *minim* [heretics] who say that the Holy One, Blessed be He, has a son. If, in the case of Abraham's son, when He saw that he was ready to slay him, He could not bear to look on in anguish, but on the contrary at once

---

[63] Stemberger 1996a:571.   [64] Justin, *Dia.* 62 Goodspeed.   [65] *Gen. Rab.* 8.3.

commanded, 'do not lay your hand on the lad'; had He had a son, would He have abandoned him? Would He not have turned the world upside down and reduced it to *tohu v'bohu* [unformed and void]?[66]

2. The same scriptural quotations

The second indication of an exegetical encounter occurs when, in the course of their interpretations, Jewish and Christian exegetes refer to the same scriptural quotation. Although it is possible that the exegetes may have chosen the same quotation separately, the choice is unlikely to have been purely coincidental.

Example

Both the *Epistle of Barnabas* and the *Mishnah* (*Rosh ha Shana*) quote Numbers 21.8 in their respective interpretations of Exodus 17.11. For *Barnabas*, the image of Moses holding up his hands when the Israelites were in battle was symbolic of the cross; for the rabbis, the lifting of Moses' hands indicated the Israelites turning towards God.

According to the *Mishnah*,

Whenever Moses held up his hand, Israel prevailed . . . (Ex. 17.11). Do Moses' hands then make or break a war? Rather, this passage is meant to tell you that whenever Israel looked on high and subjugated themselves to their Father in Heaven, they were victorious, and if not, they fell. Similarly you find, *Make a seraph figure and mount it on a standard. And if anyone who is bitten looks at it, he shall recover* (Num. 21.8). Does a serpent give life or death? Rather, when Israel looked on high and subjugated themselves to the father in heaven they were healed, and if not, they fell.[67]

According to *Barnabas*,

And he says again to Moses, when Israel was warred upon by strangers . . . the Spirit speaks to the heart of Moses to make a representation of the cross, and of him who should suffer, because, he says, unless they put their trust in him, they shall suffer war forever. Moses therefore placed one shield upon another in the midst of the fight, and standing there raised above them all kept stretching out his hands, and so Israel began to be victorious; then whenever he let them drop they began to perish. Why? That they may know that they cannot be saved if they do not hope on him . . . Again Moses makes a representative of Jesus showing that he must suffer and shall himself give life . . . Moses therefore makes a graven serpent, and places it in honour and calls the people by a proclamation. So they came together and besought Moses that he would offer a prayer on their behalf for

---

[66] *Agg. Ber.* 31 (with reference to Gen. 1.1).   [67] *M. RHS* 3.8.

their healing. But Moses said to them, 'Whenever one of you,' he said, 'be bitten, let him come to the serpent that is placed upon the tree, and let him hope, in faith that it though dead is able to give life, and he shall straightaway be saved.'[68]

The two interpretations indicate that Jewish and Christian exegetes sometimes approach the same biblical text with a similar exegetical method. Although it is possible that the authors reached the same conclusion separately, the likelihood that an exegetical encounter took place increases when we take into account that the *Epistle of Barnabas* has a number of other affinities with the rabbinic literature and deals with a number of contentious issues between Judaism and Christianity.[69]

3. The same literary form

The third indication of the existence of an exegetical encounter is the use of the same words, symbols and images, especially if the interpretations share the same extra-biblical descriptions. Clearly, the literary form can be chosen without recourse to another exegete's interpretations, since the literary form includes telling stories, asking questions, offering instruction and so on. However, the third criterion is especially significant in the interpretations of exegetes such as Origen, who expressed concern about Christians attending synagogue, which increases the likelihood that they were aware of Jewish literary form.

Example
The adoption by Melito of Jewish liturgy in *Peri Pascha* illustrates this criterion. Melito's Easter homily exhibits a number of parallels with the Jewish *Haggadah* story, which is recounted at Passover and appropriates some of its features. These include the structure of the homily, which parallels the reading of the *Haggadah*, as well as explicit references to Passover rituals such as discussion of the *afikomen* and an exposition of the unleavened bread and bitter herbs.[70]

Although Melito's homily is influenced by Jewish liturgical practice in late second-century Sardis, he denied vehemently that there was any value to the Jewish celebration of Passover. Indeed, he was unrestrained in his vilification of Jews and Judaism.[71]

---

[68] *Barn.* 12.2–7 Lake. Cf. Carleton Paget 1994.   [69] Visotzky 1995:12–17.
[70] Eg. *PP* 68 and *M. Pes.* 10.5. The reference to *afikomen* is found in *PP* 66 and 88; the exposition of the unleavened bread and bitter herbs in *PP* 93.
[71] For further discussion, see Werner 1966:200–9, Hall 1979:xxiv–xxviii, Wilson 1995:241–56.

Israel Yuval argues that Melito's homily influenced Jewish Passover liturgy. He suggests that the *Haggadah* represents a Jewish response to the Christian interpretation of Passover. For example, Yuval claims that the *Dayyenu* prayer ('it would have been enough') was influenced by Melito's *Improperia*, which condemns Israel for failing to recognize Jesus as the messiah. Yuval makes a strong case for the existence of a liturgical encounter and for a Christian influence on Judaism.[72]

4. The same or opposite conclusions

The fourth indication of an exegetical encounter occurs when Jewish and Christian exegetes reach the same or opposite conclusions (if those conclusions are not dependent upon the literal meaning of the text). It can be argued, of course, that exegetes may reach the conclusion by separate means but this criterion becomes particularly relevant when found alongside other criteria.

Example
Christian and Jewish interpreters came to the same conclusion in their interpretation of Genesis 1.28, when they argued that the verse referred to the triumph of their own religion. The Christian interpretation refers to existing church rule and the Jewish to a future messianic age when Israel would be redeemed and would rule both the heavenly and earthly realms. Their conclusions were not based upon a literal reading of the text and may demonstrate an exegetical encounter.[73]

5. Use of a well-known controversial theme for Jews and Christians

The fifth indication of an exegetical encounter, and probably the most important, consists of a reference to a well-known subject of controversy between Jews and Christians. The appearance of such references in Jewish literature provides an argument against the supporters of von Harnack's thesis: if the *Adversus Iudaeos* literature were directed either internally towards Christians or externally towards pagans, one would expect little or no evidence of Jewish interest. If, however, Jewish interpretations indicate an awareness of the Christian polemic, one could conclude, first, that Jewish attention was being paid to Christian interpretation and that, second, Jews believed that a response was required.

---

[72] Yuval 1999:99–124.   [73] Cohen 1989:119, 268.

Example

The identification of the true Israel was a well-known subject of controversy between Christians and Jews. As we saw above, Justin Martyr argued that Jews no longer possessed the Scriptures because they had been taken over by the church who possessed the true understanding of Scripture. In the same *Dialogue* Justin stated that 'the prophetical gifts remain with us, even to the present time. And hence you ought to understand that [the gifts] formerly among your nation have been transferred to us.'[74]

The rabbis responded to Christian claims about the ownership of Scripture. They were aware that the church had adopted the Greek translation of the Bible and complained that as a consequence Christians pretended to be Israel. This view is illustrated by the following interpretation from *Tanhuma*.

When the Holy One, Blessed be He, said to Moses 'write' (Ex. 34.27), Moses wanted to write the Mishnah as well. However the Holy One, Blessed be He, foresaw that ultimately the nations of the world would translate the Torah into Greek and would claim, 'We are Israel'.[75]

The passage indicates that the rabbis were familiar with the Christian claim to the Hebrew Bible and believed it necessitated a Jewish response. Further evidence of the Jewish complaint can be seen in the *Dialogue of Timothy and Aquila*, in which the Jewish interlocuter protests that 'you Christians, according to your will, wrested the Scriptures'.[76] Both the rabbinic passage and the patristic quotation show that Jews were aware of and reacted to such Christian claims.

THE BIBLICAL TEXT – GENESIS 22.1–14

The successful outcome of the exegetical approach is dependent upon the choice of an appropriate biblical text. I have chosen the story of Abraham's near sacrifice of his son Isaac as a test case, for a number of reasons. First, this story is treated only once in the Hebrew Bible and there exists no internal biblical exegesis that may serve to complicate the examination of post-biblical exegesis.[77]

Second, there are few differences between the various Greek translations, particularly the LXX and the Hebrew text. The LXX often offers a free

---

[74] Justin, *Dia.* 29 and 82 Goodspeed.   [75] *Tan. Y. Ki Tissa* 34. Cf. *Pe. R.* 5.1.

[76] *Dialogue of Timothy and Aquila* (Conybeare 1898:89). Cf. Lahey 2000:281–96, Hirshman 1996:13–22.

[77] Batten (1913:365–6) suggests that Nehemiah associated Abraham's faithfulness with the Akedah. Although Neh. 9.8 states that God found Abraham's heart faithful the association is tenuous.

translation of the Hebrew text and was viewed by the church fathers as reflecting the words of God more precisely than the Hebrew Masoretic Text. This is made clear by Justin Martyr in his *Dialogue with Trypho*, where he complains to Trypho, his Jewish interlocutor, that the words 'from the wood' have been removed from Psalm 96.

> For when the passage said, 'Tell the nations, the Lord has reigned from the wood', they have left out, 'Tell the nations, the Lord has reigned'. Now, not one of your people has ever been said to have reigned as God and Lord among the nations, with the exception of Him only who was crucified . . . Here Trypho remarked, 'whether or not the rulers of the people have erased any portion of the Scriptures, as you affirm, God knows; but it seems incredible.'[78]

However in the case of Genesis 22, Jews and Christians read, almost word for word, the same story whether in Hebrew or Greek. Thus Jewish and Christian exegetes started with a common text, which ensures that the reasons for an exegetical encounter cannot be explained by textual transmission.

Third, Genesis 22 was an important and controversial story for both Jews and Christians from a very early period. For example, Philo attacks a number of 'quarrelsome critics who misconstrue everything' and do not consider Abraham's actions in connection with the Akedah to be great or wonderful.[79] Although the identity of the critics is unclear, it is evident that their views are well known and sufficiently important to demand a response. Pseudo-Philo also mentions that the biblical story is a source of controversy and attacks those who 'malign' God.[80]

As a result of the large number of interpretations in the early writings, Jewish and Christian exegetes inherited an exegetical tradition that allows us to identify the process of the exegetical development. We are therefore in a good position to examine how much Jewish and Christian commentators were dependent upon a shared tradition, how much new interpretation they offered, and what motivated their exegetical choices. This deals with the need to take into account an earlier common heritage.

Fourth, a wide variety of controversial themes, central to both Judaism and Christianity, emerge from the biblical story. These include the prediction of Christ and the fulfilment of Scripture, the significance of both Abraham and Isaac, and the concepts of atonement and forgiveness.

Fifth, the story continues to be of fascination to Jews and Christians. For example, in the last hundred years or so, theologians, historians,

---

[78] Justin, *Dia*. 73 Goodspeed.
[79] *De Ab*. 178. Sandmel (1971:128) believes the critics to be Jewish assimilationists.
[80] Ps. Ph. (*LAB* 32.4).

psychologists, novelists, poets, artists and musicians have all wrestled with Genesis 22. Although the biblical account is compressed into fourteen verses, they have created numerous studies, novels, poems, plays, works of art and musical compositions. The Akedah continues to bring tension and drama, arousing both terror and pity. It is a paradigm of Aristotle's catharsis, dealing with the biggest themes and touching the deepest emotions. Some of the modern works on the subject question whether, as it seems to, it has a happy ending. Is there an immediately apparent, morally acceptable and topically relevant message? How could Abraham reconcile the bizarre demand to sacrifice his son against the divine promise that he would be the ancestor of a people who would spread throughout the world?

Bound by the Bible follows the order of the biblical story and examines the interpretations verse by verse. In order to obtain an insight into the Jewish–Christian encounter through the exegetical writings of the church fathers and rabbis, the account of the Sacrifice of Isaac is considered sequentially, rather than thematically, which focuses on individual themes such as atonement, fulfilment of Scripture and so on. This is a different approach to previous studies, which considered, on a chapter-by-chapter basis, pre-Christian interpretation, rabbinic interpretation, early Christian interpretations and so on.

Each chapter begins with an examination of the writings of the early interpreters, such as Philo and Josephus, whose views sometimes provide the foundation for later writings. This is followed by an examination of the interpretations of the rabbis and the church fathers, which will demonstrate the extent to which exegesis developed in the first six centuries of the Common Era and whether it is possible to ascertain the occurrence of an exegetical encounter. By considering successive stages of the biblical story it is easier to identify and analyse the existence of an exegetical encounter.

In addition to an examination of the writings of the church fathers and the rabbis, interpretations in liturgy and art are also taken into account, for these forms of interpretation can shed light on biblical interpretation in late antiquity. An examination of artistic and liturgical interpretation provides a contrast with the more traditional patristic and rabbinic commentaries. Artistic interpretation in particular demonstrates exegetical traditions, which differ significantly from the written interpretations. The Sacrifice of Isaac was of great interest to Jewish and Christian artists, which demonstrates that biblical interpretation was not limited to homily, poetry and prayer. Biblical interpreters wore a number of guises – they were not only preachers, teachers and liturgists, but also artists. A full examination of

Jewish and Christian interpretations requires a consideration of the artistic interpretations, for only then will biblical interpretation be fully appreciated in its true coat of many colours. It is only after the examination of all elements of biblical interpretation has been completed that we will be in a position to gain a full insight into Jewish and Christian biblical interpretation and their possible relationship.

As far as liturgical texts are concerned, unlike many of the commentaries and sermons of the church fathers and the rabbis, which can be approximately dated before the mid-seventh century CE, much of the liturgy, particularly the Jewish liturgy, cannot be dated from this period because it was part of a primarily oral tradition. As a result of the lack of written evidence during the period under examination, I have analysed texts dated to approximately the tenth century CE. The problem is illustrated by the rabbinic dictum that 'those who write down blessings are like those who burn the Torah',[81] and it is unsurprising to learn that the first Jewish prayer-book, *Seder Amram Gaon*, was only written in the ninth century. The oral liturgical tradition lasted longer than other oral genres, which were written down later.

One of the consequences of the stress on the oral tradition is that new prayers, particularly *piyyutim* (Jewish religious poetry), flourished. Jewish and Christian liturgical poetry, particularly the *piyyutim* and the *kontakia* (Christian hymns which deal mainly with biblical events) of Romanos, provide us with the opportunity to make direct comparisons. It is generally agreed that the geographical origin of the *piyyut* lies in Palestine. Although there is some debate about the dating of the beginnings of the *piyyutim*,[82] the earliest known poets are Yose ben Yose, Yannai and Eleazar ha-Kallir, all of whom were Palestinian and lived before the Arab conquest of Palestine in 635 CE. As a Palestinian phenomenon the *piyyutim* were influenced by Christian Byzantine cultural models. It is surely no coincidence that Romanos, one of the most important early Christian liturgical poets, flourished in the Eastern Church of the sixth century, which was precisely the period that saw the labours of the Jewish poet Eleazar ha-Kallir. The possibility that an exegetical encounter took place is alluded to by Stefan Reif who, in his magisterial study of Hebrew prayer, emphasizes that Judaism had an 'excellent digestive system'. Reif argues that its liturgy was capable of absorbing all manner of content at different periods.[83]

---

[81] JT *Shab.* 15c.
[82] Heinemann (1977:139–55) argues that the oldest Temple prayers can be classified as *piyyutim* and suggests that the *hosanot* and *selichot* were used in the Temple, a view supported by Reif (1993:80–7).
[83] Reif 1993:19.

Another reason why it is important to include liturgy in our examination of the Sacrifice of Isaac is because from biblical times prayer was closely associated with sacrifice[84] and with the forgiveness of sins. Sacrificial rites were central to Jewish practice during and after the Second Temple period as they were to the Christian liturgy from the beginning. According to Hans Lietzmann, in the first three centuries, the Eucharist was conceived as a sacrifice in a threefold sense, consisting of first the prayers, second the bread and wine laid on the altar, and third the sacred action at the altar itself (paralleling the sacrificial death of Christ).[85] It is therefore not surprising to discover references to the Sacrifice of Isaac in the Christian and Jewish liturgies. It is also worth noting that Genesis 22 was an important scriptural reading in both church and synagogue from well before the fifth century CE.

Finally, the epilogue briefly considers more recent interpretations of the Sacrifice of Isaac and to what extent it continues to play a role in Jewish–Christian relations. For many people, Genesis 22 represents 'that story' which still causes controversy and alarm. The modern reception history begins with Kierkegaard's classic work *Fear and Trembling* and, to the present day, commentators continue to remark on its significance. In today's interfaith world, it is one of the few stories that crosses religious boundaries.

PREVIOUS STUDIES OF GENESIS 22

Before beginning an examination of Jewish and Christian interpretations of Genesis 22, earlier studies on this subject need to be considered. These, for the most part, have examined it from a historical perspective and addressed, in particular, the question of whether rabbinic interpretations originated before or after the beginning of Christianity. The focus has primarily been on the rabbinic writings and the New Testament, although a few studies have been devoted to the writings of the church fathers.[86]

The dating of the rabbinic interpretations has been the focus of many of these studies, and two schools of opinion exist. One school argues that the sum and substance of the rabbinic interpretations had already come

---

[84] The Bible recounts that prayers were offered alongside sacrifice, e.g. Gen. 13.4, 26.25; Isa. 56.7.

[85] Lietzmann (1979:68).

[86] The exceptions include Lerch (1950), who offers a sweeping historical survey of the study of the Akedah in Christianity, Daniélou (1950), who examines the Akedah in terms of patristic typology, and Harl (1986), who produced a detailed study on the significance of the Greek word *symbodizo*, which is the Greek translation of 'binding' in the LXX.

into existence by the first century CE and, existing before the beginning of
Christianity, probably influenced it. The second body of opinion argues for
a later, probably third-century CE dating, and suggests that rabbinic interpretations should be viewed as a reaction to the teachings of Christianity.

The first modern scholarly study by Geiger[87] argues that the rabbinic
interpretations were a vehicle through which foreign ideas sought liturgical
(and therefore legitimate) Jewish expression. Geiger suggests they originated in Babylonia in the third century CE and were influenced by Syriac
Christianity. This view is rejected by Lévi, who suggests that, since the
Palestinian Amoraim were particularly interested in the biblical story, their
provenance was Palestinian and must have influenced early Christianity
and, in particular, Paul. Lévi suggests that the *musaf* for Rosh ha-Shana
was influenced by 'Akedah merit'.[88] Schoeps, following Lévi, argues that
'[Paul] built the doctrine of the expiatory power of the sacrificial death of
Christ on the binding of Isaac, as interpreted in the familiar Rosh Hashana
liturgy'.[89] Schoeps is particularly important in the modern study of the
Sacrifice of Isaac in early Judaism and Christianity because he was widely
respected among New Testament scholars. His support for Lévi resulted in
greater awareness of the relevance of the Sacrifice of Isaac among Christian
scholars.

Lohse[90] challenges Lévi's conclusion and argues that the rabbis were
influenced by Christian teachings concerning the atoning death of Jesus.
In other words, Jewish interpretations were influenced by a controversy
with Christians over the significance of Christ's atoning death. Rabbinic
interpretations should, therefore, be viewed as a reaction to, rather than an
instigator of, early Christianity.

Shalom Spiegel[91] puts forward a third- rather than first-century CE date,
and his own view, which he admits is 'speculative', suggests that interpretations were derived from a pagan motif that influenced both Judaism and
Christianity. Spiegel offers a more tentative approach to the question of
dating and anticipated the uncertainty of dating rabbinic texts that came
to prominence many years afterwards.

---

[87] Geiger 1872:1–10.   [88] Lévi 1912:179. Akedah merit will be discussed below.
[89] Schoeps 1946:391. Riesenfeld (1947:87) is also influenced by Lévi and states that 'the importance
  given to the Sacrifice of Isaac in Jewish literature cannot be attributed to a rabbinic reaction to
  the Christian dogma of redemption because it is of much earlier origin. This is evidenced by the
  significant position given to the Sacrifice of Isaac in pre-Christian texts.'
[90] Lohse 1955:91.
[91] Spiegel 1967:83. *The Last Trial* was originally published in Hebrew in 1947 but became more accessible
  and influential when it was translated into English in 1967.

In 1961, Geza Vermes[92] and Roger Le Déaut[93] published works that support the early-dating school of thought, and both scholars emphasize the importance of the Palestinian Targums. Vermes argues that the Palestinian Targums contain first-century interpretations, which can be isolated, and believes that they are the most important model with which to understand New Testament texts dealing with the meaning of the death of Jesus. In 1996 Vermes published a fragment from Qumran that, he argues, supports his view of an early date for rabbinic interpretations. Unfortunately, the manuscript he examines is extremely fragmentary and his interpretation is based upon a single extant Hebrew letter.[94]

In response to Vermes and Le Déaut, Davies and Chilton defend the late dating of rabbinic interpretations of Genesis 22, and scholarship today would accept a later dating of the Palestinian Targums. According to Davies and Chilton there is 'no trace of Akedah doctrine' in any pre-Christian literature.[95] These rabbinic interpretations replaced rites and practices that were extinguished after the destruction of the Temple. At the same time they represented a response to the Christian teaching of atonement. Their view is rejected by Robert Hayward, who supports the Vermes/Le Déaut position arguing that the 'basic substratum of the Targumic Aqedah was in existence by the first century A.D.'[96] American theologian Paul van Buren agrees and argues that 'the pre-Pauline gospel was the result of a highly creative application of the early Jewish interpretations of the binding of Isaac to the crucifixion of Jesus and to the events (or discovery) occurring perhaps on the first day of the next week so as to turn those days into Good Friday and Easter'.[97] He considers the implications for biblical study of the fact that Christianity began as a Jewish sect and concludes that the church's faith and identity is grounded in Jewish faith and identity.

Alan Segal offers a middle position and argues that the Sacrifice of Isaac 'was heavily used in Jewish exegesis and had already gained a firm grip on Jewish sensibilities by the time of Jesus' but, importantly, was 'nowhere used as a prototype of messianic suffering'.[98] It was the addition of this element that gave to the existing interpretations a Christian dimension. Jon Levenson, in one of the latest scholarly works to examine the issue of early versus late dating, argues that the biblical story influenced Christianity in terms not of atonement, but of supercessionism. The church's claim that it superseded Judaism was partly based upon its interpretation of the blessing

[92] Vermes 1961.   [93] Le Déaut 1961.   [94] Vermes 1996:140–6. See below, vv. 6 to 8.
[95] Davies and Chilton 1978:515.   [96] Hayward 1981:149.   [97] Van Buren 1998:48
[98] Segal 1984:179 and 1996:110.

Abraham receives at the end of the story. Levenson suggests that for the rabbis, the blessing 'renders the very existence of the Abrahamic peoples upon their ancestor's obedience', whereas for Paul it implies an extension of the blessing 'to all the nations of the earth'.[99]

[99] Levenson 1993:1. See comments by Segal (1996:99–116) and Moberley (2000: 154–61).

CHAPTER I

Verses 1–2: God tests Abraham

v. 1 And after these things God tested Abraham, and said to him, 'Abraham!' And he said, 'Here am I.' v. 2 He said, 'Take your son, your only son Isaac, whom you love, and go to the land of Moriah, and offer him there as a burnt offering upon one of the mountains which I shall tell you.'

ויהי אחר הדברים האלה והאלהים נסה את אברהם ויאמר אליו אברהם ויאמר הנני:
ויאמר קח נא את בנך את יחידך אשר אהבת את יצחק ולך לך אל ארץ המריה
והעלהו שם לעלה על אחד ההרים אשר אמר אליך:

Καὶ ἐγένετο μετὰ τὰ ῥήματα ταῦτα ὁ θεὸς ἐπείραζεν τὸν Αβρααμ καὶ εἶπεν πρὸς αὐτόν Αβρααμ, Αβρααμ· ὁ δὲ εἶπεν ἰδοὺ ἐγώ. καὶ εἶπεν λαβὲ τὸν υἱόν σου τὸν ἀγαπητόν, ὃν ἠγάπησας, τὸν Ισαακ, καὶ πορεύθητι εἰς τὴν γῆν τὴν ὑψηλὴν καὶ ἀνένεγκον αὐτὸν ἐκεῖ εἰς ὁλοκάρπωσιν ἐφ᾽ ἓν τῶν ὀρέων, ὧν ἄν σοι εἴπω.

EARLY INTERPRETATIONS

Many of the early interpreters were anxious to answer critics of Judaism who cited Genesis 22 when reproaching Jews for portraying God as desiring human sacrifice. Accusations concerning the divine desire for human sacrifice were levelled at Jews on numerous occasions. Later these accusations were directed at both Christians and Jews, as evidenced by many examples in pagan literature. According to Josephus, for example, Posidonius, Apollonius Molon and Apion all denounced Judaism[1] and Minucius Felix reproduced pagan charges against Christianity.[2]

The necessity to refute pagan accusations can be seen in the interpretations of the opening verses that stress that, although God tested Abraham, God did not desire human sacrifice. For instance, Josephus responds to the charge that Jews practised human sacrifice and goes to great lengths to

---

[1] *Contra Ap.* 2.91–6.   [2] *Octavius* 9.1–7.

point out that God does not require human blood. God was not capricious in taking away what he had given and had made the command only to 'test Abraham's soul and see whether such orders would find him obedient'.[3]

Philo also offers a defence of Abraham in his interpretations of the Akedah. He attacks 'quarrelsome critics' who did not consider Abraham's actions great or wonderful[4] and is clearly angered by these critics, using vitriolic language in his polemic.[5] Philo's opponents contend that child sacrifices had been carried out by others and Abraham's action therefore was not special. Philo responds by showing that Abraham's action differs enormously from any others who, for example, might have sacrificed their children for lower motives than those of Abraham as a result of local custom or in order to appease the gods or simply to attain personal glory. None of these reasons are true of Abraham: neither custom, love of honour or fear mastered Abraham; rather he was driven by his obedience to God.

In his defence of Genesis 22, Philo is one of a number of early interpreters who explain the benefits of the test. These interpreters pursue three approaches in their explanations, each of which is developed in more detail by later interpreters. First, they point to the significance of Abraham's obedience to God and emphasize the importance of his faith. They note that the Bible itself comments on Abraham's faithfulness to God (for example, Genesis 15.6 and Nehemiah 9.8[6]) and suggest that the purpose of the Akedah was simply to highlight the extent of Abraham's faithfulness. This approach is illustrated by the book of *Jubilees*, which states that 'I [God] have made known to all that you [Abraham] are faithful to me in everything which I say to you'.[7] Pseudo-Philo also explains that the test took place as an example to others, for it 'made you [Abraham] known to those who do not know you'.[8] Abraham is, therefore, portrayed as a heroic figure to be admired by all people. The benefit of Abraham's action is extended to the Jewish people as a whole and is the reason why they are chosen by God. According to Pseudo-Philo, 'in return for his blood I chose them'.[9]

Abraham's obedience to God is also emphasized by the fact that Genesis 22 was listed in *Jubilees* as the last and most severe of a series of divinely inspired tests.[10] The Akedah illustrated Abraham's faithfulness for, despite

---

[3] Ant. 1.233; cf. *LAB* 32.4; *De Ab.* 178–91.   [4] *De Ab.* 178.

[5] *De Ab.* 191, 'Let them, therefore, set bolt and bar to their unbridled evil speaking mouths, control their envy and hatred of excellence and not mar the virtues of men who have lived a good life, virtues which they should help to glorify by their good report.'

[6] Gen. 15.6, 'And he believed the Lord and He reckoned it to him as righteousness'. Neh. 9.8, 'And You [God] found his [Abraham's] heart faithful'.

[7] *Jub.* 18.16. Cf. 4Q225.   [8] *LAB* 32.4.   [9] *LAB* 18.5.   [10] *Jub.* 17.17–18, 19.8.

the severity of the test, he retained his faith in God and fulfilled God's command. Philo, for example, explains firstly that he made a practice of obedience to God, secondly that this was 'a totally new and extraordinary procedure' and thirdly that he loved Isaac greatly because he was the only child of his old age. 'All the other actions which won the favour of God are surpassed by this'[11] and, as a result, the test was 'unprecedented'.[12]

Second, the early interpreters discuss in detail the role of one of the angels, Mastema. Both *Jubilees* and a Qumran fragment (4Q225) explain that God tested Abraham because of the accusation of Mastema. The fragment states that after Abraham named his son 'the prince of Ma[s]tema came [to G]od, and he accused Abraham regarding Isaac'.[13] It is also worth referring to Pseudo-Philo who, rather than describing Mastema as the instigator of the test, explains that 'all the angels were jealous of him [Abraham]' and that at their prompting God tested Abraham.[14] The purpose of these interpretations was to remove God from being viewed as the instigator of the test and consequently to minimize the possibility of God being criticized for initiating the trial.

Third, interpreters mention the Akedah in response to those who are tempted to blame God for their sufferings. They offer a stern warning not to put God to the test. For instance, in the book of Judith the heroine refers to the Akedah during an impassioned plea against the decision made by the rulers of a besieged city to surrender to their enemies if God does not deliver them within five days. She argues that it is not appropriate for humans to 'put God to the test' by establishing a time limit.[15] Judith explains that the trial through which the elders were passing was not as extreme as the trials through which God put Abraham, Isaac and Jacob. 'He has not tried us with fire, nor has He taken vengeance on us.'[16] According to Judith, the proper response is not to question God but to remain faithful, give thanks and wait for deliverance.[17]

Although there is no explicit reference to verses 1–2 in the New Testament, a number of scholars have argued that the title 'Beloved Son' (υἱός ἀγαπητός),[18] conferred to Jesus at his baptism, was influenced by the biblical description of Isaac as 'your son, your only son, whom you love' (τὸν υἱόν σου τὸν ἀγαπητόν, ὃν ἠγάπησας). This view, promoted by both Le Déaut and Vermes, is expressed forcefully by Daly. In his view, 'the presence of genuine Akedah motifs . . . is such as to remove practically all

---

[11] *De Ab.* 167.   [12] *De Ab.* 197.   [13] *Jub.* 17.16; 4Q225.   [14] *LAB* 32.1–2.
[15] Jdt. 8:12.   [16] Jdt. 8.27.   [17] E.g. *Ecc. Rab.* 8.4. Cf. Jas. 1.13.
[18] Mk 1.11 (and par.); cf. Mk 9.7 (and par.); Mk. 12.6 (and par.).

doubt that the Akedah forms an essential, if not the most essential, part of the background of the synoptic voice from heaven'.[19]

In order to consider this argument, it will be helpful to examine the LXX rendering of 'your son, your only one, whom you love, Isaac' (בנך את יחידך אשר אהבת). The first point to notice is that the LXX equates 'only one' (יחיד) with 'beloved' (ἀγαπητός). The adoption of ἀγαπητός is not unusual and appears on three occasions in Genesis 22 and four times elsewhere.[20] Although ἀγαπητός is the most common rendering of יחיד, the Psalms primarily use 'only one' (μονογενής), thus indicating an overlap between the two terms.[21] Further evidence of an overlap is provided by a number of Greek translations that also use μονογενής instead of ἀγαπητός such as Aquila and Symmachus. Isaac is also described as μονογενής by Josephus,[22] and Harl argues that ἀγαπητός and μονογενής are equivalent.[23]

The equivalence of, or at the very least the overlap between, these two Greek words is a warning to take care before assuming that the description of Isaac in Genesis 22 provides the context to ἀγαπητός and to the Beloved Son imagery that is applied to Jesus in Mark 1.11 (and parallels). Although the New Testament text is similar to LXX Genesis 22.2, it is unwise for Daly and others to offer a firm conclusion on such little evidence. One is reminded of Sandmel's warning about 'parallelomania' mentioned in the introduction. Mark's choice of words provides an echo[24] of the Akedah but, on their own, they fail to prove a dependency on Genesis 22.2.

The need for extra care is reinforced by the existence of other biblical passages, which might also have provided the New Testament authors with metaphors such as Psalm 2.7, 'I will tell of the decree of the Lord: He said to me, "You are my son, today I have begotten you"'. It is also possible to uncover beloved son imagery elsewhere in the LXX, such as the rendering of Isaiah 3.25. The LXX offers 'your most beautiful son whom you love shall fall by the sword' (ὁ υἱός σου ὁ κάλλιστος, ὃν ἀγαπᾷς, μαχαίρα πεσεῖται) which is a free translation of the Hebrew text, 'your men will fall by the sword' (מתיך בחרב יפלו). Beloved son imagery can also be found in the Apocrypha,[25] Philo[26] and Josephus. For instance, Baruch 4.16 refers to the 'dear beloved children of the widow', while Philo calls Isaac 'the dearly loved, the only true offspring of the soul' (τὸ ἀγαπητὸν καὶ μόνον τῆς

---

[19] Le Déaut 1961:203–4; Vermes 1961:222–3; Daly 1977:67–74.

[20] Jud. 11.34; Jer. 6.26; Amos 8.10; and Zech. 12.10.

[21] LXX Jud. 11.34 illustrates the overlap between μονογενής and ἀγαπητός. This verse describes Jephthah's daughter as 'his only child and his beloved' (αὕτη μονογενὴς αὐτῷ ἀγαπητή), which is a translation of ורק היא יחידה.

[22] *Ant.* 1.222.   [23] Harl 1994:192.   [24] Using Hays's terminology (1989).

[25] Bar. 4.16.   [26] *Deus Imm.* 4. Cf. *Mig. Abr.* 140; *De Somn.* 194; *Alleg.* 3.209.

ψυχῆς). For his part, Josephus describes how Abraham 'passionately loved' (ὑπερηγάπα) Isaac.[27]

Since the vocabulary of Scripture would have been imprinted deeply in the minds of the early exegetes, Mark's description is likely to have been influenced by a variety of biblical texts of which Genesis 22 is but one example. Thus, an association between New Testament Beloved Son imagery and Genesis 22 remains to be proven.

INTERPRETATIONS OF THE PALESTINIAN RABBIS AND THE GREEK CHURCH FATHERS

The rabbis were particularly concerned that the biblical story appeared *in vacuo* and paid keen attention to what preceded the Akedah, a subject of almost no interest to the church fathers. Consequently, they discuss events that took place beforehand and which were understood as contributing to God's test of Abraham.

A number of interpretations discussed the role of angels and their involvement in the test. The rabbis, perhaps influenced by the early interpreters' interest in Mastema, discuss in some detail the contribution of the angels. Examples of rabbinic interest in angels can be found scattered throughout the rabbinic writings. Their views were mixed, and on numerous occasions they suggested that the angels were jealous of humankind's special relationship with God. For instance, it was on account of the angels' jealousy that, when God consulted with them before the creation of humanity, they expressed opposition to the creation of Adam because of the harm he would bring.[28]

This attitude provides the context for the rabbinic interpretation that the angels were resentful of Abraham and made a number of specific accusations against him, which they brought to God's attention. The most commonly mentioned accusation is that Abraham had failed to provide a thanksgiving sacrifice to God or to offer thanks at the birth of Isaac.[29] As a result, God commanded him to sacrifice his son. This explanation was based on an interpretation of the word for God in v. 1, והאלהים, which is normally written as אלהים. In this verse the rabbis interpreted the additional letters וה to mean that God took this action in consultation with His Court.

---

[27] *Ant.* 1.222.
[28] *Gen. Rab.* 8.6 with reference to Ps. 8.5. Cf. *Gen. Rab.* 8.4; *Lev. Rab.* 29.1; *BT San.* 38b; *Lam. Rab.* Pr. 25; *Ecc. Rab.* 7.23.1.
[29] *Gen. Rab.* 55.4; *BT San.* 89b.

This interpretation is not only based upon an exposition of והאלהים, but also takes into account the legal aspect of the verb 'to try' (נסה), emphasizing its judicial overtones. The angels, therefore, are portrayed as prosecutors who made their accusations against the defendant (Abraham) in a court trial (נסיון) before the Judge (God). The rabbis also describe the angels accusing Abraham before the Divine Judge on the charge of having previously made 'a covenant with the peoples of the world' when he made a partnership with the heathen, Abimelech (Genesis 21.27–32).[30]

As well as using legal imagery, this interpretation takes into account the double meaning of דברים, which can be understood as 'words' (or 'exchange of words') as well as 'deeds'. The LXX follows the former understanding, translating דברים in terms of words (ῥήματα). This translation, also taken up by the rabbis, is the basis upon which they outlined the angels' oral accusations before God. Similar accusations were made by the angels against Job and, as we shall see later, there are a number of rabbinic interpretations that contrast the testing of Abraham and the testing of Job.

It is noteworthy that these accusations by the angels were intended as a criticism of Abraham. However, the rabbis also criticized Abraham themselves suggesting, for example, that the trial arose as a result of Abraham's failure to offer a thanksgiving sacrifice after the birth of Isaac. According to one interpretation, Abraham had 'misgivings', which are explained in the Talmud as misgivings over Isaac's weaning feast.[31] Another interpretation, also based upon the opening phrase 'and after these words', explains that God tested Abraham because he questioned aloud God's justice. The rabbis suggest that Abraham wondered whether he had already received his reward from God as a result of his previous escape from the furnace.[32] In other words, he doubted whether God would fulfil his promise and as a result he was required to undergo this trial.

These interpretations show a readiness on the part of the rabbis to criticize Abraham, as they understand the Akedah to be a consequence of Abraham's failings of one sort or another. It is important to point out that rabbinic willingness to criticize Abraham stands in marked contrast to the attitude of the church fathers, who never once attached any blame to Abraham.

Another interpretation to examine the events preceding the Akedah considers the actions and words of Isaac. The rabbis explain that 'after these words' referred to a disagreement between the brothers Isaac and Ishmael about whom their father loved more. Ishmael appeared to have won the

---

[30] *Tan. Eli.* 45. [31] *Gen. Rab.* 55.4, expanded in *BT San.* 89b.
[32] *Tan. B. Lech Lecha* 13; *Tan. Y. Lech Lecha* 10. Cf. Mann (1940, I: 306–7) [Heb. section].

argument because he was circumcised at the age of thirteen years, whereas Isaac was circumcised at eight days – Ishmael's circumcision, unlike Isaac's, was a matter of choice. As a result, so Ishmael argued, he was more beloved than Isaac in the eyes of Abraham. At the moment of Ishmael's apparent triumph, Isaac, twenty-six, thirty-six or thirty-seven years old according to different interpretations, cried plaintively that he would even give up his life should God command it. It was, therefore, 'after these words' that God decided it was time for the test.[33]

This interpretation makes it clear that Isaac's offer to sacrifice his life as an adult was superior to Ishmael's willingness to offer a few drops of blood at the age of thirteen. The rabbis emphasize Isaac's superiority in order to explain why Isaac was chosen, rather than Ishmael, as the designated heir of Abraham. The interpretation on the one hand extols the virtues of Isaac and legitimizes his election and, on the other, condemns the actions of Ishmael and de-legitimizes his position as eldest son. Consequently, Abraham decided to 'give all that he had to Isaac'. These were necessary interpretations to rabbis compelled to explain why the biblical command of Deuteronomy 21.15–21, of the priority of the first-born, even if hated, over the second child, even if loved, was not applicable in the case of Isaac.[34]

The rabbinic interpretations also show that Genesis 22 continued to be a source of controversy in this period. For example, the rabbis explained that one of the purposes of the Akedah was to reply to sceptics who said, 'God will make rich whomsoever He wants to make rich'. The response to such critics was simply 'can you do what Abraham did?'[35] It is unlikely that these sceptics were Christian since the same criticism could be levelled at Christian exegetes. It must, therefore, be assumed that they were pagans who possibly held similar views to the critics attacked by Philo.

The church fathers, for the most part, were not concerned with what might have happened before the Akedah took place. One exception, however, was John Chrysostom who, like the rabbis, did consider the opening phrase 'and after these words' in some detail. Chrysostom, as mentioned previously, is well known for his polemic against Jews and Judaism in the *Adversus Iudaeos* sermons. However, his intimate knowledge of some contemporary Jewish practices is less well known. For example, Chrysostom shows a keen awareness of a variety of Jewish customs in fourth-century

---

[33] *Gen. Rab.* 55.4. Cf. *Tan. B. Ve-yera* 42; *Tan. Y. Ve-yera* 18; *BT San.* 89b. Note that Josephus identifies his age as twenty-five years old.

[34] Gen. 25.5. Cf. *SoS. Rab.* 3.6.2. For a detailed study of the relationship between Ishmael and Isaac as older and younger brothers see Levenson 1993:111–42.

[35] *Gen. Rab.* 55.1.

Antioch, such as the timing of the fasts and dancing in the streets during certain festivals. These writings betray a close attention to the life of
the Jewish community. Chrysostom's polemic illustrates familiarity in the
Christian community of Antioch with contemporary Judaism.[36] Indeed,
the existence of the anti-Jewish polemic in his sermons makes the possibility of a close relationship between Christians and Jews more rather than
less likely.

It is therefore not wholly surprising to discover that he asks the same
question as the rabbis: what was it that occurred before the Akedah that
could elucidate its purpose? In Chrysostom's view, the opening phrase
should be interpreted as 'despite these words' rather than simply 'after
these words'. He suggested that the test could only be understood when
it was appreciated that it took place despite God's promise to Abraham.
This interpretation is supported with reference to Genesis 21.12, indicating that, despite God's promise, he tested Abraham.[37] Although the rabbis
mentioned Genesis 21.12 in passing, the association between this verse and
the Akedah was a minor element in an interpretation critical of Abraham.
For Chrysostom, however, it was central. Since the Sacrifice of Isaac was
recounted shortly after God's promise to Abraham, its purpose was to
instruct people 'in the same love as the patriarch and in showing obedience
to the Lord's commands'.[38] Although Chrysostom's emphasis on obedience mirrors the interpretations of Philo and Josephus, his approach is
similar to that of the rabbis as he is concerned with events that preceded
the test. This does not prove the existence of an exegetical encounter but
illustrates a common approach to Scripture among the church fathers and
rabbis.

This is reinforced by the church fathers sharing with the rabbis a number
of interpretations that explain the reasons for the test. Most of these shared
interpretations can be readily explained with reference to earlier inherited
interpretations rather than to the occurrence of an exegetical encounter.
However, the shared interpretations provide another illustration of a common exegetical framework in Jewish and Christian biblical interpretation.

Examples include patristic and rabbinic concern with, and a desire to
respond to, external criticism of the Akedah and, in particular, to the charge
that God desired human sacrifice. We have noted the rabbinic concern
above but similar interpretations can be found in the writings of a number of
church fathers who felt the need to state explicitly that God does not require

---

[36] E.g., Yom Kippur (*Adv. Iud.* 1.2 Migne); Sukkot (*Adv. Iud.* 7.1 Migne). Cf. Wilken 1983:73–9.
[37] Chry., *Hom. in Gen.*, PG 54 428.   [38] Chry., *Hom. in Gen.*, PG 54 428.

human sacrifice.[39] These interpretations illustrate the continuing concern with pagan criticism, as voiced by Philo, Pseudo-Philo and Josephus.

Diodorus, for example, explains to his audience that 'Moses is going to narrate that God asked Isaac to be sacrificed to him, and in order that you, thinking correctly, be not suspicious about human sacrifice, he says, "He was testing": he was not asking earnestly but was showing the notable faith of this man'. In other words, the test did not demonstrate God's desire for human sacrifice but highlighted Abraham's faithfulness.[40]

Although anxiety about human sacrifice was shared by both the rabbis and the church fathers, specific criticism of Abraham was restricted to the rabbis. It is worth emphasizing that rabbinic criticism of Abraham was not influenced by an inherited tradition – none of the earlier interpretations criticized Abraham.

Another shared interpretation explains that the Akedah enabled Abraham to be honoured throughout the world. Both the church fathers and the rabbis explained that its purpose was to exalt Abraham. For instance, Cyril of Alexandria explains the reason for the Akedah as follows:

This was necessary not in knowledge which alone resides with God to illuminate the head of this just man, but rather to augment his good reputation as most apparent, and in the recognition of all have his fame witnessed by means of the test itself . . . It had to be proclaimed through the sacred writings that so much obedience was in him and his regard for the command of God was so great and that nothing could be greater.[41]

The rabbis also stated that the purpose of the Akedah was to educate the world about the excellence of Abraham. One interpretation declares that the Akedah took place to 'make known to the nations of the world that it was not without good reason that I [God] chose you [Abraham]'.[42]

Although the rabbis also exalted Abraham, the church fathers placed a greater emphasis on Abraham's faithfulness.[43] They stressed his faithfulness more than the rabbis partly as a result of the New Testament referring to the Akedah as an example of Abraham's faithfulness to God.[44] The purpose of the rabbinic interpretation is significantly different because it links the

---

[39] Diodorus, Frg. 203 Petit. See also Chry., *Hom. in Gen.*, PG 54 431 and Basil of Sel., *Orat.* 7 Migne.

[40] Diodorus, Frg. 203 Petit.   [41] Cyril of Alex., *Glaph. in Gen.*, PG 69 144D–146A.

[42] *Tan. B. Ve-yera* 46; *Tan. Y. Ve-yera* 22. Cf. *Tan. B. Behukotai* 7; *Tan. Y. Behukotai* 5. Note the similarities with *LAB* 18.5. Salvesen (1991:43–4) has suggested that the translation of Symmachus might have been influenced by this interpretation. Rather than using ἐπείραζεν, Symmachus rendered נסה as ἐδόξασεν, i.e. God glorified Abraham.

[43] E.g., Chry., *Hom. in Gen.*, PG 54 428; Rom., *In Ab.* 20 Grosdidier de Matons; Cyril of Alex., *Glaph. in Gen.*, PG 69 141C–D.

[44] See v. 3.

Akedah with God's choice of Israel as his people. Thus, rabbinic praise for Abraham is, to a certain degree, dependent upon God's choice of Abraham and his children, the Jewish people. This is illustrated by another interpretation, which explains how the Akedah ensured that the nations of the world could not complain that 'God had made them [Israel] great but did not test them'.[45]

The election of Israel and the granting of God's covenant provide the context for another interpretation, which considers whether the Akedah implied that God would be willing to break his covenant with Israel. If God were willing to ask Abraham to sacrifice his son would he be willing to break his covenant with Abraham's children, the Jewish people? Since the subject of covenant, and especially ownership of the covenant, was a controversial topic in Jewish–Christian relations from the beginnings of Christianity, we should consider whether the interpretation shows signs of being part of an exegetical encounter. It certainly fulfils one criterion (a controversial subject) but little else suggests an encounter.

There are two stages to the interpretation. Firstly, the rabbis compare God's command to Abraham to sacrifice Isaac with other divine commands concerning sacrifice. Just as God did not command Jephthah to sacrifice his daughter,[46] nor the king of Moab to sacrifice his son,[47] so God did not intend Abraham to sacrifice his son. This view is based on an interpretation of the phrase 'and sacrifice him (והעלהו) there for a burnt offering' (לעלה), in which the verb עלה is understood in terms of 'ascending' rather than 'sacrificing'. In other words, the rabbis suggested that God simply commanded Abraham to lead Isaac to the top of Moriah and, having fulfilled this command, both Abraham and Isaac should descend the mountain. The rabbis suggested that such was God's abhorrence of human sacrifice that Abraham must have misunderstood the command. God was described by the rabbis as telling Abraham, 'I did not tell you to slaughter him but to take him up to a beloved place. Now that I have commanded you and you have fulfilled My words, bring him down.'[48] Thus, they conclude, the Akedah did not illustrate a desire on God's part for sacrifice; rather God abhorred sacrifice.[49]

Immediately, one is reminded of the suggestion of Josephus, who also expressed concern about whether or not God required human sacrifice. Likewise, the rabbis stated vehemently that the purpose of the Akedah was not connected with whether God desired human sacrifice.

---

[45] *Tan. B. Ve-yera* 43.   [46] Jud. 11.29–40.   [47] 2 Kgs 3.27.
[48] *Gen. Rab.* 56.8. Cf. *Tan. B. Ve-yera* 40.
[49] This interpretation is expressed in most detail in *Tan. B. Ve-yera* 40. Cf. *Gen. Rab.* 56.8.

The second stage of the interpretation closely associates the Akedah with God's covenant with his people, Israel. The rabbis explain that on account of the Akedah God would not, for any reason, break his covenant with Abraham or his seed. They quote Psalm 89.35 as a proof-text, 'I will not defile my covenant', emphasizing the continuation of God's covenant with Abraham and his children (the Jews). Israel's relationship with God will endure in perpetuity. This psalm was chosen because v. 30–9 describe how God ensures that David's seed will endure forever. Even if Israel transgresses and is punished, 'My mercy will I not break off from him . . . My covenant will I not profane.'

Although this interpretation does not fulfil any criteria other than tackling a controversial subject, the next interpretation we shall consider deserves consideration because it fulfils two of the five criteria outlined in the introduction – the same imagery and the same conclusion. It is repeated in a number of different rabbinic writings and also in an oration of Basil of Seleucia, a fifth-century church father. Both explain that the purpose of the Akedah was to exalt Abraham in the world, and both use nautical imagery in their analysis.

Abraham is described by Basil as an able helmsman who could be compared to a man steering a ship safely in stormy seas in order that his actions might became known in the world. Basil states that God 'drives the ship about with winds so that you might be amazed by the skill of the helmsman. He raises the impact of the waves in order that you might be amazed that the hull is unmoved.'[50]

The rabbis, using similar imagery, explain that God tested (נסה) Abraham so that his actions would become known like a banner or sail of a ship (נס) throughout the world. This interpretation associates the test (נסה) with a ship's ensign (נס) suggesting that the Akedah should be seen like the ensign of a ship.

'You have given a banner (נס) to those who fear You so that it may be displayed (להתנוסס) because of the truth' (Ps. 40.6). This means, trial upon trial, greatness upon greatness, in order to try them in the world and exalt them in the world like a ship's ensign [flying aloft].[51]

Although these interpretations fulfil two of the five criteria, there is insufficient evidence of an exegetical encounter to offer a firm conclusion.

---

[50] Basil of Sel., *Orat.* 7 Migne. Pseudo-Ephrem also offers nautical imagery in an interpretation of the Akedah, *Sermo. in Ab.* Mercati.

[51] *Gen. Rab.* 55.1.

Nevertheless, they demonstrate similarities in Jewish and Christian approaches to Scripture.

Another similarity is that the church fathers and rabbis sometimes asked the same question of the biblical text. This occurred because both the rabbis and the church fathers were very close readers of the biblical text and interested in the detail of Scripture. Without necessarily being aware of each other's interpretations Jewish and Christian exegetes would have immediately noticed any unusual form. A close reading of the biblical text is illustrated by the comment of Origen in a homily on Genesis. Origen commended his community to 'observe each detail of Scripture, which has been written. For, if one knows how to dig into the depth, he will find a treasure in the details, and perhaps also the precious jewels of the mystery lie hidden where they are not esteemed.'[52] It is not entirely by chance that Origen uses the metaphor of 'digging' beneath the text to make sense of it. The metaphor also aptly describes rabbinic hermeneutical methodology, which seeks to derive meaning from the detail of Scripture. For example, the term midrash (מדרש)is derived from the verb 'to enquire' (דרש). Origen is representative of both the patristic and rabbinic commentators when he writes that 'the wisdom of God pervades every divinely inspired writing, reaching out to each single letter'.[53] Attention to the detail of a text can be noted throughout the rabbinic writings as exemplified by Ishmael's list of the thirteen methods of interpretation (*Sifra* 1), the significance of which is emphasized by its incorporation into the daily Jewish service.

The shared attention to the detail of the biblical text is illustrated by another series of interpretations, which fulfils more than one criterion and which concerns God's command to Abraham. In particular, both the rabbis and the church fathers were interested in God's choice of words, 'your son, your only son, whom you love, Isaac'. They asked the same question – why did God not simply say 'Isaac'? – and came to the same conclusion, agreeing that the purpose of the drawn-out description of Isaac was to increase Abraham's affection. According to the rabbis, God's words not only indicated the extent of Abraham's love for Isaac, but also made the test even more severe. Their purpose was 'to make Isaac more beloved in his eyes'.[54] Gregory of Nyssa offered a similar interpretation, which can also be found in the writings of a number of church fathers including Origen, Chrysostom and Romanos:

---

[52] Origen, *Hom. in Gen.* 8.1 Doutreleau.   [53] Origen, *In Ps.* 1.4 PG 12 1081A.
[54] E.g., *Gen. Rab.* 55.7; *Pes. R.* 40.6. Cf. *Gen. Rab.* 39.9.

See the goads of these words, how they prick the innards of the father; how they kindle the flame of nature; how they awaken the love by calling the son 'beloved' (υἱὸν ἀγαπητὸν) and 'the only one' (μονογενῆ).[55] Through these names the affection towards him [Isaac] is brought to the boil.[56]

The patristic exegetes also suggest that Abraham's test was increased in other ways. For instance, Gregory suggested that Isaac's words to Abraham in v. 8 extended 'the test of Abraham's soul', and Basil of Seleucia, probably influenced by Origen, proposed that God's delay in telling Abraham exactly where to slaughter Isaac extended the test still further.[57]

Another example of a shared interpretation is the common use by Jewish and Christian exegetes of dialogue as a means of interpreting the verse. Both the rabbis and the church fathers used dialogue to explain the reason for God's command. The church fathers created an imaginary account of what Abraham might have said to God, but did not. The rabbis, on the other hand, constructed a conversation that Abraham did have with God. The shared use of dialogue offered a number of benefits, not least of which was to add a theatrical dimension to the sermon, which helped retain the interest of the congregation. Chrysostom, known as the 'golden mouth' because of his skill as a preacher, emphasized the importance of maintaining the interest of a congregation who tended 'to listen to a preacher for pleasure, not for profit, like critics at a play or concert'. He warned that if the sermon did not match their expectation, the speaker would leave the pulpit 'the victim of countless jeers and complaints'.[58]

Although the common use of dialogue does not prove the existence of an exegetical encounter, it provides another example of a shared approach to Scripture and indicates that some of the interpretations of the rabbis and church fathers could be understood by both communities. As far as the specific dialogues themselves were concerned, we refer once again to Gregory of Nyssa. Having quoted Genesis 22.2, Gregory proposed the following imaginary words, spoken by Abraham to God:

'Why do You command these things, O Lord? On account of this You made me a father so that I could become a childkiller? On account of this You made me taste the sweet gift so that I could become a story for the world? With my own hands will I slaughter my child and pour an offering of the blood of my family to You? Do you call for such things and do you delight in such sacrifices? Do I kill my son

---

[55] Note the use of both μονογενής and ἀγαπητός.
[56] Greg. of Nys., *De Deitate*, PG 46 568B–C; Chry., *Hom. in Gen.*, PG 54 428; Rom., *In Ab.* 2 Grosdidier de Matons; Origen, *Hom. in Gen.* 8.2 Doutreleau.
[57] Greg. of Nys., *De Deitate*, PG 46 568B–C; Basil of Sel., *Orat.* 7 Migne.
[58] Chry., *De Sac.* 5 Malingrey.

by whom I expected to be buried? Is this the marriage chamber[59] I prepare for him? Is this the feast of marriage that I prepare for him? Will I not light a marriage torch for him but rather a funeral pyre? Will I crown him in addition to these things? Is this how I will be a "father of the nations" – one who has not produced a child?'

Did Abraham say any such word, or think it? Not at all![60]

The dialogue enabled Gregory to force the fathers in his congregation to consider what their reaction might have been had they received such a command. He suggests that, had Abraham hesitated and challenged God, his reaction would have been representative of that of the fathers in his congregation. However, as befits a theatrical performance, Gregory brings Abraham's imaginary questioning to an end with the closing statement that, unlike those fathers, Abraham said no such thing. He did not complain nor think similar thoughts. The dialogue enabled Gregory to reinforce the prevalent patristic exaltation of Abraham. Gregory's stress on the exemplary nature of Abraham allowed him to promote Abraham as a model to admire and to follow.[61] Whilst fathers in Gregory's congregation would 'argue with the command', Abraham 'gave himself up wholly to God and was entirely set on [fulfilling] the commandment'.[62]

The rabbis also used dialogue in their interpretation and, like Gregory, developed an element of theatre:

God said to Abraham: 'Please take your son.'
Abraham said: 'I have two sons, which one?'
God: 'Your only son.'
Abraham: 'The one is the only son of his mother and the other is the only son of his mother.'
God: 'Whom you love.'
Abraham: 'I love this one and I love that one.'
God: 'Isaac.'[63]

The purpose of the rabbinic dialogue was quite different from that of Gregory and it is clear that the rabbis did not offer this interpretation in order to promote Abraham as an ideal figure. In addition to arousing the amusement of the audience, the interpretation reveals that Abraham

---

[59] This is one of many examples of imagery borrowed from Euripedes' *Antigone*. Like Abraham, Antigone lamented the fact that she would have no wedding-song and that her marriage chamber would be her tomb. See v. 3.

[60] Greg. of Nys., *De Deitate*, PG 46 568D.   [61] Cf. Origen, *Hom. in Gen.* 8.7 Doutreleau.

[62] Greg. of Nys., *De Deitate*, PG 46 569A.

[63] *Gen. Rab.* 39.9, 55.7; *BT San.* 89b; *Tan. Y. Ve-yera* 22; *Tan. B. Ve-yera* 44; *Pes. R.* 40.6, 48.2. The rabbis presented (e.g. *BT Baba Metzia* 87a) a similar dialogue between Abraham and the angels in their interpretation of Gen. 18.1, suggesting that the purpose of the biblical text was to make Sarah more beloved in the eyes of Abraham (כדי לחבבה על בעלה).

either deliberately misunderstood the command or attempted to delay its implementation. Whilst the rabbis offered a similar hermeneutical method, in other words the use of dialogue, its purpose is in marked contrast to the conclusion of the church fathers, who did not once question Abraham's desire to fulfil God's command. Thus, although commonality in Jewish and Christian biblical interpretation is, in this instance, illustrated by the joint use of the same mechanism of interpretation (i.e. dialogue), the purpose of the dialogue was quite different.

Another difference between the church fathers and rabbis worth noting is that, although the fathers paid attention to Abraham's (internal) struggle with obedience to the divine command, they did not suggest that he was tempted to challenge God. Origen, for example, simply described it as a conflict between the 'spirit' and the 'flesh'[64] and none of the church fathers suggested that Abraham's internal struggle resulted in objection to God's command. They drew a single portrait of Abraham: a man who suffered upon hearing God's command but who readily and without question fulfilled it. Throughout the ordeal, Abraham is portrayed as a model for Christians to follow as illustrated by the comment of Irenaeus, who commends his community to 'have the faith of Abraham . . . [and] follow him'.[65] At no time did the church fathers criticize Abraham or suggest that he tried to avoid fulfilling the command.

The rabbis, on the other hand, did not draw a single portrait of Abraham, nor did they describe him exclusively as an ideal figure. Rather, they offered a variety of descriptions of Abraham's response to God's command, some of which were critical. Others were notably similar to those of the church fathers, such as their description of Abraham's internal struggle and, in the words of the rabbis, Abraham needed 'to suppress his compassion' for Isaac before being able to fulfil God's command.[66]

Thus, some rabbinic interpretations, unlike those of the church fathers, portrayed Abraham not as a model of faith and obedience, but as a model of reluctance and hesitation. The rabbis' readiness to criticize Abraham was consistent with the interpretations discussed above, according to which the Akedah was the result of Abraham's failure to offer a sacrifice of thanksgiving for the birth of Isaac.

---

[64] Origen, *Hom. in Gen.* 8.3 (Doutreleau) stated that 'in all these things there might be a period of struggle between affection and faith, love of God and love of the flesh, the charm of things present and the expectation of things future'.

[65] Iren., *Catena* 1233 Petit; Cyril of Alex., *Glaph. in Gen.*, PG 69 144D; Cyril of Alex., *Catena* 1237 Petit; Origen, *Hom. in Gen.* 8.7 Doutreleau.

[66] *Gen. Rab.* 56.10. Cf. *Tan. Y. Ve-yera* 23; *Tan. B. Ve-yera* 46.

The significance of the contrast between the rabbinic readiness to criticize Abraham and the church fathers' unqualified admiration will be considered in more detail when we examine the interpretations of v. 9. However, it is worth summarizing the significant differences between the interpretations of vv. 1–2. First, unlike those of the rabbis, there is no hint of any criticism being levelled at Abraham in the writings of the church fathers. Second, the fathers interpreted Abraham as an ideal figure, whose actions were to be wholly admired and imitated. These two differences will become increasingly important as our examination of the interpretations of Genesis 22 continues.

The last interpretation of these verses that we shall consider deals with the subject of priesthood, a well-known source of controversy between Jews and Christians. This disputed subject was central to the interpretations of both the church fathers and the rabbis, although, not surprisingly, their conclusions were diametrically opposed.

The rabbis considered the subject of priesthood in a discussion of Abraham's response to God's command. They depicted Abraham asking God whether he had the authority to sacrifice Isaac. This did not imply that Abraham attempted to delay or postpone the command. He was concerned not with the death of Isaac but with whether he possessed the authority of a priest to sacrifice him.

He [Abraham] said to Him, 'Sovereign of the Universe, can there be a sacrifice without a priest?' 'I have already appointed you a priest' said the Holy One, Blessed be He, 'as it is written "You are a priest forever." (Ps. 110.4)'

Thus, God explains to Abraham that he had already been appointed a priest and cited Psalm 110.4 as clarification.[67] In the previous interpretation, the rabbis had considered Abraham's suitability for priesthood and kingship and concluded that he fitted the position of priest and king.

On two occasions Moses compared himself to Abraham and God answered him, 'do not glorify yourself in the presence of the king and do not stand in the place of great men' (Prov. 25.6). Now Abraham said, 'Here I am' – ready for priesthood and ready for kingship and he attained priesthood and kingship. He attained priesthood as it is said, 'The Lord has promised and will not change: you are a priest forever after Melchizedek' (Ps. 110.4); kingship: 'you are a mighty prince among us' (Gen. 23.5).

Once again, a comparison is made with Melchizedek, but this time the rabbis offer a favourable description of Abraham because, unlike Moses,

---

[67] *Gen. Rab.* 55.7.

he was not asked by God to remove his shoes before the divine presence (cf. Exodus 3.5).[68] The reason why Melchizedek is important to the rabbis is because the priesthood was taken away from him and bestowed upon Abraham.[69] The rabbis suggest that Melchizedek's priesthood was taken away because he blessed Abraham before he blessed God. Another interpretation identifies Melchizedek with Shem thus implying that no priesthood was admitted outside of Judaism.

The interpretations of Origen provide an interesting contrast. Origen begins by describing Isaac not only as the victim, but also as the priest,[70] because whoever carried the wood for the burnt offering must also have borne the office of priest. Origen's interpretation was probably influenced by Philo, who stated that Abraham began 'the sacrificial rite as priest with a son as victim'.[71] Origen suggested that, as a result, Isaac was like Christ, yet Christ was a priest 'forever, according to the order of Melchizedek' (Psalm 110.4).[72]

Interestingly, in direct contrast to Origen's description of Isaac as equal to Abraham in terms of the sacrificial function, the rabbis paid no attention to Isaac's suitability as priest. Rather they emphasized his role in the sacrifice in terms of the offering itself and described him as 'a burnt offering (עולה) without blemish' in accordance with the requirements of a burnt offering.[73]

Origen's reference to Psalm 110.4 is significant; it parallels the rabbis' quotation and, at the same time, mentions Melchizedek, an important figure in the early church. Melchizedek's significance is illustrated by the fact that he is mentioned on nine occasions in the letter to the Hebrews and highlights the superiority of Christ's priesthood over the Levitical priesthood.[74] Hebrews also quotes Psalm 110.4 to reveal the obsolete character of Temple worship and ritual which followed the Levitical order. Since Christ was viewed as high priest 'after the order of Melchizedek' and 'not after the order of Aaron', Christ's priesthood was superior to that of the Levites.

Melchizedek was also an important figure in the Qumran texts. The Melchizedek Scroll, for example, describes Melchizedek passing judgement at the end of the last jubilee.[75] He was also important in the writings of the

---

[68] *Gen. Rab.* 55.6. Cf. *Tan. B. Shem.* 16.

[69] *Lev. Rab.* 25.6, *BT Ned.* 32b; *Mid. Teh.* on Ps. 76.3. Petuchowski (1957:127–36) suggests that the rabbinic interpretation was originally a polemic against the Hasmonean dynasty but was later applied to Christians.

[70] Origen, *Hom. in Gen.* 8.6 Doutreleau.   [71] Philo, *De Ab.* 198. Cf. Runia 1993:157–83.

[72] Origen, *Hom. in Gen.* 8.9 Doutreleau. Note the comment of Eph. Grae., *De Ab.*, Mercati, 80, who stated that 'through the sacrifice he [Abraham] was made a priest (διὰ γὰρ τῆς θυσίας ἱερεὺς ἐγένετο)'.

[73] *Gen. Rab.* 64.3.   [74] Heb. 7.1–11, 17–21.   [75] Horton 1976:60–82.

early church fathers, as illustrated by the following quotation from Justin
Martyr, who explains that the priesthood of Melchizedek was continued
by the priesthood of the early church

Melchizedek, the priest of the Most High was uncircumcised, to whom Abraham,
the first to receive circumcision after the flesh, gave tithes, and Melchizedek blessed
him. It was according to his order that God declared through David that he would
make him a priest forever.[76]

The significance of Melchizedek and of Psalm 110.4, especially its apologetic
overtones, would not have been lost on either Origen or the rabbis. As far as
Origen was concerned, the eternal priesthood of Christ was foreshadowed
by the priesthood of Abraham and Isaac, while in contrast the rabbis argued
that Abraham, rather than Melchizedek, was a priest forever and that this
authority could not be transferred elsewhere. It is worth pointing out that
Abraham is commonly referred to as 'our father Abraham' (אברהם אבינו)
in the rabbinic writings.[77] This rabbinic interpretation might therefore be
understood as a riposte to Christianity because it argued that if Moses, the
greatest prophet of all, was not worthy to be called king and priest, no-one
else (i.e. Jesus) could be king and priest.

    As well as quoting Psalm 110.4, Origen also made the same comparison as
the rabbis between Abraham (and Isaac) and Moses. Abraham, he stated,
was superior to Moses because, among other reasons, he was not asked
to remove his shoes when God gave him the command to sacrifice Isaac,
whereas Moses was asked to remove his shoes when God spoke to him in
the burning bush.[78] Origen did not take the comparison further, which
may also imply exegetical influence. The rabbis, on the other hand, used
the comparison to show that Abraham was suitable not only for priesthood,
but also for kingship, implying presumably that no other person could be
chosen. Abraham, and by extension the Jewish people, would retain this
authority forever and it could not be taken away or appropriated by another
figure.

    There are a number of reasons why we should conclude that these inter-
pretations of Origen and the rabbis illustrate an exegetical encounter:
1. The same scriptural quotations are used (i.e. Psalm 110.4; Exodus 3.4–5) –
   criterion 2.
2. The same literary form is used (i.e. a comparison between Moses and
   Abraham) – criterion 3.

---

[76] Justin, *Dia.* 19, 33 Goodspeed. Cf. Bowker 1969:196–9.   [77] Cf. Jn 8.56.   [78] Ex. 3.5.

3. The opposite conclusions are reached (i.e. Abraham is priest forever; Christ replaces Abraham as priest) – criterion 4.
4. A well-known controversial theme is discussed (i.e. priesthood and authority) – criterion 5.

Thus the interpretations of Origen and *Genesis Rabbah* illustrate four of the five criteria, which suggests that we have uncovered an example of an exegetical encounter.

CONCLUSION

As might be expected, the reason for the test was of interest to both the early interpreters as well as the rabbis and church fathers. The early interpreters explained that the test exemplified Abraham's obedience to God as well as the significance of his faith. They stressed the exemplary nature of Abraham's response and portrayed him as a hero. They emphasized that humankind should not question God, even when being tested. An alternative series of interpretations depicted the angels as the initiators of the test.

One of the rabbinic concerns dealt with whether the Akedah implied that God would break his covenant with Israel. If God were willing to ask Abraham to sacrifice his son he might also be willing to break his covenant with Abraham's seed, the Jewish people. The rabbis explain first that God abhorred sacrifice and second that God would not, on any account, abandon his covenant.

Many of the rabbinic interpretations focused on what took place beforehand and a significant number criticized Abraham. The rabbis suggested that the test occurred because of Abraham's failures and their willingness to criticize Abraham stood in marked contrast to the attitude of the church fathers. The rabbis also offered a number of interpretations that depicted a disagreement between Isaac and Ishmael that resulted in the test.

The rabbis shared a number of interpretations with the church fathers, many of which are to be explained with reference to earlier inherited interpretations rather than to the existence of an exegetical encounter. In particular, they offered similar responses to external criticism of the apparent divine desire for human sacrifice. They also jointly agreed that one of the purposes of the Akedah was to highlight the faithfulness and obedience of Abraham. Abraham was not merely to be admired by both Jews and Christians but was to be exalted throughout the world, and the Akedah provided the justification for such exaltation. This illustrates a common ground between Jewish and Christian exegetes.

Another common interpretation examined God's words 'your son, your only son, whom you love, Isaac'. The rabbis and church fathers asked the same question of the biblical text because they were both interested in the detail of the text and noticed the unusual form. Thus they agreed that the description made Isaac more beloved in the eyes of his father and made the test more severe. Thus, vv. 1–2 illustrate a number of examples of shared interpretations, which demonstrate that the rabbis and church fathers could understand some of each other's interpretations.

The fathers, like the early interpreters, depicted Abraham as a model for Christians to follow and, influenced by New Testament accounts, placed heavy emphasis on Abraham's faithfulness. The rabbis, on the other hand, drew a variety of portraits of Abraham and offered different interpretations of his response to God's command.

Our study of these verses has highlighted one possible and one probable example of an exegetical encounter. The example of a possible encounter exhibited two of the five criteria. First, Jewish and Christian exegetes agreed that the Akedah served to exalt Abraham, and second they both used nautical imagery in their interpretations.

The example of a probable exegetical encounter occurred in a discussion of Abraham's response to God's command and fulfilled four of the five criteria outlined in the introduction. The rabbis portrayed Abraham as a priest appointed forever by divine command, while in contrast the church fathers explained that the priesthood had been transferred from Abraham to Christ. In their interpretations, the rabbis and the fathers not only came to opposite conclusions in their interpretations of a controversial subject, but they also quoted the same scriptural verse (Psalm 110.4), and offered the same comparison (between Abraham and Moses).

CHAPTER 2

Verse 3: The response

v. 3 So Abraham rose early in the morning, saddled his ass and took
two of his young men with him, and his son Isaac; and he cut the
wood for the burnt offering, and arose and went to the place of which
God had told him.

וישכם אברהם בבוקר ויחבש את חמרו ויקח את שני נעריו אתו ואת יצחק בנו ויבקע
את עצי עלה ויקם וילך אל המקום אשר אמר לו האלהים

ἀναστὰς δὲ Αβρααμ τὸ πρωὶ ἐπέσαξεν τὴν ὄνον αὐτοῦ· παρέλαβεν
δὲ μεθ᾽ ἑαυτοῦ δύο παῖδας καὶ Ισαακ τὸν υἱὸν αὐτοῦ καὶ σχίσας
ξύλα εἰς ὁλοκάρπωσιν ἀναστὰς ἐπορεύθη καὶ ἦλθεν ἐπὶ τὸν τόπον,
ὃν εἶπεν αὐτῷ ὁ θεός (τῇ ἡμέρᾳ τῇ τρίτῃ).[1]

EARLY INTERPRETATIONS

In the early interpretations, Abraham was the focus of concern and his
response to God's command was regarded as exemplary in every way.
Indeed, his model response to divine testing exemplified steadfastness and
obedience to God. The Wisdom of Solomon, for instance, explains that
his ability to overcome a father's affection for his son in obedience to God
provided proof of Abraham's righteousness:

> Wisdom also, when the nations in wicked agreement had been put
>   to confusion,
> recognized the righteous man
> and preserved him blameless before God
> and kept him strong in the face of compassion for his child.[2]

---

[1] The LXX assumes that 'on the third day' (ביום השלישי) belongs to v. 3 for it concludes with τῇ ἡμέρᾳ
τῇ τρίτῃ, i.e. Abraham reached Moriah on the third day. The Masoretes included this phrase at the
beginning of v. 4 before וישא, i.e. on the third day Abraham looked up and saw Moriah. The Hebrew
text had no verse numbers and it is, therefore, not possible to be sure of its original location. For
further discussion, see Wevers 1993:318.
[2] Wis. of Sol. 10.5 cf. 4 Mac. 14.20.

A similar interpretation was offered by Ben Sira, who portrayed Abraham as a living example of obedience to God whose faithfulness climaxed in the Akedah.

> Abraham was the great father of a multitude of nations,
> and no-one has been found like him in glory.
> he kept the Law of the Most High,
> and entered into a covenant with him;
> he certified the covenant in his flesh,
> and when he was tested (πειρασμῷ) he proved faithful.[3]

The emphasis on obedience is repeated in 4 Maccabees, which is an examination of 'religious reason's mastery over the emotions'.[4] The author appeals to a number of biblical characters, and especially Abraham and Isaac, and refers to a variety of biblical events, and especially the Akedah. It is clear that, through his description of the martyrdom of Eleazar and a mother with her seven sons, the author views the Akedah as a model to be followed by martyrs. Their torture is described as a 'test' (adopting LXX Genesis 22.1 – πεῖρα) and the seven sons are portrayed in a manner reminiscent of the biblical story. For example, the first child is described as 'bound by his hands and arms' and a 'true son of Abraham'; his brother exhorts the others to 'remember whence you came, and the father by whose hand Isaac gave himself to be sacrificed for piety's sake'.[5]

Comparing themselves to the biblical heroes, they tell the tyrant, Antiochus Epiphanes,

If the aged men of the Hebrews died for religion's sake while enduring torture, it would be even more fitting that we young men should die despising your coercive tortures, which our aged instructor also overcame. Therefore, tyrant put us to the test (πείραζε); if you take our lives because of our religion, do not suppose that you can injure us by torturing us. For we, through this severe suffering and endurance shall have the prize of virtue and shall be with God on whose account we suffer.[6]

Not only are the seven children called true descendants of Abraham[7] but their mother is 'of the same mind as Abraham' and described as a 'daughter of God-fearing Abraham'.[8] She is called 'mother of the nation', another allusion to Abraham, who is similarly called 'father of the nation'.[9] Like the interpretations of the patriarch mentioned above, she remains obedient to God, and her sympathy for her children is overwhelmed by 'devout reason'.

A similar emphasis on Abraham's obedience can also be found in the writings of Philo and Josephus. Philo states that, when Abraham received

---

[3] Ecc. 44.20:   [4] 4 Mac. 1.1, cf. 1.7, 9, 13; 2.24; 3.16.   [5] 4 Mac. 9.11, 21 and 13.12.
[6] 4 Mac. 9.6–8.   [7] 4 Mac. 9.21.   [8] 4 Mac. 14.20 and 15.28.   [9] 4 Mac. 15.29 and 17.20.

the command to sacrifice Isaac, 'though devoted to his son with a fondness which no words can express, [Abraham] showed no change of colour nor weakening of soul but remained as steadfast as ever with a judgment that never bent nor wavered'. Philo explains that his love for God overcame his affection for his son.[10] In his view, Abraham's response to God's command was unique, 'a totally new and extraordinary procedure'[11] and the Akedah was his 'greatest action'.[12] He offers a variety of explanations why the deed really deserves such praise, suggesting among other reasons that, although other people may have sacrificed their children, none had done so for such commendable motives. They might have been influenced by local custom, intended to appease the gods or simply to attain personal glory. None of these reasons are true of Abraham, who made a practice of obedience to God.

Josephus viewed Abraham's willingness to sacrifice Isaac as a great example of faith in God: Abraham believed that 'nothing would justify disobedience to God' since all things had been divinely ordained.[13] Like Philo, Josephus views Abraham's action as his greatest example of faith in God. The virtues of Isaac – obedient to his parents and zealous for God – serve to amplify Abraham's affection for his son. His great love for Isaac, who was born 'on the threshold of old age' emphasizes his faith in God still further. This expression, familiar to all readers of Homer, associates Abraham with Priam, who addresses his son Hector before the latter goes off to battle with Achilles and his death. Josephus does not use this expression by chance – note, for example, that both Abraham and Priam are aged fathers, and Hector and Isaac are both promising sons who are about to die in their youth. Josephus applies another description commonly used of Greek and Roman heroes such as Heracles, Oedipus and Romulus when he describes Isaac as being 'born out of the course of nature'.

These examples illustrate the influence of the style and conventions of Greek literature on Josephus. Spilsbury identifies Josephus' depiction of Abraham as a Hellenistic sage, which is intended to impress an audience of his peers and patrons drawn from the small circle of Roman aristocracy.[14]

The early exegetes shared a number of other interpretations that served to reinforce Abraham's obedience to God. These could often be inferred logically from the biblical text, such as the suggestion of Pseudo-Philo who explained that Abraham set out immediately upon receiving the command[15]

---

[10] Philo, *De Ab.* 170.

[11] *De Ab.* 167. In the same verse Philo states that 'all the other actions which won the favour of God are surpassed by this'.

[12] Philo, *De Ab.* 192–7.   [13] Ant 1.225.   [14] Spilsbury 1994: 9.   [15] Ps. Ph., LAB 32.2.

or, according to *Jubilees*, left before daybreak.[16] Second, Abraham told
neither Sarah nor any of his household of his intentions,[17] and third, because
Abraham did not argue with God, he must have gladly given his consent
to the sacrifice.[18]

1 Maccabees presents a slightly different emphasis in its interpretation of
Abraham's response to God's command. During Mattathias' final speech,
the dying man commends his sons to live their lives like biblical heroes
who achieved fame through their deeds. Mattathias lists a series of examples
and describes both the deed and its reward. For example, although Joseph
suffered trials and tribulations, he kept the commandments and, as a reward,
became lord over Egypt.

Abraham is mentioned first in the list, and Mattathias asks, 'was not
Abraham found faithful when tested ($\pi\epsilon\rho\iota\alpha\sigma\mu\tilde{\omega}$) and it was reckoned to
him as righteousness?'[19] The interpretation associates Abraham's response
to the divine command with faithfulness and links his action in Genesis 22.3
with Genesis 15.6 'he believed the Lord, and it was reckoned to him as righteousness'. In Genesis 15.6, the 'reckoning of righteousness' was associated
with Abraham's belief in God's promise of the birth of a son. The author of
1 Maccabees, however, links it to the Akedah and understands the declaration of righteousness to have resulted from Abraham's trust in God and in
his willingness to perform the sacrifice on Moriah. Thus the interpretation
emphasizes first and foremost Abraham's obedience to God and secondarily
his trust in God, most notably in God's promise. 1 Maccabees changes the
emphasis from praising Abraham's obedience to praising his trust in God.[20]

Before we examine the writings of the church fathers and the rabbis, we
shall consider the only New Testament passages that explicitly comment on
Abraham's response to God's command: the epistle of James and the epistle
to the Hebrews. We should bear two points in mind from the outset. First,
Genesis 22 is central neither to the New Testament writings in general nor
to these epistles in particular. Second, both these New Testament passages
follow the earlier interpretations and provide no change of emphasis.

The lack of references to the Sacrifice of Isaac in the New Testament
deserves comment. Although one has to be cautious about basing arguments
ex silentio, the absence of imagery from Genesis 22 suggests that the biblical

---

[16] E.g., *Jub.* 18.3.   [17] E.g., Jos, Ant 1.225; Philo, *De Ab.* 170.

[18] Pseudo Philo (LAB 40.2), for example, explains that 'the father placed the son as a burnt offering
and he did not dispute him but gladly gave consent to him, and the one being offered was ready
and the one who was offered was rejoicing'.

[19] 1 Mac. 2.52.

[20] This can also be observed in Dan. 3.13–30, which describes how the faithfulness of Shadrach, Meshach
and Abed-nego resulted in their being saved from the furnace.

story was either not of special importance and/or lacked significance to Jesus and his first followers. Since biblical quotations are commonly found throughout the New Testament, one can assume that the authors saw little value in referring to Genesis 22. As a consequence, there is no hint in the New Testament that the Akedah has value in terms of an atoning sacrifice.

It is also worth pointing out that, by emphasizing Abraham's faith and obedience, both James and Hebrews repeat earlier interpretations found in Philo, Josephus and the apocryphal literature. James and Hebrews are important because they provide the context for the later patristic interpretations. Once again however, we should note what is *not* mentioned:

1. A typological interpretation of Genesis 22
2. a reference to fulfilment of Scripture
3. an association between Genesis 22 and salvation through Christ.

We begin with James, who was concerned primarily with encouraging the early Christian community in the face of trials. The theme of testing is central to the epistle,[21] and the author argues that trials produce 'steadfastness'. James associated testing with the eschatological wait (5.7), the need to bring back those who erred (5.19–20) and with the defection of believers (4.1–10). He is concerned with the breakdown of unity, love and charity within the church. The tests of faith were breaking the church apart and Christians were yielding under pressure. In response, the epistle calls for internal unity and charity in the face of outward collapse and raises eschatological expectations. As a result of overcoming the present hardship, James explains, in a term remarkably similar to Philo, that Christians would become 'perfect and complete'.[22] It is also worth mentioning that James 2.22–24 follows 1 Maccabees 2.52 by associating Genesis 15.6 with the Akedah:

Was not Abraham, our Father, justified by works when he offered his son Isaac upon the altar? You see that faith was active along with his works and faith was completed by his works and the scripture was fulfilled which says, 'Abraham believed God and it was reckoned to him as righteousness'; and he was called a friend of God. You see, man is justified by works and not by faith alone.

The significance of the Akedah was that it demonstrated that faith and works were inseparable – faith was worthless unless accompanied by works. The author explains that faith not accompanied by practical action was false and hollow.[23] The Akedah is cited primarily because it illustrated Abraham's

---

[21] E.g., Jas 1.2 and 12.
[22] Jas 1.2–4. Cf. Philo, *De Ab.* 177, who states that Abraham's action, though not resulting in the intended ending was nevertheless 'complete and perfect'.
[23] Cf. Chester and Martin 1994:20–28.

faith alongside his works. It demonstrates that Abraham believed in God's promise of a son and numerous progeny at the same time as he fulfilled God's command to offer his son as a sacrifice. Thus Abraham's faith in God was completed through his practical action in fulfilling God's command.[24] It is worth pointing out the example of the Akedah is followed by a reference to the faith and action of Rahab.

In addition to reinforcing the emphasis on faith, the Akedah might also have been mentioned by James because the significance of Abraham's role caused disagreement in the early church. This passage, therefore, may represent one side of an internal Christian debate about the significance of Abraham's actions with reference to faith and works.[25] Other New Testament passages also discuss the subject of Abraham's faith such as faith in the promise of a son (Romans 4.17–22) or faith in leaving his own land for an unknown country (Hebrews 11.8–9). James, however, is of particular interest because he refers to the same figure as did Paul (i.e. Abraham) and cites the same biblical quotation (Genesis 15.6[26]) to emphasize an aspect of Christian faith in direct contrast to Paul. Although there has been some debate about whether James was responding to Paul's teaching or whether he misrepresented or misunderstood Paul's teaching or even responded to a later form of Paulinism,[27] this passage shows that James clearly has Paul's writings in mind and disagrees with them. James 2.22–4 illustrates an important debate in the early church. It is interesting to note that Paul fails to refer explicitly to the Akedah, and his single allusion to the story, which will be discussed later, deals primarily with the exemplary nature of Abraham's faith.

Returning to James, we discover other signs of a dependency on earlier exegesis. For instance, the description of Abraham as a 'friend of God' (φίλος θεοῦ) was a common expression from biblical times.[28] Interestingly, the author makes no reference to Jesus in the context of faith and when he uses the term 'faithful' it refers exclusively to Abraham's relationship with God. Indeed, the only two references to Jesus are located in the opening verse and in 2.1. Finally, it should also be noted that Isaac plays no role at all in the exegesis and the author fails to draw a Christological conclusion from Genesis 22.

---

[24] Cf. Heb. 11.30.   [25] Cf. Siker 1991:98–102.

[26] Paul quotes Gen. 15.6 in a discussion on Abraham in Rom. 4.3, 9 and 22.

[27] For a helpful discussion, see Chester and Martin 1994:46–53.

[28] Isa. 41.8; 51.2 (LXX = 'whom I have loved', ἠγάπησα); 2 Chron. 20.7; Dan. 3.35 (LXX = 'beloved', τὸν ἠγαπημένον). Other early post-biblical references include *Jub.* 19.9; 2 Esd. 3.14; Philo, *De Ab.* 273; *Sobr.* 56. For further details, see Jacobs 1995:145–53.

A similar emphasis on Abraham's faith, trust and obedience is found in the other explicit New Testament interpretation of the Akedah, in Hebrews 11.17–19. Hebrews 11 examines the relationship between faith and suffering and cites the actions of Abraham, Isaac, Jacob and Joseph, all of whom prevailed in threatening situations. It is their act of faith in the apparent threat to the continuation of the dynasty that represents the common denominator. All four instances involve a choice by God, which demands an unusual response. These figures provide examples of faithfulness to God in the face of adversity. The Akedah is one in a list of many examples of faith, which from v. 3 onwards become increasingly explicit about the relation of faith to suffering:

By faith Abraham, when he was tested (πειραζόμενος), offered up Isaac, and he who had received the promises (ἐπαγγελίας) was ready to offer up his only son (τὸν μονογενῆ), of whom it was said, 'through Isaac shall your descendants be named' (Genesis 21.12). He considered that God was able to raise men even from the dead; hence, figuratively speaking (ἐν παραβολῇ), he did receive him back.

Hebrews 11.17–19 preserves the earlier interpretations, as witnessed by its emphasis on the importance of faithfulness to God in response to suffering, and, like James, we notice no typological or Christological interpretation. The epistle was tailored to Christians, who were suffering on account of their faith, whose lives were being threatened and whose faith was being assailed.[29] In addition, the author was concerned that a number of Christians were returning to Judaism. This served to reinforce his exhortation to Christians to remain faithful, which becomes the central theme of the epistle.[30]

Hebrews explains that the reason Abraham's response to God's command to sacrifice Isaac merited special attention was because the one who 'received the promises' was asked to kill his only son, the one in whom the promises would be realized. The drama of Abraham's test consisted of the command to sacrifice Isaac and of Abraham's willingness to sacrifice the promise. This is suggested by the location of μονογενῆ ('only son'), which parallels ἐπαγγελίας ('promises'), and the author makes clear that Isaac is the 'only son' as far as the promises were concerned. The quotation from Genesis 21.12 and the emphatic placement of ἐν Ἰσαακ ('in Isaac') reinforce his position. The problem the author has is not child sacrifice per se, but rather that the fulfilment of God's promises depends upon Isaac's survival – in other words, the author does not question the morality of God for demanding the sacrifice of a beloved son; rather, the concern of the exegete

---

[29] Cf. Heb. 10.32–9.   [30] Cf. Attridge 1989.

is directed toward a different problem: an apparent contradiction between God's promises and God's command. On the one hand God commanded the sacrifice of Isaac but, on the other, promised posterity through Isaac. How could Abraham reconcile the command of God with the promise of God? According to Hebrews, Abraham realized that the fulfilment of God's promises depended upon Isaac's survival, yet he showed his faith in God by his desire to fulfil God's command.

Thus for Hebrews the Akedah exemplified a trial of faith, in which Abraham was proven true through his obedience and trust. He was a figure to emulate, and his ability to overcome his test provided strong encouragement to Christians who were facing tribulations.[31] Throughout the passage the emphasis is on Abraham and his willingness to overcome the trials through faith and especially his belief in God's power to effect resurrection from the dead.

There is no Christological interpretation in either Hebrews or James that demonstrates that they viewed Genesis 22 as Christologically significant. The expression ἐν παραβολῇ ('figuratively speaking') has sometimes been viewed as pointing towards the future death and resurrection of Christ and therefore providing evidence of a Christological concern in the epistle. However, the expression implies that so dramatic was the story that, for the author of Hebrews, it were as though Isaac had really died and had been raised to life again.[32]

INTERPRETATIONS OF THE PALESTINIAN RABBIS AND THE GREEK CHURCH FATHERS

The writings of the Greek church fathers and those of the Palestinian rabbis show a significant difference in the understanding of Abraham's response to God's command. The church fathers, heavily influenced by James 2.22–4 and Hebrews 11.17–19, follow the earlier interpretations by emphasizing Abraham's obedience and portraying him as a model to follow, particularly in times of difficulty. The rabbis, however, emphasize the consequence of Abraham's obedience and, in particular, *zecut avot* (merit of the fathers). This term means that God remembers the righteous deeds of biblical heroes, particularly the patriarchs, and that, as a result, their children benefit.

The effects of *zecut avot* provide numerous benefits to the Jewish people by, for example, contributing towards the forgiveness of sins and the

---

[31] Cf. Heb. 6.16–19. Cf. Cosby 1988:34–40.

[32] For a summary, see Swetnam 1981:119–23. Interpretations that suggest that Isaac may have been sacrificed will be discussed in more detail below. See vv. 9–12.

redemption of Israel. The rabbis declare, 'Happy are the righteous! Not only do they acquire merit, but they bestow it upon their children, and children's children to the end of all generations'. Another interpretation offers a comparison between Israel and a vine: 'as the vine itself is alive but supported by dead wood so Israel is living but leaning upon the righteous deeds of the deceased fathers'.[33] *Zecut avot* refers primarily to the actions of the three patriarchs, and the rabbis suggest that the deeds of each patriarch provided enough merit for the world 'to be suspended in its position'.[34]

The merit of Abraham was the most significant of the three, and such was its value that, 'notwithstanding all the follies and lies in which Israel engages in this world, Abraham is of sufficient merit to win expiation for all of them'.[35] The rabbis stated that Abraham underwent ten trials and that each of his ten trials (נסים) resulted in some miracle (נס) for his descendants. They explain that the ten tests not only mirror the ten plagues of Egypt but also enable Abraham's descendants to escape them.[36] Although the rabbis failed to agree which they were, they did agree that the Akedah was Abraham's greatest test.[37] The fourth-century church father Basil of Seleucia came to the same conclusion.[38]

Other examples of the beneficial consequences of Abraham's merit include God's Presence (*Shekhina*) dwelling in the Temple and the blood of his circumcision evoking divine mercy. Unsurprisingly, the effect of the 'merit of the fathers' underlies many of the rabbinic interpretations of the Akedah, and since it represented Abraham's greatest test, so it was also the source of the greatest merit to his descendants. The rabbis suggest that the mere recollection of the Akedah is sufficient to evoke God's mercy:

I call heaven and earth to witness that whether Gentile or Israelite, man or woman, slave or handmaid, reads this verse [Leviticus 1.11], the Holy One, Blessed be He, remembers the Binding of Isaac, as it is said 'northward (צפנה) before the Lord.[39]

Although we noted that some of the rabbinic interpretations of vv. 1–2 criticize Abraham, an examination of v. 3 demonstrates eagerness among the rabbis to extol him. Each of the following examples continues the theme of *zecut avot*. For instance, Abraham's enthusiasm to fulfil God's command, by rising early in the morning and by saddling his own ass (rather than allowing his servants to accomplish the task), forestalled the wicked plan of

---

[33] BT *Yoma* 87a; LevRab 36.2.   [34] LevRab 36.5.   [35] PRK 23.8.
[36] ARN 33; LevRab 31.4; TanY *Ve-yera* 4.   [37] E.g., *M. Avot* 5.3; *Neofiti* 22.1; PRE 26.
[38] Basil of Sel, *Orat.* 7 Migne.
[39] LevRab 2.11. Cf. Tan Eli 36. The interpretation understands צפנה as referring to God, who was reminded of the Akedah by the daily sacrifice of the ram. Cf. Vermes 1961:209–11.

Balaam, who also rose early in the morning and likewise saddled his own ass (Numbers 22.21).[40] This interpretation is one of a number that describe the benefits of Abraham's actions. Another mentions that when Abraham stretched out his hand he nullified Pharaoh stretching out his hand against the Israelites as he pursued them in the desert.[41]

The rabbis also discuss the consequences of Abraham cutting his own wood, and, following the standard rabbinic hermeneutical practice of explaining Scripture by Scripture, they compared Genesis 22.4 with Exodus 14.21. Using the principle of *Gezerah shewa* the rabbis noted that not only was the same verb used (בקע) but both the word 'wood' (עצים) and 'waters' (מים) have plural endings in the Hebrew. Thus they associated the Akedah with God dividing the Red Sea to allow the Israelites to escape from Egypt:

[God said] 'because of the merit of the deed which Abraham their father did I will divide the sea for them'. For it is said, 'and he cleaved (ויבקע) the wood (עצים) of the burnt offering'. And here it is written 'And the waters (מים) were divided (ויבקעו)' (Exodus 14.21).[42]

Although many of the rabbinic interpretations are based on the principle *zecut avot*, the majority of the church fathers' interpretations that consider Abraham's willingness to sacrifice his son follow a typological approach. They describe the figure of Isaac as a model (τύπος) of Christ and the actions of Abraham prefiguring the actions of God. Christian typology is based on the premise that the Old Testament prefigures what God would accomplish in the New.[43] In other words, typology provides the church fathers with the means of interpreting the Old Testament in the light of Jesus. One of the primary concerns of typological exegesis is to argue for the unity of the two Testaments. As we shall shortly see, the Sacrifice of Isaac was commonly cited in order to assert the view that the Old Testament was fulfilled in Jesus. The typological approach is exemplified by the following interpretation of Pseudo-Gregory of Nyssa, which portrays God speaking to Abraham as follows:

It suffices for you [Abraham] that you have been honoured by being the type (τῷ τύπῳ). I have an only born son who is beloved. This one will live in the world; this one will be sacrificed on behalf of the world. Your son having awaited the slaughter was of no profit to the world, patriarch; the slaughter of My only born Son will be the salvation of the world.[44]

A similar typological understanding of the story can be found elsewhere. For example, according to Cyril of Alexandria, through the events on Moriah

---

[40] GenRab 55.8; MdRI *Besh.* 2; MdSbY *Besh.* 14.5; BT *San.* 105b; TanB *Bal.* 11; TanY *Bal.* 8.
[41] MdRI *Besh.* 2.   [42] MdRI *Besh.* 4. Cf. MdRSbY *Besh.* 14.15; ExRab 21.8; GenRab 55.8.
[43] E.g., Melito, *PP* 19.   [44] Ps Greg Nys, *In Ab.* Mercati.

the 'mystery of our saviour is typified'. In his *Paschal Homily* Cyril makes frequent reference to the biblical story prefiguring Christ. For instance, 'the child being led to the sacrifice by his father indicates through symbol and outline that neither human strength nor the greed of the conspirators led our Lord Jesus Christ to the cross, but the desire of the Father'.[45]

However, a different emphasis can be discerned in an interpretation of Irenaeus, which might have been influenced by the rabbinic emphasis on *zecut avot*. It differs significantly from the standard typological interpretations, as it assumes that Abraham was rewarded for his actions. It appears that Irenaeus developed a 'meritorial' understanding of the Akedah, suggesting that the willingness, even eagerness, of Abraham to sacrifice Isaac was rewarded. The meritorial approach hints at the existence of a Christian version of *zecut avot*:

And having eagerly yielded his own only-born and beloved [son] himself (τὸν ἴδιον μονογενῆ καὶ ἀγαπητὸν), as a sacrifice to God, in order that (ἵνα) God too might also be pleased to offer His own only-begotten and beloved Son (ὁ θεὸς εὐδοκήσῃ . . . τὸν ἴδιον μονογενῆ καὶ ἀγαπητὸν) on behalf of his seed as a sacrifice for our redemption.[46]

The key to this interpretation is the question whether, in the view of Irenaeus, Abraham's action resulted in God 'offering his only begotten and beloved son'. If Irenaeus understood God's saving action as a response to Abraham's action, his interpretation might be viewed as a Christian version of 'merit of the fathers' and an example of interaction between Jewish and Christian exegetes.

Let us examine this interpretation in a little more detail. The possibility that Irenaeaus' interpretation is influenced by the rabbinic concept of *zecut avot* is dependent upon whether Irenaeus believed that Abraham had some foreknowledge of the purpose of his actions. Did Abraham 'eagerly yield up his only born and beloved son' in order to receive a reciprocal response from God? Unlike the majority of the patristic interpretations, which suggest that Abraham's action was a model for the future sacrifice of Christ and a prefiguring of God abandoning his Son, Irenaeus' meritorial approach implies that Abraham was rewarded for his willingness to sacrifice Isaac by God's corresponding act.

The argument for a meritorial approach is dependent, grammatically, on the reading of the clause 'in order that' (ἵνα). The word denotes purpose and, consequently, implies that Abraham was willing to sacrifice his son for the purpose of enabling God to give up his Son. It seems that Irenaeus interpreted the Akedah in terms of merit and reward. It is true that there

---

[45] Cyril, *Pas. Hom.* 5 Migne.   [46] Iren, *Catena* 1234 Petit.

are a number of parallelisms in the interpretation, which might indicate a typological approach. However, the one reference to εὐδοκήσῃ describes God's action, not that of Abraham. It is difficult to view the interpretation of Irenaeus typologically because it does not compare the actions of Abraham with those of God. Rather, Abraham was rewarded for his response to God's command by God's willingness to give up his Son. As a result of God being 'pleased' by Abraham's action, God was willing 'to offer his only begotten and beloved Son as a sacrifice for our redemption'.

The likelihood that the rabbinic concept of *zecut avot* underlies Irenaeus' comment is further supported by an ancient Armenian version of the same interpretation. This emphasizes Abraham's reward by explicitly demonstrating a correspondence between merit and reward: Abraham was willing to sacrifice Isaac and God was willing to give up his Son. It describes Abraham as 'one who also through faith asked God that for the sake of humanity he might reward him for his son'.[47]

One of the consequences of Irenaeus' interpretation is the suggestion that God gives atonement through Christ as a reward for Abraham's willingness to sacrifice Isaac.[48] Although Paul had alluded to Genesis 22 in Romans 8.32 with reference to God's faithfulness, Irenaeus linked what Abraham was willing to do on Mount Moriah with what God actually did on Golgotha. Irenaeus' interpretation is a significant development from Paul. For Paul, the doctrine of salvation does not hinge upon the merit of Jesus because Christ acted as both righteous God and righteous man to procure victory over sin, death and the powers of darkness. The victory did not come as a divine reward but it lived with Jesus and arose with him from the dead. For Irenaeus, God rewarded Abraham by a corresponding action, not sparing his own Son, but giving him up for the descendents of Abraham.

Another example of a meritorial interpretation of Abraham's action can be found in the writings of Pseudo-Ephrem Graecus:

In your shadow I make clear the truth of all things going to happen in the heavens. I too have an only-born Son, Abraham, who is not known. Because you have given your son and did not spare him I too give My only-born Son after a short time (ὅτι σὺ τὸν υἱὸν δέδωκας μὴ φεισάμενος, κἀγὼ τὸν μονογενῆ τὸν ἐμὸν μετὰ μικρὸν ἐπιδίδωμι). You gave yours to Me and I give Mine to your race. You gave someone of the same line, I give someone of the same essence. Yours was from a childless sterile woman and Mine will soon be from a virgin.[49]

---

[47] *Qui et advocavit per fidem deum quoniam pro filio retribuit ipse.* Irenaeus, *Adv. Haer.* 4, quoted in Rousseau 1966:435.

[48] Cf. Dahl (1969), who examines the Armenian fragment but does not consider the possibility of Jewish influence and the relevance of *zecut avot*.

[49] Ps Eph Grae, *In Ab.* Mercati 103.

This interpretation begins with standard patristic typological exegesis but is not limited to a description of Abraham's actions prefiguring those of God; rather it suggests that, as a result of Abraham abandoning his son, God abandoned his. The author provides further evidence that the church fathers did not interpret Abraham's willingness to give up his only-born son solely in terms of typology. This view is reinforced by the first sentence, which offers a clear typological statement – the shadow (the Hebrew Scriptures) was made clear by the truth (the saving action of Christ). Pseudo-Ephrem Graecus, however, continues in a different vein. He suggests that the action of Abraham should not be understood solely through the prism of the action of God (by giving up his Son); rather the action should be understood as contributing to (and even influencing) God.

These interpretations provide a valuable insight into the early church's understanding of atonement. They imply that the death of Jesus, interpreted as a divine act of redemption, might be understood in terms of 'merit and reward'. The life, death and resurrection of Jesus were believed to bring redemption to Israel according to the Scriptures. The doctrine of atonement was interpreted as fulfilling what God had promised to Abraham by oath: as Abraham had not withheld his son, so God did not spare his own Son.

The interpretations of Irenaeus and Pseudo-Ephrem Graecus indicate that a number of early Jewish and Christian interpretations of Scripture shared the same hermeneutical principles. The Christian meritorial interpretation of Genesis 22 hints at an exegetical encounter.

The existence of an exegetical encounter is also suggested by interpretations that deal with Abraham's obedient response to God. I mentioned above that Gregory of Nyssa described how Abraham might have, but did not, challenge God. Gregory told his congregation that hearing the words of the divine command would strike fathers with terror. He argued that in response any father would become an 'advocate' (συνήγορος) and argue with God against carrying out the sacrifice. Similar interpretations are mentioned by other church fathers. Chrysostom, for example, states that Abraham 'transcended human nature and put all compassion and fatherly affection second to God's commands' and Cyril of Alexandria describes how Abraham 'obeyed God without concern'.[50]

As one would expect, discussion of Abraham's obedience and response to God's command is also common to rabbinic interpretations. The following

---

[50] Greg. of Nys., *De Deitate* PG 46 568C–D; Chry, *Hom. in Gen.*, PG 54 429–30; Cyril of Alex, *Hom. Pas.* 5 Burns.

interpretation describes Abraham's request to God that he be rewarded as follows:

May it be Your will, O Lord our God, that whenever Isaac's children enter into distress, and there is no-one to speak in their defence, You shall speak in their defence. ((συνηγορία) סניגוריא עליהם ילמד מי להם ואין)[51]

This passage is noteworthy because, when examined alongside the interpretation offered by Gregory of Nyssa, it fulfils a number of the criteria that identify an exegetical encounter. First, the interpretations examine the same theme – Abraham's obedience – and second, they arrive at the opposite conclusions on the subject of advocacy. Third, both Gregory and the rabbis not only use the same legal imagery but also even the same technical term *synagoria* which is a Hebrew transliteration (סניגוריא) of the Greek word (συνηγορία). סניגוריא is rarely found in the rabbinic writings[52] and its inclusion in both interpretations is significant. It is also worth mentioning that סניגוריא was removed in the parallel interpretations edited after the Jerusalem Talmud.

The theme of obedience is a common thread running throughout the interpretations of the church fathers. For example, 'learn to be submissive'[53] was the theme of *1 Clement*, which referred to the Akedah as an example of obedience and a model for Christians to follow. Clement wrote the epistle to the community at Corinth and told them that just as Abraham rendered obedience to God, so the community should also obey the words of Clement and his presbyters; just as Abraham was rewarded by God, so Christians would be rewarded for listening to the presbyters. Once again we can see an emphasis on reward, mirroring the rabbinic concept of *zecut avot*.

Emphasis on obedience is also found in the writings of Gregory of Nyssa, who described Abraham as follows:

When he saw the aim of the command, he turned towards divine love and resolutely ignored nature, and resisted much of the earthly burden which is the empathetic disposition of nature and he gave himself up wholly to God and was entirely set on [fulfilling] the commandment.[54]

Gregory's interpretation finds parallels in other patristic writings. For example, Ephrem the Greek describes Abraham as follows:

---

[51] JT *Ta'an.* 65d. Cf. GenRab 56.10; LevRab 29.9; TanB *Ve-yera* 46; TanY *Ve-yera* 23; PesR 40.6.

[52] Only the JT uses the transliteration סניגוריא in this interpretation, although the term can be found on a number of other occasions, e.g. LevRab 23.9; ExRab 15.29, 38.8, 43:1. Cf. Sperber 1984:128–9.

[53] *1 Clem.* 57:3.   [54] Greg of Nys, *De Deitate* PG 46 569A.

Having become obedient [in response to the divine command] he kindled his love more furiously than the fire and his desire sharper than the sword and cut the chains of nature, as if leaving some earthly mass of sympathetic disposition. Willingly he had given over his whole self and was completely of the commandment to slaughter his son.[55]

Following the New Testament interpretations, Gregory demonstrates how the church fathers acclaim Abraham's response to and acceptance of his trial and depict him as a model both to admire and emulate. We should remember that the persecutions of the early Christian communities were still in recent memory and that Julian the Apostate had been killed a few years earlier in 363 CE. Indeed, although the conversion of Constantine occurred in 313 CE and an orthodox Christian emperor, Theodosius I, succeeded to the imperial throne in 379 CE, Christianity did not dominate society in the late fourth century. New Testament passages that exhorted the community to remain faithful in times of difficulty possessed particular significance for these later generations. One of the reasons why the figure of Abraham retained such prominence during the period under review was that the various trials that took place during his lifetime had contemporary relevance. This was particularly true of the Akedah.

For example, Irenaeus examines Abraham's trust in God and comments on the phrase that Abraham 'believed God, and it was reckoned to him as righteousness'. He states that 'we also, having the faith of Abraham, and having taken up the cross as Isaac took up the bundles of wood, follow him'.[56] Irenaeus explains that the action of Abraham provides a model for Christians to follow. The mention of Abraham as a model is reminiscent of the rabbinic interpretation of נס (banner) and נסה (test – mentioned above), which described the testing of Abraham as a banner for the world to admire and follow. Once again we notice that interpretations shared by Christians and Jews are commonplace.

Abraham's faith in God is upheld by a number of other church fathers, such as Cyril of Alexandria, who wrote that Abraham 'conveyed his child into the sacrifice, not having been in despair over the commandments but having placed himself in the power of the Lord because he knew the promise would be fulfilled'.[57] Such interpretations should be understood as a continuation of the earlier double emphasis on Abraham's obedience and trust.

---

[55] Eph Grae, *In Ab*. Mercati. See also Cyril of Alex, *Hom. Pas*. Burns.
[56] Iren., *Catena* 1233 Petit. Cf. *Adv. Haer*. 4.5.4 Rousseau and Doutreleau. Greg. of Naz., *Orat*. 1 Bernardi.
[57] Cyril of Alex., *Glaph. in Gen.*, PG 69 145A.

Abraham's enthusiasm to carry out the command was also discussed. According to Pseudo-Gregory, Abraham 'hurried toward the mountain' upon receiving the command[58] and Origen states that 'on hearing that he was to sacrifice his son, he does not hesitate, but complies with the command'.[59] Chrysostom also offers a similar interpretation, describing Abraham as 'putting all compassion and fatherly affection second to God's commands he hastened their discharge'.[60] This represents another example of a shared interpretation, because the rabbis also maintained that Abraham set out immediately after God had spoken to him, basing this interpretation on Genesis 22.3, that Abraham 'rose early in the morning'.[61]

Other examples of shared interpretations include rabbinic discussion of how Abraham suppressed his urge to question God and overcame his love for Isaac. A number of rabbis considered Abraham's decision not to challenge God. According to one interpretation, Abraham said:

Sovereign of the Universe! When you commanded me, 'Take now your son, your only one . . .' I could have answered, 'Yesterday You promised me 'For in Isaac shall your seed be called . . .' Yet, God forbid! I did not do this but suppressed my feelings of compassion in order to do Your will.[62]

The church fathers also explained how Abraham accepted his trial without questioning God.[63] For example, Abraham's decision not to challenge God is discussed by Basil of Seleucia, who wrote:

So how did he not bristle at his voice? How did his soul not contract? How did he not anticipate the slaughter of his child by his own death? O! The strength of his soul! He did not groan. He did not weep. He did not yield to his nature (οὐκ εἶξε τῇ φύσει). He was not divided in purposes. Nor did he change his facial expression. Nor did he let out a paternal cry, refusing the slaughter of his child.[64]

As we saw in the previous chapter, Abraham's determination not to question God provided an opportunity for some church fathers to offer long and eloquent accounts of what Abraham might have said (but did not) to God.[65] Like the rabbis, they also comment on the incongruity between God's promise and Abraham's enthusiasm to fulfil God's command. Origen suggests that, even though the command would have forced Abraham

---

[58] Ps. Greg. Nys., *In Ab.* Mercati. Cf. Rom, *De Ab.* 3 Grosdidier de Matons; Origen, *Hom. in Gen.* 8.4 Doutreleau.

[59] Origen, *In Cant.*, Prol. 3.18 Brésard and Crouzel.

[60] Chry, *Hom. in Gen.*, PG 54 429.   [61] E.g., TanY *Ve-yera* 22; *Frg. Tg.*: 22.14

[62] GenRab 56.10. Cf. JT *Ta'an.* 65d; LevRab 29.9; TanB *Ve-yera* 46; TanY *Ve-yera* 23; PesR 40.6.

[63] E.g., Greg of Nys, *De Deitate*, PG 46 568D–569A; Origen, *Hom. in Gen.* 8.7 Doutreleau; PesR 40.6. Cf. Philo, *De Ab.* 170.

[64] Basil of Sel, *Orat.* 7 Migne.   [65] See vv. 1–2.

to recall the promise, he nevertheless 'does not deliberate, he does not reconsider, he does not take counsel with any man, but immediately he sets out on the journey'.[66] Other examples of interpretations common to the rabbis and church fathers include discussion of Abraham's lack of concern over accusations of being a childkiller,[67] of not being mad[68] and of his silence.

By now, it will have become clear to the reader that classical Christian and Jewish interpretations of Genesis 22 share a great deal in common. I have made it clear, however, that shared interpretations do not in themselves prove the occurrence of an exegetical encounter, since other factors may also have been involved. For example, concern about being accused a childkiller should not be considered as evidence of an exegetical encounter because such an accusation is a logical interpretation that can be derived from the text. However, shared interpretations indicate that Jewish and Christian exegetes sometimes asked the same questions of the biblical text and came to the same conclusion. This makes an encounter more rather than less likely. We should not be surprised, therefore, if we come across evidence, because shared interpretations and common conclusions are likely to provide a fertile ground for an exegetical encounter.

A study by Rowan Greer of early biblical interpretation also supports the argument that a careful reading of biblical interpretation will help us uncover an exegetical encounter. He describes how Jews and Christians were united 'in assuming the general correlation of sacred texts with the beliefs and practices of religious communities'.[69] That is, Scripture both authenticates the existence and practice of faith communities and is also formed through its interpretation. In the first three verses, we have already noticed this process in a number of shared interpretations, as well as some exegetical encounters.

Let us consider Abraham's silence in more detail. Earlier interpretations that discussed Abraham's silence were repeated by a number of church fathers, such as Basil of Seleucia, who wrote that 'having taken silence as his partner he was entirely at one with the command'.[70] The rabbis also stated that Abraham 'did not say anything but kept silent'.[71] Such was the significance of Abraham's silence that 'only for Abraham does the Holy One, Blessed be He, keep silent'.[72]

---

[66] Origen, *Hom. in Gen.* 8.4 Doutreleau.

[67] E.g., Greg of Nys, *De Deitate*, PG 46 568D; Rom, *De Ab.* 3–6 Grosdidier de Matons; GenRab 56.4; TanB *Ve-yera* 46; TanY *Ve-yera* 23.

[68] Rom, *De Ab.* 3 Grosdidier de Matons; GenRab 56.4.   [69] Kugel and Greer 1986: 126.

[70] Basil of Sel, *Orat.* 7 Migne.   [71] TanB *Ve-yera* 39.   [72] TanB *Ve-yera* 10.

The subject of silence was also discussed in some detail by the church fathers with reference to Sarah. They were particularly interested in why Abraham had avoided telling Sarah of God's intention and what Sarah might have said had she known. Their interest in Sarah is influenced by a typological understanding of Sarah as a model of Mary, as the comments of Ephrem Graecus make clear:

It was not an act of nature for her almost dead womb to conceive, and her dry breasts to furnish milk for Isaac. It was not an act of nature for the maiden Mary to conceive without a man, and to bear the saviour of all free men from mortality. He made Sarah a mother in old age, and he showed Mary to be a virgin after childbirth. An angel in the tent said to the patriarch, 'at the appointed time, there will be a son for Sarah' (Genesis 18.10). An angel in Bethlehem said to Mary, 'You will give birth to a son, having been shown grace' (Luke 1.31).[73]

For their part, the rabbis were far less interested in Sarah, although they also commented on the miracle of the milk returning to Sarah's breast.[74] Nevertheless, on those few occasions the rabbis mention her, their interpretations include a number of parallels with those of the church fathers. Like many of the church fathers, the rabbis assume that Abraham did not inform Sarah of God's command. For example, they suggest that Abraham told Sarah that he was taking Isaac to a place where he could be educated:

Abraham had asked himself: what shall I do? If I tell Sarah about it [God's command], consider what may happen. After all, a woman's mind becomes distraught over insignificant matters; how much more disturbed would she become if she heard something as shocking as this! However, if I tell her nothing at all and simply steal him away from her when she is not looking, she will kill herself. What did he do? He said to Sarah: 'Prepare some food and drink that we may eat and rejoice.' 'But why is this day different from other days?' she asked. 'What are you celebrating?' He replied: 'When a couple our age has a son it is fitting, indeed they should eat, drink and rejoice.' Whereupon she prepared the food. While they were eating, he said to her: 'When I was a child of three, I already knew my Creator, yet this child is growing up and still has no instruction. There is a place a short distance away where children are being taught, I will take him there.' She answered: 'Go in peace.'[75]

---

[73] Eph Grae, *De Ab*. Mercati. Although Mercati (1915: 46–7) argues that this poem originated from Ephrem the Syrian, no Syriac original appears and it is unclear whether any existed. Brock (1986:66) categorizes this work as that of Ephrem the Greek. It is certainly true, however, that Sarah was of significant interest to the Syriac interpreters. For a summary of the interpretations of the Syriac fathers with reference to Sarah, see Brock 1974.

[74] GenRab 53.9; TanB *Ve-yera* 37; TanY *Toldot* 3; BT *Baba Metzia* 87a.   [75] TanY *Ve-yera* 22.

Nevertheless, this interpretation concludes, although Sarah agreed with Abraham's decision, he still left early the next morning for 'he said to himself: perhaps Sarah will change her mind and not permit me to go; I will arise before she does'.

The church fathers also suggest that the main reason why Abraham failed to tell Sarah was that he feared she would attempt to stop the sacrifice. Sarah would have been overwhelmed by nature and would have tried to persuade Abraham not to fulfil the command. However, such was Abraham's faith in God that he was not put off by his nature or by what Sarah might have said. For instance, according to Basil of Seleucia, Abraham tells himself that

She is pious (φιλόθεος), he says, and although being amazed at her will and disposition, I fear her nature (αἰδοῦμαι τὴν φύσιν). Although seeing the piety, I fear the love. The woman is pious, but she is a mother. It is a terrible thing when mothers are overpowered by the weakness of nature (ἀσθενείᾳ . . .φύσεως). I fear lest she defile the sacrifice through weeping. Lest she outrage the commandment-Maker through lamenting her child. Lest beating her face, she ruins the sacrifice and does violence to God. Lest, cowering with respect to her mind, she strips the grace from the remarkable event.[76]

Gregory of Nyssa was more critical. Abraham, he explained, 'judged the woman untrustworthy for deliberation'.[77] Once again we note the similarity with the rabbinic interpretation.

Mention of Sarah allowed Christian exegetes to create an imaginary dialogue between Abraham and Sarah, some of which demonstrates similarities with the imaginary challenge of Abraham discussed in our analysis of the interpretations of vv. 1–2. Gregory of Nyssa, for example, describes in some detail what Sarah might have said had she been informed of God's command. She is portrayed as a grief-stricken mother who would rather die than see Isaac killed. In the following passage Sarah appeals to Abraham 'to spare' (φεῖσαι) Isaac.[78] Abraham, whose strength is illustrated by his willingness to give up his son while Sarah's weakness is symbolized by her desire to withhold her son, refuses her request:

What sort of words would she have used? 'Spare (φεῖσαι) nature, husband. Do not become a wicked story for the world. This is my only-born son, my only-born in birthpangs, Isaac, alone in my arms. He is my first and last child. Whom will we see after this one at our table? Who will call his sweet voice to me? Who will call for mother? Who will attend my old age? Who will wrap up my body after my

---

[76] Basil of Sel, *Orat.* 7 Migne.   [77] Greg of Nys, *De Deitate*, PG 46 569A.
[78] This word echoes οὐκ ἐφείσω from LXX Gen. 22.14. Gregory's choice of φεῖσαι might also allude to Christ in view of the reference to μονογενής.

Table 1

Sarah	Antigone
'Is this the marriage chamber I prepare for him? Is this the feast of marriage that I prepare for him? Will I not light a marriage torch for him but rather a funeral pyre?'	Antigone laments the fact that she will have no wedding-song and that her marriage chamber will be her tomb. Creon's servants describe the tomb as 'death's hollow marriage-chamber'.
'Let the eyes of Sarah see neither Abraham as a childkiller nor Isaac killed by his father's hands.'	Oedipus blinded himself at the death of Jocasta.
'This one is the staff of our old age'.	Antigone was the staff of Oedipus.
'Who will wrap up my body after my death? Who will heap up a mound over the body? . . . Let a common burial mound stand for both of us . . . let common dust cover our bodies; let a common tombstone tell of our suffering.'	Antigone builds a burial-mound for her brother; she covers his body with dust; she explains that she washed the bodies of her father, mother, and brother and dressed them for the grave.

death? Who will heap up a mound over the body? Do you see the bloom of youth (τὸ ἄνθος τοῦ νέου), which even an enemy would see, and would wholly pity his age? This one is the fruit of a great prayer; this one is the branch of our succession; this one is the remnant of our people; this one is the staff of our old age. If you bear the sword against this one, grant me this favour: use the sword first on me and then do this thing that seems best to this one. Let a common mound stand for both of us; let common dust cover our bodies; let a common tombstone tell of our suffering. Let the eyes of Sarah see neither Abraham as a childkiller (Ἀβρααμ παιδοκτονοῦντα) nor Isaac killed by his father's hands.'[79]

This passage illustrates the strong influence of classical pagan writings such as *Antigone* and the *Iliad*, on Gregory's interpretations. These ancient stories provided the images and vocabulary, which Gregory adopted in his portrayal of the Akedah. For example, note the questions raised by Sarah which are paralleled by Antigone in Table 1.

An example of the Iliad's influence can be seen in Gregory's adoption of the Homeric phrase 'bloom of youth' (τὸ ἄνθος τοῦ νέου), which would remind the congregation of Hector, who was killed in his prime by Achilles. Hector's mother, Hecabe, warned him against going into battle with Achilles: 'If he brings you down, I shall no longer be allowed to mourn you, laid out on your bed, dear bloom of youth, born of me!'

[79] Greg of Nys, *De Deitate* PG 46 569 B–C.

Gregory incorporates the ancient Greek images into his interpretations because he is concerned to show the superiority of the biblical story to the Greek myth. For example, Abraham and Isaac were strong and survived the ordeal; Hector was strong but was killed. Unlike Priam and Hecabe, Abraham did not mourn his son. Although Sarah was weak and overcome by nature, her life, unlike Antigone's, did not end in tragedy.

Romanos, the sixth-century Byzantine poet, also examines the role of Sarah. He describes how Sarah pleaded with Abraham: 'I beg of you that he [Isaac] not leave me and kill me with grief'.[80] Abraham warns Sarah not to weep, otherwise she will 'put a blemish' (μῶμον ἐπιθήσεις) on the sacrifice.[81] A similar interpretation is offered by the rabbis who, without referring to Sarah, mention that the knife had been dissolved by the tears of the angels. Abraham, however, asked that at least he be allowed to bring forth a drop of blood, but was told not to do anything (מואמה) to Isaac, nor to inflict a blemish (מומה) on him.[82]

Basil of Seleucia comments on Sarah's weeping and takes her impending mourning so seriously that he describes Abraham meditating on which words he should use to comfort Sarah after the sacrifice of Isaac has taken place:

I will tell her, the lamenting one, after the sacrifice. I will take care of her when she is weeping. Saying such things to her as: 'Stop your crying. Do not weep for your son. He has been honoured by this sacrifice. The child was a gift that was granting pain. The father did not kill the child for the greater benefit of himself. The right hand, having dared the sacrifice, renders a service done. Whom He gave, He asked for, and whom He fashioned, He sought again, and having sought him He took him, and this one having been asked for, is the one God gave. If He wishes it, He will return him, being hindered by no-one.[83]

Although the rabbis did not adopt pagan imagery in their interpretations of Sarah, their descriptions mirror some of the patristic interpretations. Interestingly, one of the few rabbinic interpretations to mention Sarah discusses her death and suggests that she died upon learning what Abraham intended to do to Isaac:

Satan visited Sarah in the guise of Isaac. When she saw him she asked, 'What did your father do to you, my son?' He replied, 'My father led me over mountains and through valleys until we finally reached the top of a certain mountain. There he erected an altar, arranged the firewood, bound me upon the altar, took a knife to slaughter me. If the Holy One, Blessed be He, had not called out, "Lay not your

[80] Rom, *De Ab.* 8 Grosdidier de Matons.   [81] Rom, *De Ab.* 12 Grosdidier de Matons.
[82] GenRab 56.7.   [83] Basil of Sel, *Orat.* 7 Migne.

hand upon the lad" I would have been slaughtered.' He had hardly completed relating what had transpired when she fainted and died, as it is written 'And Abraham came to mourn for Sarah'. From where did he come? From Moriah.[84]

Another interpretation depicts Isaac as asking Abraham to take his ashes to his mother. 'Isaac kissed his father Abraham, and commanded him and told him, "Sprinkle my blood over the altar, assemble my dust and bring it to my mother." '[85]

Finally, we should mention a strand of patristic exegesis represented by Romanos and Pseudo-Ephrem Graecus, which suggests that Abraham told Sarah about the impending sacrifice.[86] Pseudo-Ephrem Graecus states that Abraham 'spoke to the mother of the child about the coming sacrifice [saying] "learn what is going to happen" '. The recently published fourth-century Greek Bodmer Poem also considers Abraham's comments on the impending sacrifice before it took place. Abraham tells Sarah that 'the Immortal God wishes that I should bring noble Isaac' and Sarah responds positively, advising Isaac to 'take courage'.[87] Romanos for his part offers a number of interpretations that are not found in any other writings. For instance, he writes that Sarah asked Abraham why God gave them a child if he wanted to take him back? How would it be possible for her to become pregnant again? She wanted God or the angel, not Abraham, to tell her of the command. In reply, Abraham told Sarah not to blemish the sacrifice with her tears and that they were merely returning to God what was his. Eventually Sarah accepted the necessity of the sacrifice and told Isaac to go with his father.[88]

CONCLUSION

In the early interpretations, Abraham's response to God's command was regarded as exemplary in every way. His was the model response to divine testing for it illustrated steadfastness and obedience to God. An additional element, that of faithfulness, was mentioned in 1 Maccabees. Abraham's faithfulness was illustrated by the fact that he did not challenge God, told nobody about the command and (almost) immediately set out on his journey. Abraham was portrayed as a model to admire and to follow.

---

[84] TanY *Ve-yera* 23. Cf. LevRab 20.2; TanB *Ahre Mot* 3; *Ecc. Rab.* 9.7.1.
[85] Anonymous *piyyut* reconstructed from Genizah manuscripts by Sokoloff and Yahalom (1999: 124–31).
[86] Ps. Eph. Grae., *De Ab.* Mercati 100.
[87] Hurst and Rudhardt 1999: 37–56. Cf. Hilhorst 2002: 96–108.
[88] Rom, *De Ab.* 7–14 Grosdidier de Matons.

The exemplary aspect of Abraham's response was developed in the two New Testament passages that referred briefly but explicitly to Genesis 22: James 2.22–4 and Hebrews 11.17–19. Both emphasized the traditional association between faith, trust and obedience. It is noteworthy that the Akedah was not central to the arguments of either James or Hebrews. Their dependence on earlier interpretations and the lack of detailed interpretation indicates that it was not a significant text but was primarily cited to exhort the early Christian community to remain steadfast during times of suffering. The lack of reference to the Akedah elsewhere in the New Testament is also notable.

Nevertheless, New Testament references, whilst short, provided the basis for the later interpretations of the church fathers. For the most part, the church fathers followed the traditional twofold interpretation of Abraham's response: faithfulness in a time of trial associated with trust in and obedience to God. Abraham was portrayed as a model to follow, which appeared particularly apposite during times of trial. In contrast, the rabbis did not discuss the Akedah with reference to the suffering of Israel nor did they depict Abraham as a model to follow in times of trouble.

A new development in the writings of the church fathers, not found in the rabbinic interpretations, considered the role and feelings of Sarah. Her importance was partly a result of an exegetical link between Sarah and Mary. There was disagreement about whether Sarah was told about God's command, but the church fathers agreed that she would have attempted/did attempt to persuade Abraham not to carry out the sacrifice.

For their part, the rabbis hardly mentioned Sarah nor did they portray Abraham as a model to follow. The rabbis emphasized the *consequence* of Abraham's obedience and, in particular, the concept of *zecut avot* dominated rabbinic interpretations of the Akedah. For example, Abraham's enthusiasm to fulfil God's command forestalled the wicked plan of Balaam. For the rabbis, the Akedah provided benefit to the Jewish people throughout time; for the church fathers it provided a model (Abraham), particularly helpful in times of suffering.

Our study of v. 3 has illustrated a number of shared interpretations that considered Abraham's response to the divine command. Both the church fathers and the rabbis agreed that Abraham set out immediately upon receiving the command, suppressed his urge to question God, overcame his love for Isaac, maintained a silence, was not mad and was not concerned about being accused a childkiller. These examples of shared interpretations do not necessarily illustrate an exegetical encounter because they can either be derived from the biblical text or can be found in earlier interpretations.

Nevertheless, they are important because they alert us to the commonality between Jewish and Christian interpretations as well as to the possibility of discovering examples of exegetical encounter.

This is illustrated by a Christian version of *zecut avot*, an interpretation of Irenaeus. The interpretation follows the rabbinic meritorial approach. The key to the interpretation is whether, in the view of Irenaeus, Abraham's action *resulted* in God 'offering his only begotten and beloved son'. It is significant that, according to Irenaeus, God had acted this way as a result of Abraham's action, implying that God rewarded Abraham for his action, a view that is reinforced by an Armenian version, which emphasized Abraham's reward by demonstrating correspondence between merit (Abraham's willingness to sacrifice Isaac) and reward (God's willingness to give up his Son).

A second possible example of an exegetical encounter was noted in interpretations that considered Abraham's obedience. Both Jewish and Christian exegetes used the same legal imagery in their interpretations and even the same technical term. Although it was noted that *synagoria* (סניגוריא = συνηγορία) is a technical term that can occasionally be found in rabbinic writings, it is significant that the word was cited by both the church fathers and the rabbis and that it was removed in later parallel interpretations.

CHAPTER 3

Verses 4–5: The servants and the three-day journey

v. 4 On the third day Abraham lifted up his eyes and saw the place afar off. v. 5 Then Abraham said to his young men, 'Stay here with the ass; I and the lad will go yonder, and worship, and come again to you.'

ביום השלישי וישא אברהם את עיניו וירא את המקום מרחק: ויאמר אברהם אל נעריו
שבו לכם פה עם החמור ואני והנער נלכה עד כה ונשתחוה ונשובה אליכם:

(τῇ ἡμέρᾳ τῇ τρίτῃ) καὶ ἀναβλέψας Αβρααμ τοῖς ὀφθαλμοῖς εἶδεν τὸν τόπον μακρόθεν. καὶ εἶπεν Αβρααμ τοῖς παισὶν αὐτοῦ καθίσατε αὐτοῦ μετὰ τῆς ὄνου, ἐγὼ δὲ καὶ τὸ παιδάριον διελευσόμεθα ἕως ὧδε καὶ προσκυνήσαντες ἀναστρέψωμεν πρὸς ὑμᾶς.

EARLY INTERPRETATIONS

Verses 4–5 did not receive a detailed examination in the period preceding the interpretations of the church fathers and rabbis. They were not cited by Pseudo-Philo, nor were they mentioned in the Apocryphal and Pseudepigraphical writings. Even Josephus omitted part of v. 4 in his recounting of the Akedah, probably because it conflicted with the purpose of *Jewish Antiquities*.

Although Josephus states at the beginning of his work that he 'neither added nor omitted anything',[1] it was not unusual for him to revise a biblical story. As well as omissions, Josephus also made a number of expansions. For example, in *Antiquities*, he emphasises the significance of the LXX translation of Exodus 22.28; whereas the Hebrew text reads, 'You shall not revile God' the LXX renders, 'You shall not revile the gods'. Josephus explains that 'one is expressly forbidden to deride or blaspheme the gods recognised by others out of respect for the very word "God"'.[2] Another example of

---

[1] Ant 1.17.   [2] *Contra Ap* 2.237.

Josephus' desire to revise the biblical story can be seen in his paraphrase of Genesis 22.17, 'I promise that I will give you as many descendants as there are stars in the sky or grains of sand along the seashore. Your descendants will conquer your enemies.' Josephus offers:

He moreover foretold that their race would swell into a multitude of nations, with increasing wealth, nations whose founders would be had in everlasting remembrance, that they would subdue Canaan by their arms and be envied of all men.[3]

Clearly Josephus did not wish to offend his Roman patrons. As far as Abraham was concerned, we have already suggested that Josephus portrayed him as a national hero, such as was popular in Hellenistic times.[4] His apologetic concerns are illustrated by his commentary on the Sacrifice of Isaac, for he modifies Genesis 22.4 and deletes Abraham's comment to his two servants that both father and son would return. This omission probably reflects Josephus' unease with Abraham's deception and his apparent deviousness. Its removal illustrates that his revisions were carefully thought out.[5]

Josephus' apologetic concerns might also have been shared by the author of *Jubilees*, who, whilst accurately recounting the biblical account of Abraham's words to his servants, added the comment, not repeated elsewhere, that they were left 'near a well of water'.[6]

The main concern of the early interpretations of vv. 4–5 relates to the site of the Akedah. The LXX translation of 'to the land of Moriah' (אל ארץ המריה) as 'to the high land' (εἰς τὴν γῆν τὴν ὑψηλήν) is consistent with the rendering of 'oak of Moreh' (אלון מורה) by 'the high oak' (τὴν δρῦν τὴν ὑψηλήν) in Genesis 12.6 and 'oaks of Moreh' (אלוני מרה) by 'high oak' (τῆς δρυὸς τῆς ὑψηλῆς) in Deuteronomy 11.30.[7] *Jubilees* also calls Moriah the 'high land' and describes Abraham approaching the 'mountain of God', which is identified explicitly with Mount Zion.[8] This identification is consistent with the later biblical writings, which associate Mount Zion with the Temple and describe, for example, the Lord as dwelling on Mount

---

[3] Ant 1.235.

[4] Feldman and Hata 1987:137. On the other hand, Spilsbury (1994:26) has warned 'that it should not be assumed that instances of hellenization in the *Antiquities* are always to be taken as propaganda, as Feldman seems to suggest. They are just as likely to be the genuine expressions of Josephus' own understanding of the biblical narrative.'

[5] Cf. Franxman 1979:289.   [6] *Jub.* 18.4.

[7] Wevers (1996:96) suggests the translation is derived from רום.   [8] *Jub.* 18.8 and 13.

Zion.[9] Josephus, influenced by 2 Chronicles 3.1, also connects Moriah with Solomon's Temple in Jerusalem.[10]

Philo makes no mention of Mount Zion or Moriah, although, as a result of the LXX rendering, he does express interest in the apparent contradiction between the words 'he came to the place' and, shortly after, 'he saw the place from afar'. The LXX placed 'on the third day' at the end of Verse 3 and, as a result, it modified 'came to the place'. It describes Abraham arriving on the third day. The Masoretic Text, on the other hand, located 'on the third day' at the beginning of v. 4, which implies that Abraham looked up and saw the place on the third day. The LXX, therefore, caused a difficulty for exegetes because it described Abraham as reaching his destination on the third day but, shortly afterwards, only seeing it from afar. The Masoretic Text, however, simply described Abraham as 'getting up and going towards the place' that God had told him to and, in the next verse, seeing it from afar. As a result, Philo and the church fathers wrestled with a problem of which the rabbis seemed unaware.

Philo argues that 'place', apart from its ordinary sense, might also indicate the Logos that God filled or even God himself. Philo describes Abraham as journeying along the path that would take him through knowledge and wisdom before coming into contact with divine words (λόγοι) and the realization that God would always be 'at a distance'. Having reached the divine Logos, Abraham saw God from afar[11] because God, by definition, was beyond man's capacity and the divine Logos represented the upper limit of man's possible attainment.

Finally, vv. 4–5 refer to the servants or young men (נעריו). The LXX understands נעריו as 'servants', rather than 'young men', which the Hebrew term might also mean. This interpretation is followed by both the rabbis and the church fathers. The LXX makes little distinction between 'servant' (עבד) and 'youth' (נער) and uses παῖς for both, even though נער refers to a 'youth' or 'lad' and עבד to 'servant' or 'slave'. Interestingly, the LXX renders a different translation when נער refers to Isaac (παιδάριον = youth) or to the servants (παῖς = servant).[12] The purpose of this distinction is unclear, although it is possible that the intention is to emphasize Isaac's youth

---

[9] E.g., Isa. 8.18; Ps. 9.12 and 65.2–3.

[10] Ant 1.227; 7.333. 2 Chron. 3.1, 'Solomon began building the Lord's Temple in Jerusalem on Mount Moriah, where the Lord had appeared to his father David. This was the place that David prepared at the threshing floor of Ornan the Jebusite.'

[11] *De Somn.* 66–7. Cf. *De Post.* 17–18.

[12] Note that παιδάριον renders ילד ('child') in Gen. 37.30 and 42.22 in reference to Joseph. Cf. Wright 1995:263–77, who discusses the Greek translations of עבד.

compared to that of the servants. It is worth pointing out that none of the early interpretations attempted to identify the servants, although Philo calls them 'the oldest and most loyal'.[13]

INTERPRETATIONS OF THE PALESTINIAN RABBIS AND THE GREEK CHURCH FATHERS

The interpretations of the church fathers and the rabbis can be more clearly examined when divided into two sections: the three-day journey and Abraham and the servants.

The three-day journey

The length of Abraham's journey was of interest to the church fathers from as early as the second century CE. Clement of Alexandria describes the three days as a symbol of the seal by which one believed in God.[14] Clement was one of a number of interpreters who commented on the contradiction between how Abraham could arrive at the place of sacrifice and yet afterwards see it from afar. His response was to offer an allegorical interpretation that illustrates Clement's dependence on Philo.[15] Cyril of Alexandria also examined the contradiction between the two statements and explains that 'Abraham seeing this region from afar, indicates the pre-existent foreknowledge of the Father concerning His own off-spring, Christ'.[16]

Origen called the three-day journey a 'mystery' (μυστήριον) and was one of a number of church fathers who discussed it with reference to the day of Christ's resurrection:

The third day, however, is always applied to the mysteries. For also, when the people had departed from Egypt, they offer sacrifice to God on the third day and are purified on the third day. And the third day is the day of the Lord's resurrection. Many other mysteries are also included within this day.[17]

At first glance, it seems surprising that Origen simply noted the association between the three-day period and the day of Christ's resurrection but failed to offer a more extensive interpretation. The same duration of time would seem to provide an exemplary proof-text with which to argue that the Hebrew Scriptures prefigured the New Testament. We should remember that proof-texts were commonly used in the patristic writings to show that

---

[13] *De Ab.* 170.   [14] *Strom.* 5, 11.73 Le Boulluec.
[15] *Strom.* 5, 11.73 Le Boulluec. Cf. Le Boulluec's comments (SC 278: 251–3). For a discussion of Philo's influence on Clement, see Runia 1993:132–56.
[16] Cyril of Alex, *Hom. Pas.* 5 Burns.   [17] *Hom. in Gen.* 8.4 Doutreleau.

the Hebrew Bible contained, in a veiled and hidden form, an outline, sketch or prediction of the future establishment of the Christian faith.

This argument is clearly and vehemently expressed by the second-century CE theologian Melito of Sardis:

What is said and done is nothing, beloved, without a comparison and preliminary sketch (δίχα παραβολῆς καὶ προκεντήματος) . . . The people was precious before the church arose, and the law was marvellous before the gospel was elucidated. But when the church arose and the gospel took precedence, the model is made void (ὁ τύπος ἐκενώθη), conceding its power to the reality, and the law was fulfilled (ὁ νόμος ἐπληρώθη), conceding its power to the gospel.[18]

Cyril of Alexandria also explained that the Hebrew Bible was a shadow of things, that it was 'the teacher who leads beautifully to the mystery of Christ',[19] demonstrating that the Jewish way of life had been superseded and a new way established. One of the guiding principles in the *Adversus Iudaeos* literature was that the Hebrew Bible was no longer the history of the Jewish people but, in fact, a witness to Christian truth. Christianity claimed the Jewish Scriptures and, in the words of Justin Martyr to Trypho, they 'are your scriptures, or rather, not yours but ours, for we obey them, but you, when you read, do not understand their sense'.[20]

Origen, however, appears reluctant to apply this principle to v. 4 and decided not to offer a Christological interpretation of Abraham's three-day journey. His general statement that 'the third day, however, is always applied to the mysteries', his allusion to a number of other biblical references to the third day and his mild concluding comment 'many other mysteries are also included within this day' are surprising. Is it possible that Origen might have deliberately avoided adopting the Sacrifice of Isaac as a proof-text? His interpretation needs careful consideration.

Although any argument *ex silentio* must be tentative – and we must add a further note of caution because Origen's writings survive, for the most part, in a Latin translation, of unknown quality, from a Greek original – we should consider the possibility that Origen's reluctance was influenced by contemporary rabbinic interpretations. There are a number of notable parallels between the Jewish and Christian interpretations that considered the significance of the third day. For example, like Origen, the rabbis list a series of biblical references to third day, the consequence of which, however, was to minimize the significance of the reference to the third day in Genesis 22.4. This provided the rabbis with a riposte to Christians who may have used the reference as a proof-text and applied to it a

---

[18] PP 35–42 Hall.   [19] Cyril of Alex, *De Ador*. PG 68 140A.   [20] Justin, *Dia.* 29 Goodspeed.

Christological interpretation. According to the rabbis, Genesis 22.4 is simply one of many biblical references to the third day that makes any individual reference to the third day less applicable on its own to the day of Christ's resurrection.

The rabbis mention a series of miraculous events, all of which occurred on a third day:

• the day of resurrection (Hosea 6.2)
• the words of Joseph to his brothers (Genesis 42.18 'do this and live')
• the day of the giving of the Torah (Exodus 19.18)
• the hiding of the spies (Joshua 2.19)
• Esther putting on her dress to meet Ahasuerus (Esther 5.1)
• Ezra and the exiles from Babylon, who stayed in Jerusalem for three days (Ezra 8.32).[21]

The list of examples enabled the rabbis to emphasize the miraculous life-giving consequence of each biblical story. It was the combination of biblical references to a three-day period that was important rather than any single biblical account. Abraham's three-day journey was simply one more example of a life-giving miracle. Christian exegetes, such as Origen, who might have been aware of the rabbinic interpretation because they lived in areas inhabited by Jews, would have been presented with it as an objection had they argued that Genesis 22.4 simply prefigured the resurrection of Christ. The rabbinic interpretation demonstrated that the verse was simply one among many found in the Bible that referred to a three-day period. Origen's reticence to offer a more detailed interpretation can be more easily understood when viewed alongside this rabbinic argument. The possibility of an exegetical encounter is increased further by the observation that both the rabbis and Origen referred to Exodus 19.18 in their interpretations. Thus, three criteria for a possible exegetical encounter are fulfilled by these interpretations: a controversial theme (resurrection and the fulfilment of Scripture), a similar list of examples as well as the same quotation (Exodus 19.18) and opposite conclusions.

The church fathers and rabbis not only considered the significance of the third day, but also examined the purpose of the journey. Why, for example, did the journey not last one or two days? Their answers offer a number of examples of shared interpretation. The rabbis explain that the purpose of the journey was to ensure that 'the nations of the world do not say that Abraham was in a state of confusion when he sacrificed his son' – he had three days to reflect upon the command.[22] This interpretation parallels that of Chrysostom, who suggests that Abraham's 'thinking was not deranged;

---

[21] GenRab 56.1.   [22] TanY *Ve-yera* 22. Cf. GenRab 55.6; TanB *Ve-yera* 46; PesR 40.6.

his mind not confused; he was not at a loss to cope with the strangeness of the command'.[23]

Jewish and Christian exegetes also agree that the three-day journey enabled Abraham to ponder the divine command and forced him to endure the torture of considering what lay ahead and, in the words of Origen, 'along the whole journey be torn to pieces with his thoughts'.[24] The rabbis, for their part, also suggest that the purpose of the journey was 'to afflict him' during the three days.[25] According to a number of rabbinic interpretations, Satan increased the torment further and, for example, placed obstacles on the journey to prevent Abraham and Isaac reaching the place of sacrifice.[26] He also attempted to persuade Abraham not to sacrifice his son,[27] because the nations of the world would condemn him as a childkiller. The church fathers, although they did not mention Satan, also suggested that Abraham would be called a childkiller.[28]

Another subject of mutual interest concerns the site of the Akedah. We noted above that the LXX renders 'the land of Moriah' as 'the high land', and does not mention the name 'Moriah'. This may partly be influenced by the book of *Jubilees*, which adopts the same phrase, and perhaps also because of the similarity of Moriah to *moros* (μωρός), which means folly. Pagan critics such as Apion would have taken delight in associating Moriah with folly, implying that Abraham was commanded by God to take his son to the mountain of folly![29]

The meaning, as well as the location, of Moriah became the subject of much discussion in the writings of the rabbis and church fathers, and the subject of concern to the biblical translators. The word is probably derived from the Hebrew verb 'to see', and the theme of vision was an important element in nearly all the interpretations. For example, the rabbis suggested that Moriah referred to 'the place of vision' (יהא מראה)[30] and it is worth noting that the Samaritan translation renders 'land of revelation' (המוראה). These interpretations were reinforced by the phrase in Genesis 22.14 (which is commonly translated either as 'on the mountain of the Lord he will be seen' or 'on the mountain of the Lord it will be provided' – בהר

---

[23] *Hom. in Gen.* PG 54 429.

[24] *Hom. in Gen.* 8.3 Doutreleau. Cf. Chry, *Hom. in Gen.* PG 54 330: 'Consider as well what it was likely the good man endured in the three days as he calculated the meaning of the command and pondered the fact that he was destined to put to death with his own hands the son he loved so much.'

[25] *Midrash Zuta*, Buber (1894:4).   [26] TanY *Ve-yera* 22.

[27] GenRab 56.4. Cf. BT *San.* 89b; TanB *Ve-yera* 46; TanY *Ve-yera* 22; PesR 40.6.

[28] See above pp. 75–6.

[29] Pagan use of word-plays in polemic was not unusual, e.g. Apion (*Contra Ap.* 2.20–7) suggested that the word 'Sabbath' was associated with a disease of the groin, *sabbo* (σαββώ).

[30] GenRab 55.7.

יהוה יראה) which could easily be understood as a 'mountain of vision'. The LXX and Vulgate render this phrase as 'in the mount the Lord was seen'.[31] It is also worth noting in connection with Moriah that LXX 2 Chronicles 3.1 offers the following addition to the Masoretic Text, 'the Lord appeared unto David', which reinforces the association between Moriah and vision of the Lord.[32]

Likewise, the targumic translations imply that Abraham's visionary experience provided support for the location of the Temple on Mount Zion/Moriah.[33] In other words, the visual appearance of God's Presence legitimized the Temple's position as the place of sacrifice. For example, Aquila renders 'land of Moriah' as 'that which is clearly seen'. Symmachus also offers 'vision', which may have influenced Jerome's choice of *visionis* in the Vulgate translation.[34] Onkelos offers 'land of worship', which is consistent with his addition of 'before Me' in his translation of v. 2 – in other words, Abraham was commanded to offer Isaac before God. In the Samaritan writings the site of the Akedah is identified with Mount Gerizim and is a key feature of the Samaritan argument with Judaism over the site of the Temple.[35] *Neofiti* adds 'to the land of *Mount* Moriah' rather than the 'land of Moriah', emphasizing the connection between the sacrificial site of Genesis 22 and the Temple. This interpretation is made explicit by *Targum Pseudo-Jonathan* and *Sifre* Deuteronomy 28. The former identifies the place where Isaac was bound as the 'mount of worship'.[36] The latter states that the phrase 'on the mountain of the Lord' refers to the Temple, 'for everybody calls it a mountain – Abraham, Moses (Deuteronomy 3.25), David (Psalm 24.3), Isaiah (Isaiah 2.2) and the nations (Isaiah 2.3).'

These targumic translations are similar to the rabbinic interpretations that suggested that Moriah corresponded (ראי) to the Temple on High. The theme of worship was also mentioned by the rabbis, and Moriah was described as a place of incense (מור),[37] and other rabbinic interpretations likewise emphasize its holiness. For example, it is variously described as the place of instruction (הוראה), awe (יראה) and the seat of the world's dominion

---

[31] The LXX ἐν τῷ ὄρει κύριος ὤφθη clearly provides the translation of the Vulgate 'in monte Dominus videbit'.

[32] GenRab 55.7. LXX 2 Chron. 3.1: καὶ ἤρξατο Σαλωμων τοῦ οἰκοδομεῖν τὸν οἶκον κυρίου ἐν Ιερουσαλημ ἐν ὄρει τοῦ Αμορια οὗ ὤφθη Κύριος τῷ Δαυιδ πατρὶ αὐτοῦ. The LXX addition, 'where the Lord appeared unto David', is not found in the Masoretic Text (ויחל שלמה לבנות את בית יהוה בירושלם בהר המוריה אשר נראה לדויד אביהו)

[33] Cf. comments of Levenson (1993:94–5).

[34] Salvesen 1991:44. However, Hayward (1995:177) suggests that Jerome associated Moriah with אור or אורה rather than ראה.

[35] Kalimi 2002: 48–58.   [36] *Tg.* Ps Jon on Lev. 9.2.

[37] SoS. *Rab.* 4.6.2; GenRab 55.7. Myrrh was one of the ingredients used in the preparation of the oil and incense in the Temple (cf. Ex. 30.23–9).

(מרוותה). It is even described as the place from which God shoots at (מורא) the nations and hurls them into Gehenna.[38] All of these interpretations consist of a play on words with Moriah.

The sanctity of Moriah might also have provided the context for a well-known rabbinic interpretation, which suggests that Abraham saw a cloud enveloping the mountain.[39] The appearance of the cloud, representing the Divine Presence, indicated to Abraham the site of the sacrifice. Isaac also saw the cloud, but the servants, who saw nothing, were told to stay behind, which implies that only Abraham and Isaac were granted the privilege of seeing the Divine Presence. This interpretation is somewhat similar to a Qumran fragment that refers to Abraham seeing a 'fire' on Moriah. The fire also represents a divine apparition as illustrated in a later midrash, *Pirkei de Rabbi Eliezer*, which mentions a 'pillar of fire extending from the earth to the heavens'.[40]

This interpretation provides us with another example of an exegetical encounter because Isho'Dad of Merv, the ninth-century east Syrian Christian interpreter, was clearly aware of its existence because in his commentary on Genesis he states that Abraham 'saw a column of light in that place going up to heaven. Others say that he saw the column of light in the form of a cross'.[41]

Although the Greek fathers showed no awareness of a cloud surrounding the mountain, they did share with the rabbis an exegetical interest in the site of the sacrifice and also emphasized its holiness. For example, Melito offers the following typological interpretation:

> And the Lord was a lamb like the ram
> which Abraham saw caught in a sabek tree (ἐν φυτῷ Σαβέκ)[42]
> but the tree displayed the cross,
> and that place, Jerusalem,
> and the lamb, the Lord fettered for slaughter.[43]

---

[38] GenRab 55.7; PesR 40.6.

[39] GenRab 56.1 and 2; LevRab 20.2; TanB *Ve-yera* 46; TanY *Ve-yera* 23; PRK 26.3; PesR 40.6. Cf. Klein 1986:34; Grelot 1957:12–13.

[40] 4Q225 and PRE 31. Cf. Fitzmyer 2002:211–29.

[41] CSCO 126:173. Cf. Parmentier 1996:111; Brock 1981a:10.

[42] 'Bush' (סבך) is transliterated in the LXX σαβεκ, indicating that it was the name of the bush. *Neofiti* uses 'tree' (אילנא) as did Onk (although it is worth noting that Onk also uses אילנא in the translation of שיח (Gen. 2.5)). *Tg.* Ps-Jon gives 'branches of a tree' (רחישותא דאילנא), Aq has 'thicket' (συχνῶνος) and Sym offers 'net' (δίκτυον), which, according to Salvesen (1991:45), was adopted to avoid a Christological interpretation.

[43] Melito Frg. 11 Hall. This may explain why Melito stated elsewhere that 'Isaac was offered in the midst', i.e., in view of many people, even though the biblical account clearly explained that Abraham and Isaac were alone on Moriah. The reason for this discrepancy can probably be found in Melito's emphasis on typology: the site of the sacrifice was Jerusalem and Jesus was crucified in front of many people.

Melito's interest in the location, which might have been influenced by his pilgrimage to the Land of Israel, serves to emphasize Christ's fulfilment of Scripture.[44]

The next interpretation we shall consider develops further the traditional association between Moriah and Jerusalem. According to Eusebius, as a result of the journey to Moriah, 'God showed Abraham where Christ was crucified'.[45] Another version of the same interpretation states, 'where the temple is established, there Isaac is sacrificed; but it is perhaps better said, where the Son of God is crucified'.[46]

Eusebius was the first church father to identify the site of the Akedah with that of Christ's sacrifice. The exegetical development from an association of Moriah with Jerusalem (and/or the Temple) to the site of Christ's crucifixion illustrates Eusebius' emphasis on sacrifice and holiness.

Eusebius' interpretation also sheds light on Christian sixth-century travel accounts offering a description of an altar that stood against the slope of Golgotha and that was thought to have been built by Abraham for the sacrifice of Isaac.[47] Isho'Dad of Merv commented that 'the altar was built on the spot where Solomon would build the Temple, where Adam lay buried and where our Lord would be crucified'. A remarkably similar interpretation is found in *Targum Pseudo-Jonathan*, which explained that the Temple was located on an altar built by Adam, destroyed by the flood, rebuilt by Noah and finally destroyed by the generation of the division. The Targum describes how Abraham rebuilt the altar, and this interpretation suggests that the sanctity of the Temple stretched back to the time of Adam.[48]

The rabbinic interpretations that examine the association between the site of the Akedah and Jerusalem or the Temple consider the reasons for the destruction of the Temple in 70 CE. This event, as well as the expulsion of Jews by Hadrian after the Bar Kochba revolt in 135 CE, were commonly cited by the church fathers (and pagans) as a demonstration of God's rejection of the Jewish people. For instance, according to Origen, the dispersal of the Jews invalidated Jewish practice because it was bound to the city of Jerusalem.[49] In response, the rabbis offered a number of

---

[44] Frg. 3 Hall, cf. Harvey 1967:401–4.
[45] Euseb, *Catena* 1242 Petit.   [46] Euseb, *Catena* 1260 Petit.
[47] Theodosius mentions (CSEL 39:140) that the place of the Sacrifice of Isaac was also the site of Calvary. This interpretation may explain the representation on the Bury St Edmund's Cross on which the cross of Christ is planted on the grave of Adam. Cf. Milgrom 1988:97, n. 1.
[48] *Tg.* Ps Jon 22.9. Isho'Dad of Merv CSCO 126:172–6. Cf. Parmentier 1996:111; Brock 1981a:8–9.
[49] *Contra Celsum* 4.22 Borret; *Hom. in Josh.* 17.1 Jaubert. For a summary of Christian comments on the destruction of the Temple and the dispersal of the Jewish people, see Wilken 1983:134–8.

explanations for the disaster, which served both to encourage the Jewish community and reply to external criticism. They explained that Jerusalem was destroyed because, for example, the Sabbath was profaned, the Shema was neglected, the rabbis were despised and because there were no people of faith.[50]

One attempt to explain the destruction is found in a detailed exegesis of a number of key words from vv. 4–5 (מרחק 'from afar', פֹּה 'here', שבו 'stay' and חמור 'donkey'). The rabbis offered the following interpretation, which examines whether the destruction of the Temple signalled the end of the covenant between God and Israel:

In the future this place will be alienated from its Owner (לירחק בעליו). Will this last forever? No, for it is written, 'This is my resting place for ever; here (פֹּה) will I dwell (אשב) for I have desired it' (Psalm 132.14); when he comes of whom it is written, 'Lowly, and riding upon an ass (חמור)' (Zechariah 9.9).[51]

This interpretation demonstrates the rabbis' perennial concern with the destruction of Jerusalem and with how long the city and the Temple would be separated from God. The answer of the rabbis was that, just as Abraham saw the mountain from afar (מרחק) and reached the site soon after, so God would not be alienated (לירחק) from the Temple forever but would return (אשב) to his home (פֹּה). In other words, Jerusalem would return to its previous glory, and Jews, who only saw Jerusalem from a distance, would also return to their home (Zion).[52] The rabbis quote Psalm 132.14 partly because it emphasizes God's promise to Israel and partly because it refers to God's eternal choice of Zion and to his messiah. The messianic theme is reinforced by a quotation from Zechariah 9.9, which predicts that the messiah would arrive on an ass; just as Abraham and Isaac would return from the mountain to the ass so the messiah would arrive on an ass.

This interpretation makes clear that there was a divine purpose behind the destruction of the Temple and the dispersion of the Jewish people. The destruction had messianic consequences and did not imply the end of the covenant between God and Israel, for God would remain faithful to his promise. The rabbinic interpretation fulfilled a role similar to the epistle to the Hebrews and the epistle of James, encouraging the faithful to cling onto their faith in the face of trials.

---

[50] BT *Shab.* 119b. Cf. BT *Yoma* 9b. [51] GenRab 56.2. Cf. Tos *Ber.* 1 and ExRab 31.10.
[52] Cf. *Midrash Zuta* Buber (1894:4): "'Stay here . . .' – why is this written? To teach that the site for the Temple had been chosen as indicated by the use of "here"', (פֹּה), Ps. 132.14.

Abraham and the servants

Both the rabbis and church fathers considered in some detail the role of the servants, and especially Abraham's words to them.

As mentioned above, the rabbis suggested that, because the servants were unable to see the cloud that surrounded the mountain, they were told to stay 'with' (עם) the ass. By changing the vocalization of עם, the rabbis interpreted 'with' as 'people'. The servants were therefore described as a 'people of an ass' (עם החמור),[53] for they represented people who 'see and do not understand'.[54] The rabbis were clearly concerned with their spiritual, rather than any physical, blindness and concluded that, as a result, the servants had not been allowed to continue the journey.

The church fathers also associated the servants with the ass, likewise suggesting that they could not see. For their part, they linked the blindness of the servants with the blindness of Jews. Cyril of Alexandria, as we shall shortly see, offers an interpretation of why the servants were not entrusted to go up to 'the highest and sacred (ἱεράν) land'.[55] This is of particular interest because it offers a number of sharp criticisms, which may reveal a contemporary fifth-century argument between Jews and Christians.

The Alexandrian Jewish community was of concern to Cyril who, according to a study by Haas, emerged 'as one of the principal players on the urban scene of fifth-century Alexandria'.[56] Cyril's ruthless dealings with the Jewish community (and others) were reported in the eyewitness account of Socrates and, in 415 CE, Cyril expelled the Jewish community from the city.[57] Since Cyril also mentioned ongoing Jewish activity in his *Paschal Homily* of 416 CE,[58] the expulsion probably affected only one section of the community, or perhaps Jews were allowed back into the city soon afterwards. The fact that the Jewish and Christian communities had good relations clearly irked for he rages:

Since it is possible to bear fruit spiritually in the churches of Christ, what reason could there be for wanting to be joined, as it were, and to be in communion with profane synagogues, and to provoke the God of the universe against us?[59]

It is likely that he faced the same problems as John Chrysostom, who observed Christians attending synagogue on Saturday and church on

---

[53] GenRab 56.2.   [54] TanB *Ve-yera* 46; TanY *Ve-yera* 23.

[55] It is possible that ἱεράν referred to Jerusalem, thus emphasizing the holiness of the site of the Akedah.

[56] Haas 1997:91.

[57] Socratis Hesmiale Sozomeni, *Hist. Eccl.* 7.13 Migne. Cf. Wilken 1971:54–7; Haas 1997:297–305.

[58] *Hom. Pasco.* 3 Burns.   [59] Cyril of Alex., *Hom. in Mal.* Migne, cf. O'Keefe (1993:143–144).

Sunday.[60] Cyril's complaint that Judaism attracted Christians from his community suggests that he was also well acquainted with Jews[61] and that many in his community had close relations with their Jewish neighbours. There is a striking parallel between Antioch and Alexandria, since it seems that good relations existed between ordinary Jews and Christians in both cities. Indeed, so good were the relations that local Christian leaders such as Cyril and Chrysostom felt sufficiently threatened that they condemned Jews and Judaism, as well as the Christians who admired them.

Although relations between the communities may have been good, Cyril clearly felt that his position was being undermined, and his response was to denigrate Jews and Judaism, following the *Adversus Iudaeos* tradition. In his homilies he argued that many biblical passages highlighted Jewish infidelity to God and hostility to Christ.[62] His interpretation of the Akedah provided him with another opportunity to condemn Jews and Jewish exegesis. According to Cyril, the command to the servants to remain behind illustrated that Jews had been hindered by many errors:

Israel having followed God by means of law until the time of the coming of our saviour, was not willing by means of faith to follow Christ, who went to his death on behalf of all, but rather were hindered by many errors. For 'from part of Israel there was rigidness' (Romans 11.25), which is signified by means of the ass present with the servants. For the ass is the representation (εἰκών) of their final unreasonableness. And their rigidness is the child of unreasonableness.[63]

Thus, like the rabbis, Cyril suggested that the ass signified the servants' 'unreasonableness' or spiritual blindness, which, in his view, referred to Jewish stubbornness. The two servants symbolized 'slavery to the law', which was especially noticeable in Jewish interpretation, or misinterpretation, of Scripture and in a failure to realize that the biblical prophecies were fulfilled by Christianity.[64]

Another aspect of the relationship between Abraham and his servants that was commented upon by both Jewish and Christian interpreters concerns Abraham's comment to the servants, 'we will return to you'. This phrase caused difficulties as Origen makes clear:

---

[60] Chry, Adv Iud 1.5 Migne.

[61] Wilken suggests that Cyril learnt of Jewish interpretations directly from Jews. Cf. Wilken 1971:54–68.

[62] For a list of examples, see Kerrigan 1952:385–7, who asks whether 'his censures of the Jews [were] occasioned by real worries that the Jewish community at Alexandria caused him'.

[63] *Glaph. in Gen.*, PG 69 141B–C.

[64] *Glaph. in Gen.*, PG 69 140D. Cf. Justin, *Dia.* 34 Goodspeed.

Tell me, Abraham, are you saying to the servants in truth that you will worship and return with the child, or are you deceiving them? If you are telling the truth, then you will not sacrifice him. If you are being deceitful, it is not fitting for so great a patriarch to deceive. What disposition, therefore, does this statement indicate in you?[65]

The rabbis and the church fathers were aware of the problem and suggested a number of solutions. Origen, for example, answered his own question by creating the following speech delivered by Abraham: 'I am speaking the truth, he says, and I offer the child as a sacrifice. For this reason I both carry the wood with me, and I return to you with him. For I believe, and this is my faith, that "God is able to raise up even from the dead" (Hebrews 11.17.)' The rabbis offered a number of their own suggestions. First, they linked Abraham's statement to the servants with the promise of Genesis 15.5 (based on the repetition of 'there' (כה) in Genesis 15.5 and 22.5), suggesting that Abraham believed that he would soon discover the outcome of God's promise. Second, they suggested that God informed Abraham that Isaac would return safely from Moriah. Third, they suggested that they would return safely because of the merit of Abraham's worshipping.[66]

The most obvious solution, shared by both Jewish and Christian exegetes, was that Abraham spoke prophetically without realizing that he was fore-telling the future. For example, one rabbinic interpretation simply stated that it was 'his mouth which proclaimed he would come back and return as it is written, "to a man belongs the thought of the heart but the reply of the tongue belongs to the Lord" (Proverbs 16.1).'[67] Successus makes a similar point:

Beautifully the prophecy heralded what was going to be. On the one hand, he expected to sacrifice, but he was making clear what was going to be with the prophetic word. Not willingly, he said, 'we will return'. For his character was considering the slaughter, but his faith declared and spoke the truth about the outcome.[68]

Other church fathers offered similar interpretations. Chrysostom, for exam-ple, explained that, although Abraham foretold the future, he was unsure whether what he said would happen and spoke these words only to ensure

---

[65] *Hom. in Gen.* 8.5 Doutreleau.
[66] First suggestion: GenRab 56.2. Cf. TanB *Ve-yera* 46; TanY *Ve-yechi* 7; PesR 40.6; second, GenRab 56.2, PesR 40.6; third, GenRab 56.2.
[67] TanB *Ve-yera* 46; TanY *Ve-yera* 23. Cf. BT *Mo'ed Katan* 18a.
[68] Succen., *Catena* 1250 Petit. Cf. Euseb, *Catena* 1251 Petit. 'He said "we will return" as a prophet although he did not know this.'

that the servants stayed behind.[69] Gregory of Nyssa was possibly more real-istic when he suggested that Abraham's deception was required to ensure that the servants did not attempt to prevent the sacrifice. Abraham 'left the slaves so that they would not plot something most low in their slavish nature and hinder the sacrifice of the child'.[70]

According to Cyril, Abraham's words were to be understood in two different ways. First, like Gregory of Nyssa, Cyril held that Abraham's words were a 'pretext' to ensure that the servants remained behind with the ass and, at the same time, they illustrate the inability of Jews to understand the mystery of Christ. Jews were not to be trusted with the mystery nor did they deserve to receive the truth. Their disbelief, he told his congregation, was matched by their inability to understand:

And the blessed Abraham did not say clearly that he brought his son with the intention of sacrificing him, but offered the pretext of 'we will come back here'. This was a clear sign that the mystery of Christ would not be believed by the Jewish people. And this explanation appears true when we see Jesus speaking to the Jews in parables and through riddles, and saying to his disciples, 'to you it has been given to know the secrets of the kingdom of God, but for the rest [it has been given] in parables' (Matthew 13.11).[71]

Second, Abraham's words to his servants were for Cyril an indication of the future conversion of the Jewish people. Cyril argued that the separation of Jews from God would be 'temporary' and that their 'future return' would be accomplished 'by means of faith in Christ'. Thus 'we will return to you' prefigured not only the 'unreasonableness' of Jews but also their eventual conversion:

The servants' separation and the father's departure at the same time as his son, while saying that he will return again . . . indicate the temporary separation of God from the children of Israel, and the future return at the end of the ages to them, accomplished by means of faith in Christ 'for when the full numbers of Gentiles come in, then all Israel will be saved' (Romans 11.25).[72]

As well as predicting the eventual conversion of the Jewish people, Cyril also criticized them for their literal interpretation of the Bible and, following standard patristic criticism, attacked them for their inability to interpret Scripture correctly. He complained that Jews took the text of the Bible literally because they only saw the outward meaning and missed its true significance. Cyril disparaged Jewish interpretation of Scripture and criti-cized Jews for 'examining only the flesh' and being restricted to the literal

[69] *Hom. in Gen.*, PG 54 430.   [70] *De Deitate*, PG 46 569D.
[71] *Glaph. in Gen.*, PG 69 141C–D.   [72] *Glaph. in Gen.*, PG 69 141C. *Hom. Pas.* 5 Burns.

interpretation. In other words, Jews fundamentally misunderstood the Scriptures because they did not interpret the biblical text as Christians! He makes this explicit when he asks, 'Having been taught by the divine Scripture, did you not know the one who was owed to you from the promise? Did you not know that the Word of God was about to dwell with us?'[73]

It should be noted that neither Cyril nor the church fathers ignored the literal meaning of biblical texts when it suited their interpretations. For example, in his commentary on Isaiah he states that 'those who wish to make clear the subtle and hidden breath of spiritual insights must hasten to consider thoroughly, with the eye of the mind especially, on the one hand, the exact literal meaning and, on the other, the interpretation resulting from spiritual contemplation'.[74] Yet, the charge of literalism was a useful stick with which to attack Jewish exegesis.

In addition to incorporating standard *Adversus Iudaeos* arguments, Cyril's interpretations also reveal an insight into a fifth-century argument in Alexandria. The following interpretation discloses the background to his polemic against the 'unholy Jews':

And the two servants following him and travelling with him up until the third day, are a model of the two peoples who have been called into slavery as a result of the law, the two peoples of Israel and Judah, I mean. They [the two peoples] thought it necessary to follow solely the commandment of God, the Father, just as these [the two servants] followed Abraham, not believing in the Son through whom all things are, nor recognising the heir of the Father, of whom [Isaac] furnishes the most beautiful likeness (οὕπερ ἂν εἰσφέροι καλλίστην ἡμῖν τὴν εἰκόνα), small and lying in the breast of his own father, and in no way bearing power fitting for a lord. For the Son was and is always Lord and perfect God. By not being apparent to all, and, most of all, to the unholy Jews who look only at the flesh, He was considered to be a small and random figure (μικρός τις εἶναι καὶ ὁ τυχὼν ἐνομίζετο). And analogously their knowledge about Him corresponds to their opinions of all [things]. For little is the knowledge found among little peoples and great among the great peoples.[75]

Cyril's polemic seems to have been directed against a Jewish criticism of Jesus as 'a small and random figure'. He may also have been aware of Tertullian's treatise in the incarnation, which emphasized Jesus' humanity in an argument against Marcion and some Valentinians.[76] Cyril's mention of μικρός . . . καὶ ὁ τυχὼν would have reminded the listener of his previous comment that biblical events in general, and the words of Paul in particular, did not occur by chance but rather were planned by God. Yet Jews still

[73] *Hom. Pas.* 5 Burns Cf. O'Keefe 1996:144–5.   [74] *In Isa.*, PG 70 9A.
[75] *Glaph. in Gen.*, PG 68 140D–141A.   [76] Tertullian, *De Carne Christi*.

believed that Jesus was an insignificant figure who 'came by chance', even though Jesus was a Jew and preached to Jews. If our conjecture is correct, this Jewish criticism would have demanded a Christian response. Thus Cyril stressed that Jesus was not an incidental figure but was clearly foretold in the Hebrew Scriptures. Consequently, Jews had little excuse for not realizing that Jesus was part of God's saving plan, or failing to recognize Isaac in the likeness of Christ. Cyril's interpretation was part of this argument between Jews and Christians.

His criticism that Jews failed to appreciate the significance of Isaac was repeated by Athanasius, who also complained about the Jews' interpretations of Isaac. According to Athanasius, Jews rejected 'the prophetic declaration concerning our Saviour, but especially those spoken by the Psalmist, "sacrifice and offering you would not accept; a body you have prepared for me" (Psalm 40.6), and should refer all such things to the son of Abraham'.[77] Athanasius' statement provides further evidence that Jews and Christians were involved in an exegetical encounter – in this example, a polemical encounter that concerned to whom the biblical sacrificial language should be applied. The comments of Athanasius, which will be discussed in more detail during our examination of vv. 9–12, indicates that Jewish and Christian exegetes were aware of each other's interpretations. Athanasius' complaint also provides support to the view that Cyril's interpretation of vv. 4–5 represents an example of a contemporary exegetical argument between Jews and Christians in fifth-century Alexandria.

CONCLUSION

We have seen that the interpretations of the church fathers and rabbis considered in detail the length of time of Abraham's journey as well as the role of the servants. Neither was a subject of great interest to the earlier interpreters.

The writings of the church fathers and the rabbis highlight a number of shared interpretations. They both explain that the reason why the journey to Moriah lasted three days was so that no one could suggest that Abraham was in a state of confusion when he reached the sacrificial site. Jewish and Christian exegetes also agree that the three-day journey forced Abraham to endure the torture of considering what lay ahead. Moriah was likewise of interest to the exegetes. The church fathers shared with the rabbis an exegetical interest in the site of the sacrifice and emphasized its

---

[77] *Epist.* 6 Migne.

holiness. Both Jewish and Christian interpreters were also concerned with Abraham's deceptive words to the servants. Unlike Josephus, they did not delete Abraham's words but attempted to justify them by emphasizing, for example, that Abraham spoke prophetically but did not realize that he was foretelling the future.

Our examination has also highlighted examples of a possible exegetical encounter. For instance, it is significant that Origen failed to develop the potential Christological implications of the three-day period, even though there was an obvious link with the resurrection of Jesus. This may have been influenced by the rabbinic interpretation, which emphasized the life-giving consequence of a number of different biblical stories, all of which were linked by a three-day period. It was the combination of biblical references to the three-day period that the rabbis stressed rather than any single biblical account, and Abraham's three-day journey was simply another example of a life-giving miracle. As a result, the rabbinic interpretation effectively reduced the possibility of this verse being used as a Christian proof-text.

Interpretations that consider the meaning and location of Moriah might provide another example. The location of the site of the Akedah was of interest to the church fathers as well as to the rabbis. The interpretation of Isho'Dad of Merv identified a column of light on Moriah and mirrors the rabbinic description of a column of cloud, indicating clear exegetical interaction. Eusebius' interpretation is also suggestive as it contains a combination of the rabbis' dual emphasis on sanctity and sacrifice. Eusebius was the first church father to identify the site of the Akedah with the site of the crucifixion.

In the course of their interpretations the rabbis considered the reasons for the destruction of the Temple and the expulsion of the Jewish people from Jerusalem. Although the rabbis needed to encourage their own communities, whether external criticism existed or not, the fact that their interpretations discussed well-known subjects of controversy between Jews and Christians (such as the ongoing covenant between Jews and God) is suggestive. The rabbinic emphasis on God's eternal faithfulness to Israel was combined with a stress on God's messianic promise. The quotation from a familiar Christian proof-text, Zechariah 9.9, indicates that the rabbinic interpretation might have been influenced by Christian exegesis.

Our analysis of the interpretations of Cyril of Alexandria showed that, as well as using standard *Adversus Iudaeos* polemic (such as the inability of Jews to understand Scripture properly, i.e. Christologically), the Alexandrian bishop also shared a number of interpretations with the rabbis, such as the ass and the servants, representing spiritual blindness. Most interestingly,

Cyril's polemic may exhibit an awareness of a contemporary Jewish criticism that suggested that Jesus was not part of God's saving plan but was simply an incidental figure. Cyril's response was intended, on the one hand, to denigrate Jewish exegesis and, on the other, to stress that Jesus was prefigured in the Hebrew Scriptures in general, and by Isaac in Genesis 22 in particular. Since Cyril had elsewhere complained about the influence of Judaism on Christians, and Athanasius had acknowledged Jewish and Christian disagreement over the figure of Isaac, it is possible that we have uncovered a contemporary argument between Jews and Christians in fifth-century Alexandria.

CHAPTER 4

Verses 6–8: Abraham and Isaac's journey to Moriah

v. 6 And Abraham took the wood of the burnt offering, and laid it on Isaac his son; and he took in his hand the fire and the knife. So they went both of them together. v. 7 And Isaac said to his father Abraham, 'My father!' And he said, 'Here I am, my son.' He said, 'Behold, the fire and the wood; but where is the lamb for a burnt offering?' v. 8 Abraham said, 'God will provide himself the lamb for a burnt offering, my son.' So they went both of them together.

ויקח אברהם את עצי העלה וישם על יצחק בנו ויקח בידו את האש ואת המאכלת
וילכו שניהם יחדו: ויאמר יצחק אל אברהם אביו ויאמר אבי ויאמר הנני בני ויאמר
הנה האש והעצים ואיה השה לעלה: ויאמר אברהם אלהים יראה לו השה לעלה בני
וילכו שניהם יחדו:

ἔλαβεν δὲ Αβρααμ τὰ ξύλα τῆς ὁλοκαρπώσεως καὶ ἐπέθηκεν Ισαακ τῷ υἱῷ αὐτοῦ· ἔλαβεν δὲ καὶ τὸ πῦρ μετὰ χεῖρα καὶ τὴν μάχαιραν, καὶ ἐπορεύθησαν οἱ δύο ἅμα. εἶπεν δὲ Ισαακ πρὸς Αβρααμ τὸν πατέρα αὐτοῦ εἴπας πάτερ. ὁ δὲ εἶπεν τί ἐστιν, τέκνον; λέγων ἰδοὺ τὸ πῦρ καὶ τὰ ξύλα· ποῦ ἐστιν τὸ πρόβατον τὸ εἰς ὁλοκάρπωσιν; εἶπεν δὲ Αβρααμ ὁ θεὸς ὄψεται ἑαυτῷ πρόβατον εἰς ὁλοκάρπωσιν, τέκνον. (πορευθέντες δὲ ἀμφότεροι ἅμα).[1]

EARLY INTERPRETATIONS

Although Abraham plays the central role in the biblical account in vv. 6–8, many of the early interpretations stressed the figure of Isaac. This is illustrated by the writings of Josephus, who stated that he was a grown man of twenty-five years[2] and possessed practically every virtue.[3] As a result of his maturity, Isaac was no longer depicted by Josephus, or the other early interpreters, as a minor figure, but became a key actor in the drama.

---

[1] The LXX locates πορευθέντες δὲ ἀμφότεροι ἅμα at the beginning of v. 9 rather than at the end of v. 8 subordinating the phrase to ἦλθον. In the Masoretic Text, ויבא marked the beginning of v. 9 and וילכו שניהם יחדו the end of v. 8.

[2] Ant 1.227.

[3] Ant 1.222. Cf. Philo (De Ab. 168) describes Isaac as 'showing a perfection beyond his years'.

It is highly likely that Josephus intended to contrast his own portrayal of Isaac with Euripides' portrayal of Iphigenia.[4] Both Isaac and Iphigenia approached their sacrifice with enthusiasm, and Isaac could no more consider rejecting God's command than Iphigenia could stand in the way of Artemis. Both were of noble birth, neither flinched before the impending sacrifice, and a hind was laid before Artemis just as a ram was offered by Abraham to God. However, there are also a number of significant differences. Since Isaac was a grown man, whereas Iphigenia was a young girl, Josephus suggested that his virtue outweighed hers. In addition, the God of Isaac was superior to the goddess Artemis, who contrasted poorly because she rejoiced in human sacrifice, whereas God, Josephus explained, had 'no craving for human blood'.[5]

For his part, Philo adopts a double approach to this passage and offers both an allegorical and a literal interpretation. He is by no means rigid about this division, which can cause difficulty when reading his writings. Not only does there regularly occur a rapid shift of subject but often inconsistencies and even contradictions.

For Philo, there is a literal Isaac and an allegorical Isaac. The literal Isaac is the historical character of the biblical story who, born in extraordinary circumstance, survived the Akedah experience, married Rebecca, fathered Jacob and Esau, and passed away in old age. The allegorical Isaac represents the perfect mind achieved through nature or intuition. In other words, he was self-taught. While Philo differentiates between the literal and allegorical figures, he is unable to present one without the intrusion of the other. As a result, even the literal Isaac is more than a recasting of the biblical character.

In contrast to Abraham and Jacob, Isaac possessed the ability to teach himself and was 'born good by nature'.[6] For example, his name remained the same and he was also the only patriarch to stay in Canaan. Indeed, Isaac was praised by God before being born and is described as perfect at birth.

What is it, then, that has made this one too to be praised before his birth? . . . Joy, not only when present, but when hoped for, causes the soul to overflow with gladness, God fitly held Isaac, even before he was begotten, worthy of his great name and therein of a vast endowment.[7]

Intriguingly, Isaac was the only patriarch to be called a son of God (υἱὸς θεοῦ).[8] Although Philo mentions a number of women who became pregnant 'through no mortal agency'[9] (Leah, Rebecca, Tamar and Zipporah), it is startling that he explicitly describes that God is the father of Isaac.

---

[4] Feldman 1984:220–46. [5] *Ant* 1.223. [6] *De Somn.* 171. [7] *Leg. Alleg.* 3.86–7.
[8] *De Mut. Nom.* 131. [9] *De Cher.* 45–7; *De Mut. Nom.* 132–6.

He mentions this on more than one occasion. For example: 'Isaac is not a product of created beings, but a work of the Uncreated One' and again, 'God may with perfect truth be said to be Isaac's father'.[10] Elsewhere Philo explains that God taught Abraham but fathered Isaac, 'giving one the rank of pupil, the other that of son'.[11]

These interpretations at first glance are similar to the title of Jesus as Son of God. It is extremely unfortunate, and perhaps not a coincidence, that Philo's major treatise on Isaac was not copied. Although the vast majority of Philo's works survived, only three, as far as we know, are lost. Philo's comments on Isaac are only found sporadically located throughout his copious writings. Goodenough, one of the most important scholars of Philo, has suggested that this treatise had been censored by Christian copyists.

Philo's treatment of the life of Isaac has so largely vanished that I long ago suspected it to have been for some purpose suppressed by Christians for the reason that it said so much about the sacrifice and atoning value of Isaac which Christians wanted to say of Christ alone.[12]

Isaac, unlike Abraham and Jacob, did not need to strive for perfection. Eventually, the two patriarchs became equal in virtue to Isaac, but both Abraham and Jacob needed to improve themselves in order to achieve this stage. Each patriarch was especially associated with one virtue: Abraham represented instruction, Isaac intuition and Jacob practice.[13] Philo interpreted the phrase 'and they went off together' as a demonstration of how the perfection of Abraham, although acquired, equalled the natural perfection of Isaac.

It is clear that Isaac increases in significance in the eyes of the early interpreters, and it is possible to discern his growing importance even in the LXX translation of vv. 6–8. For example, the LXX deletes the Hebrew suffixes and renders 'my father' (אבי) as 'father' (πάτερ) rather than offering a literal translation, πάτερ μοῦ ('my father'). Similarly, 'here I am, my son' (הנני בני) is translated as 'what is it, son?' (τί ἐστιν, τέκνον).[14] This change of emphasis is further emphasized by the repetition of 'son' (τέκνον) for 'my son' (בני) in v. 7. The removal of the suffixes increases the formality of the conversation and reduces the intimacy produced by the Hebrew construction (particularly by the repetition of 'my son' (בני)) and, as a result, the conversation between Abraham and Isaac is depicted as less affectionate. We can be sure these were deliberate changes because in v. 1

---

[10] *Quod Det.* 124.   [11] *De Somn.* 173. Cf. *Leg. Alleg.* 3.219.
[12] Goodenough 1953–68, IV:191.   [13] *De Praem. et Poen.* 28–40.
[14] Cf. Wevers 1993:501. The same translation renders Gen. 31.11; 46.2; Ex. 3.4.

'here I am' (הנני) is rendered literally as ἰδοὺ ἐγώ. Also, the childlike question in v. 7, 'where is the lamb for the burnt offering?' (ואיה השה לעלה) is translated as a more formal and adult question, 'where is the lamb which is to be sacrificed?' (ποῦ ἐστιν τὸ πρόβατον τὸ εἰς ὁλοκάρπωσιν). The increased formality and the removal of the childlike language suggests that the LXX did not wish to portray Isaac as a helpless child but preferred to describe him as a more mature figure.

The maturity of Isaac is also demonstrated in the Apocrypha and Pseude-pigrapha. The book of Judith, for example, was written in the second century BCE and is contemporary with the LXX translation. Judith deals with the confrontation between the Assyrians and Persians on the one hand and Jews on the other. It is written to encourage Jews to remain loyal to Judaism during the persecutions of the Maccabean period. The heroine, Judith, refers to Genesis 22 during an impassioned plea against the decision made by the Jewish rulers of a besieged city to surrender to their enemies if God does not deliver them within five days. The trial through which Judith and the elders were passing was not as extreme as the trials by which God singled out Abraham, Isaac and Jacob. 'Remember what He did with Abraham, how He tested (ἐπείρασεν) Isaac and what happened to Jacob . . .' It is interesting that it is only Isaac who is explicitly mentioned as being tested.[15] Although there is no explicit reference to the Akedah, the use of the same verb as in the LXX suggests that this test (perhaps one amongst many) is in the mind of the author. It is interesting to note that in the Greek text Isaac is described as being 'tested', whereas in the Vulgate, Abraham is the object of God's testing. Assuming the Greek version to be based on the Hebrew original, we may suggest that in the original text of Judith Isaac was the representative of the tested patriarchs.[16] It was only later that Abraham became wholly associated with being tested.

Pseudo-Philo also demonstrates the increased importance of Isaac. Although he does not explicitly mention Isaac's age, he does state that 'the one being offered was ready', accepted God's command and was willing to be sacrificed.[17] In another passage, Isaac was informed in advance that he was going to be sacrificed and was depicted as being equal to Abraham:

As he [Abraham] was setting out he said to his son, 'behold now, my son, I am offering you as a burnt offering and am delivering you into the hands that gave you to me.' But the son said to the father, 'Hear me, father. If a lamb from the flock is accepted as a sacrifice to the Lord with an odour of sweetness, and if for the wicked deeds of men animals are appointed to be killed but man is designed to inherit the

---

[15] Jud. 8.26.   [16] Jud. 8.22.   [17] LAB 40.2.

world, how is it that you do not say to me, 'Come and inherit life without limit and time without measure?' But have I not been born into the world to be offered as a sacrifice to Him who made me? Now, my blessedness will be above that of all men because there will be nothing like this – about me future generations will be instructed and through me the peoples will understand that the Lord has made the soul of a man worthy to be a sacrifice.'[18]

Isaac's initial reaction was one of reluctance – surely animals provided atonement for man's sins. What would have happened, Isaac asked, if he had not been born? However, after initially questioning his father, Isaac accepted the command and offered himself freely to Abraham. Although this is a rather difficult passage to understand and perhaps derives from a corrupt text, it seems likely that the author intended to show Isaac playing a full part. He is not portrayed as a helpless victim but as a full and active participant, and his eventual willingness to accept the command to be sacrificed confirms active participation.

In another passage, Pseudo-Philo recounts the biblical horror story in Judges 11, when Jephthah, the soldier who fought successfully against the Ammonites, sacrificed his daughter Seila. Jephthah had made an oath to God that, should he be victorious, he would sacrifice the first animal that came out of the city to meet him. Seila, his only child, was the first to leave the city walls to greet him on his return from the victorious battle. Soon afterwards, Jephthah sacrificed his daughter to fulfil his vow. Seila, in both the biblical story and Pseudo-Philo's account, accepts her fate with equanimity. When Seila was about to be sacrificed by her father, Pseudo-Philo explains that, like Isaac, she was ready to be offered and that her father, like Abraham, should be happy to sacrifice her:

Seila his daughter, said to him [Jephthah], 'And who is there who would be sad to die, seeing the people freed? Or have you forgotten what happened in the days of our fathers when the father placed a son as the burnt offering and he did not dispute him but gladly gave his consent to him and the one being offered was ready and the one who was offering was rejoicing?'[19]

This interpretation emphasizes Isaac's willingness to be sacrificed. It also associates Genesis 22 with martyrdom, for it views the Akedah as a voluntary sacrifice. Isaac is depicted as an exemplary martyr and a model to be followed by martyrs. The fact that Isaac is not sacrificed is not important; his willingness to be sacrificed is sufficient.

The introduction of the theme of martyrdom represented a new development in the interpretation of the Akedah. This theme is developed in

---

[18] LAB 32.2–3, following Jacobson's emendation (1996:864).   [19] LAB 40.2.

4 Maccabees, which describes the torture of a number of heroes at the hands of Antiochus Epiphanes. For example, Eleazar and the seven brothers were compared explicitly to Isaac and were able to withstand torture. Like them, Isaac 'did not shrink when he saw the knife lifted against him by his father's hand'.[20] The brothers encouraged each other to accept their death like Isaac, who also accepted his fate as a sacrifice. Isaac, like these martyrs, exemplified the desire for a life of devout reason and 'offered himself to be sacrificed for the sake of righteousness'.[21]

The author of 4 Maccabees argues that the suffering and death of righteous martyrs had redemptive efficacy for all Israel and secured God's pardon for his people. As a result of their martyrdom 'our enemies did not prevail against our nation, and the tyrant was punished and our land purified, since they became, as it were, a ransom for the sin of our nation'.[22] Thus the suffering and death of the martyrs resulted in purification of the land as well as in atonement for the people's sins. It is significant that 4 Maccabees makes an association between the suffering and death of the righteous and the atonement that results. This association is also found in the *Testament of Levi* 15.4 and elsewhere in apocryphal and pseudepigraphical writings.[23]

It is unclear however whether 4 Maccabees views the Akedah itself or the figure of Isaac in terms of atonement. It seems to simply depict Isaac as a model in order to encourage other righteous martyrs whose actions have atoning value (this will be examined in more detail in vv. 13–14). This is significant because some scholars view 4 Maccabees as propounding an Akedah theology that is vicariously atoning. However, it is more likely that 4 Maccabees views Isaac as the ideal and the righteous martyrs who follow as atoning.

4 Maccabees certainly influenced the description of the martyrdom of Polycarp, which is reminiscent of the Akedah. Polycarp was compared to a 'noble ram out of a great flock for an offering, a burnt offering made ready and acceptable to God'. The allusion to the Akedah was reinforced by the description of the martyr being bound, rather than nailed.[24] In 4 Maccabees Isaac is portrayed as a martyr who consciously accepted the role of the sacrificial animal.[25]

We will consider one final example of an increased role for Isaac in a Qumran fragment 4Q225, which is dated between 30 BCE and 20 CE[26] and offers further evidence of the voluntary nature of Isaac's sacrifice. The

---

[20] 4 Mac. 7.14.   [21] 4 Mac. 13.12.   [22] 4 Mac. 17.20–2.
[23] Cf. Van Henten 1997:140–63; Seeley 1990:92–9.
[24] In *Martyrdom of Polycarp* 14.1 Lake. Note that προσδέω is used in the description.
[25] Cf. Hayward 1981:148.   [26] Milik 1994:141–55.

fragment has been classified as 'Pseudo-Jubilees' because aspects of the text are characteristic of the book of *Jubilees*; for example, both describe Mastema as making a Job-like 'accusation' to God against Abraham and initiating the test (rather than God) – thus removing any possible criticism of God. Significantly, however, 4Q225 differs from *Jubilees* when, according to one scholar, it describes Isaac as offering himself voluntarily for the sacrifice.

The fragment presents Isaac asking his father about the lamb for the burnt offering. Words or letters in the square brackets do not exist in the fragment but represent the deduction of the editor:

Isaac said to Abraham [his father, 'Here are the fire and the wood, but where is the lamb] for the whole burnt offering?' Abraham said to [his son, Isaac, 'God will provide the lamb]
for himself'. Isaac said to his father 'T[ie me well . . .]
The angels of holiness were standing weeping above [the altar . . .]
his sons from the earth. The angels of the Ma[stemah . . .]
being happy and saying, 'Now he will perish'. And [in all this the Prince of the Mastemah was testing whether]
he would be found weak, and whether A[braham] should not be found faithful [to God].[27]

The importance of this fragment lies in Isaac's words 'tie me well', which are not found in the biblical story. If the editor's emendations are correct, this fragment represents the earliest example of Isaac being informed in advance about the sacrifice, as well as the earliest record of his willingness to be sacrificed. It would support the argument put forward by some scholars that 4 Maccabees links Isaac with voluntary martyrdom that was vicariously atoning. However, the number of editorial additions should make us cautious. They argue that the Akedah was viewed as atoning in these early interpretations and may have influenced the self-understanding of Jesus and the development of the early church.

Although 4Q225 appears to emphasize the voluntary nature of Isaac's sacrifice and the significance of Isaac's role at the Akedah, only one Hebrew letter, *kaph* (כ), is visible in the extant manuscript in the crucial sentence. The editor has produced an emended translation, which wholly relies on the later rabbinic interpretation – in which Isaac asked Abraham to bind his hands כפתני ('bind me') – to fill the gap. This seems based more on conjecture and hope than firm evidence, and even one of its main proponents, Milik, admits 'it is thus *not improbable* [my emphasis] that the

---

[27] 4Q225 Frg. 2, col. 2.

present fragment attributed to Isaac a shorter statement that began with *kaphot*.[28] We should be more cautious than Vermes and Milik and refrain from offering any conclusion based on this limited evidence. Interestingly, Fitzmyer, although he follows Milik's emendations, rejects the conclusions of Vermes.

INTERPRETATIONS OF THE GREEK CHURCH FATHERS AND THE PALESTINIAN RABBIS

In the interpretations of the church fathers, following the biblical account, Isaac remains a youth. They ignore the portrait of Isaac as an adult in the earlier post-biblical writings. This change is particularly noticeable when the patristic interpretations are compared with the rabbinic writings, which still consistently portray him as an adult. Jewish and Christian discussion concerning Isaac's age represents a clear example of an exegetical encounter. We begin with the church fathers.

Isaac was described by a number of church fathers as childlike. Cyril, for example, emphasizes Isaac's youth by describing him as 'small and lying in the breast of his own father'.[29] Origen explains how, during the tortuous three-day journey, Abraham viewed Isaac as 'the child who might weigh in his father's embrace for so many nights, who might cling to his breast, who might lie in his bosom . . .'[30] Romanos, in his description of the task that lay ahead of Abraham, describes how Abraham would make speechless 'Isaac's prattling tongue'.[31] Eusebius comments that Genesis 22.13 'did not say, "a lamb", young like Isaac, but "a ram", full-grown, like the Lord'.[32] Each of these interpretations depicts Isaac as a boy.

Other church fathers, such as Chrysostom, portray Isaac as slightly more mature, but who nevertheless retained his youthfulness: 'Isaac had come of age and was in fact in the very bloom of youth.'[33] Gregory of Nyssa states that Isaac was old enough to be considered for marriage when God commanded Abraham to sacrifice his son. According to Gregory, Abraham had believed that when God summoned him (Genesis 22.1) he was about to be told to prepare a marriage and the wedding chamber. This would fulfil the blessing that through Isaac Abraham's seed would be as numerous as the stars in heaven.[34] Similarly, the fourth-century Bodmer poem describes

---

[28] Milik 1994:152. Cf. *Tg.* Ps Jon; *Neofiti*; GenRab 56.8; PesR 40.6; TanB *Ve-yera* 46; TanY *Ve-yera* 23.
[29] *Glaph. in Gen.*, PG 69 140D. [30] *Hom. in Gen.* 8.4 Doutreleau.
[31] *De Ab.* 5 Grosdidier de Matons. [32] *Catena* 1277 Petit. [33] *Hom. in Gen.*, PG 54 429.
[34] *De Deitate*, PG 46 568B. Although it is outside of our timescale, it is worth noting the description in the medieval collection of rabbinic interpretations, *Midrash Ha-Gadol* (Margulies 1947: 253), which portrays Abraham preparing the altar like a bridegroom's father.

how Isaac tells his parents that they should 'prepare a blooming bridal chamber'.[35]

Indeed, the reason Abraham placed the wood for the burnt offering on his shoulders was that Isaac had 'already matured in age for the more burdensome of tasks'.[36] Ephrem Graecus summarizes this view:

The child grew up, reached the age of blossoming adolescence and was joyful. At this age, the virtues of his soul and the beauty of his body increased and he was pleasing to his parents.[37]

Thus two opinions existed in the writings of the church fathers. The first saw Isaac as a child and the second viewed him as a youth or young man. It is clear that, although there is a discrepancy between the two, the church fathers agreed that, whilst Isaac played an important role, he remained young and had not yet reached full adulthood.

The rabbinic position was quite different. The rabbis stated that 'Isaac was 37 years of age when he was offered upon the altar'.[38] Another interpretation gave his age as twenty-six years[39] and a third proposed thirty-six years.[40] It is significant that, whilst the precise age varied, the rabbis were consistent in their portrayal of Isaac as an adult. None of the rabbinic interpretations, in direct contrast to those of the church fathers, hinted that Isaac might have still been a child. For the rabbis, perhaps influenced by the portrayal of Isaac's age in the earlier post-biblical writings, Isaac was a fully developed and mature adult.

Two noteworthy factors suggest that interpretations over Isaac point to an exegetical encounter. They also provide the reason why Athanasius commented (as mentioned in the previous chapter) that interpretations about Isaac were a source of dispute between Jews and Christians.[41] The figure of Isaac is the key with which to unlock the reasons for the existence of exegetical encounters in the patristic and rabbinic writings. Isaac's age was one topic of particular interest to the rabbis and church fathers as was the significance of his carrying the wood for the sacrifice. Isaac is the subject of, and sheds light on, the Jewish–Christian debate.

The interpretations of the church fathers consider in some detail the reason Abraham placed the wood on Isaac as well as the significance of Isaac carrying the wood. Their interpretations cannot have been influenced by the early interpretations because none of the early interpreters comment

---

[35] Hurst and Rudhardt 1999:37–56. Cf. Hilhorst 2002:96–108.   [36] *De Deitate*, PG 46 569D.
[37] *Sermo. in Ab.* 28 Mercati.   [38] GenRab 55.4; 56.8; TanB, *Ve-yera* 42 and 46; TanY *Ve-yera* 23.
[39] GenRab 56.8.   [40] *Tg.* Ps Jon.   [41] Athan, *Epist.* 6 Migne.

on it. Unsurprisingly, the church fathers viewed this action as a model of Jesus carrying the cross. Evidence of an exegetical association between the wood of Isaac and the cross of Christ can already be seen at least as early as the second century CE. This is illustrated in the writings of Melito, bishop of Sardis, who lived in one of the oldest and possibly largest Jewish communities of Asia Minor.[42]

Melito was familiar with Judaism not only from the local Jewish community in Sardis and the many other Jewish settlements in Asia Minor, but also from a visit to Palestine. His writings on Jews and Judaism are, like those of Chrysostom, polemical and contemptuous of Judaism.

The writings of Melito have generally been understood by scholars as a defensive response to the activity of the Jewish community, possibly a reaction to a powerful local Jewish community, which Melito felt forced to attack.[43] This view has been questioned recently with the suggestion that they should be seen simply as theological documents unconnected with local circumstance. Taylor, for instance, has argued that Melito was simply emphasizing Christological issues, and that, as bishop, he saw it as part of his ministry to instil in the members of his congregation a sense of the momentous significance of the Easter event. According to this argument, Melito's accusations form an integral part of this endeavour and have little to do with the Sardian Jews of his day, however prominent or influential.[44]

His writings illustrate a concern not with issues associated with faithfulness, but with the fulfilment of Scripture. In Melito's view, the life, death and resurrection of Jesus had already been foretold, for what has occurred had already been made clear and merely required elucidation: 'if you look carefully at the model, you will perceive him through the final outcome'. The words and deeds of Christ are anticipated by previous comparisons and models, and, following a literal interpretation of biblical personalities, Melito describes Christ as being 'in Abel murdered' and 'in Jacob in exile'. Christ had made 'prior arrangements for his own sufferings in the patriarchs and in the prophets and in the whole people'.[45]

Melito's major extant work is a liturgical homily on the Passion, *Peri Pascha*, which was influenced by the festival of Passover as well as the Jewish Haggadah. The Sardis community was Quartodeciman and celebrated Easter on 14 Nissan – the Jewish Passover. Consequently, it would have been natural for the Sardis Christian community to show interest

---

[42] Wilken 1976:53–5; Trebilco 1991:37–54.
[43] Kraeling 1956:77–85, followed by Wilson 1995:241–55.
[44] Taylor 1995:73. Cf. criticism of Carleton Paget 1997:195–225.   [45] PP v 57 Hall.

in Jewish liturgy and ceremony. Melito's interpretation of Jewish symbols such as *afikomen* and the exposition of unleavened bread and bitter herbs illustrates an intimate knowledge of Passover ritual. Melito clearly possessed detailed knowledge of the contemporary Jewish celebration of Passover.

The theological argument of the homily centres on the superiority of Christianity over Judaism. The homily deals with two mysteries: firstly, the Exodus from Egypt, secondly, the redemption through Christ. The death and resurrection of Jesus insured a Christian's escape from sin and mortality just as the slaughtered Passover lamb secured the escape of Jews from Egypt. However, there is a clear difference between Judaism and Christianity because the latter is not wholly new but is the wholly new Israel. In other words, Christianity replaces Judaism. In this way the Jewish people gives way to the church and the Torah concedes power to the gospel.

In the following passage found in fragmentary form, Melito describes Isaac as foreshadowing Christ and his interpretation is representative of many of the church fathers.

> For as a ram he was bound
> and as a lamb he was shorn
> and as a sheep he was led to slaughter
> and as a lamb he was crucified;
> and he carried the wood on his shoulders . . .
> as he was led up to be slain like Isaac by his Father.
> For it was a strange mystery to behold,
> a son led by his father to a mountain for slaughter,
> whose feet he bound and whom he put on the wood of the offering
> preparing with zeal the things for his slaughter.
> But Isaac was silent bound like a ram,
> not opening his mouth nor uttering a sound.
> For not frightened by the sword
> nor alarmed at the fire
> nor sorrowful at the suffering,
> he carried with fortitude the model of the Lord.[46]

Since Melito's interpretation is one of the earliest patristic writings on the Akedah, as well as one of the most significant interpretations since the epistle to the Hebrews and the epistle of James were written, it is worth noting his exegetical nuances. Melito shows a great interest in Isaac, indicating an awareness of the increasing emphasis on Isaac in the earlier post-biblical and

---

[46] *PP.* Frg. 9 Hall.

rabbinic interpretations. The importance of Isaac to Melito is illustrated by his reference to a large number of parallels between Isaac and Jesus:

- Isaac carrying the wood to the place of slaughter was understood as a reference to Christ carrying the cross.
- Both remaining silent indicated their acceptance of the will of God.
- Melito, like Clement of Rome,[47] stressed that Isaac 'carried with fortitude the model of the Lord'.
- Isaac, like Jesus, knew what was to befall him.
- Both Isaac and Jesus were bound.[48]
- Both were led to the sacrifice by their father, an act that caused great astonishment.
- Neither was sorrowful at their impending sacrifice.

We can see that Melito's interpretations indicate an encounter with Jewish exegesis, which is likely to have been the result partly of his concern with the Christian message in a Jewish environment. In his view, the 'battle' had, to some extent, to be fought on 'Jewish soil'. He exhibits a twofold approach to interpreting Genesis 22. Firstly, it foreshadows the sacrifice of Christ and secondly, it is incomplete. Isaac represents Christ and is a model of Christ, who was going to suffer. On the one hand, Isaac paralleled Christ; on the other, he looked forward to Christ.

Melito's interpretation not only reinforces the efficacy of the Christian gospel but also replies to Jewish exegesis. Melito's writings show that the figure of Isaac is central to the Jewish–Christian debate about the significance of the Akedah. Melito's typological interpretation of Isaac was commonplace elsewhere in the writings of the other church fathers. For instance, Pseudo-Gregory of Nyssa relates that

When he [Abraham] reached the foot of the mountain, he placed the wood of the burnt offering on Isaac, and at once made his son the victim and altar. Beautifully, with respect to our concerns, as if making an outline, Abraham was branding the things of the only-born [Christ] in his only-born [Isaac]. Isaac being led away to sacrifice and being burdened with the wood of the sacrifice on his shoulders carries an autograph of the only-born carrying this cross on his shoulders.[49]

Thus Isaac was viewed as a type of the redemptive sacrifice of Christ, and the Akedah is once again viewed as a biblical example of an earlier comparison with (παραβολῇ) and a model of (τύπος) the words and deeds

---

[47] *1 Clem.* 31.3 Lake. 'Isaac, with confident knowledge of the future, was gladly led as a sacrifice.'

[48] It is interesting that Melito used the Jewish description of Isaac being bound, which may be an example of his use of Jewish categories as well as of exegetical influence. This will be discussed in the next chapter.

[49] Ps Greg Nys, *Sermo. in Ab.* Mercati 108.

of Christ. As a result the Akedah became known in Christian exegesis as the Sacrifice of Isaac, looking forward to the Sacrifice of Christ, as opposed to its Jewish title, the Binding of Isaac. In the words of Gregory of Nyssa, 'one can see in the story all the mystery of the true religion'.[50] Chrysostom states that 'truth was sketched out ahead of time in shadow' and, slightly later on in his commentary, that 'everything was prefigured in shadow: an only-begotten son in that case, an only-begotten in this; dearly beloved in that case, dearly beloved in this'.[51] Similarly, Melito explains: 'If you therefore wish to contemplate the mystery of the Lord look at Abel who is similarly murdered, at Isaac who is similarly bound.'[52] For the church fathers, therefore, the Akedah represented a sketch that was required before the completion of the 'final picture'.

Typological interpretations of the Akedah became as important to the church fathers as *zecut avot* (merit of the fathers) was to the rabbis. In some ways, this division fulfils the maxim proposed by James Kugel: Jews and Christians are divided by a common Bible.[53]

Isaac's carrying of the wood was one of the most frequently mentioned examples of typological interpretations found in the writings of the church fathers. For instance, Clement of Alexandria stated that

Isaac . . . is a type (τύπος) of the Lord, a child just as the Son; for he was the son of Abraham as Christ is the Son of God. He was a sacrificial victim as was the Lord. Yet he was not sacrificed as the Lord. Isaac did at least carry the wood of the sacrifice, as the Lord carried the wood of the cross.[54]

Other examples include: Irenaeus' exhortation of the Christians to carry their cross with the faith of Abraham and like Isaac who carried the sacrificial wood;[55] Origen's comment 'that Isaac who carries on himself the wood for the sacrifice is a figure, because Christ also himself carried his own cross';[56] Cyril of Alexandria's explanation that 'the mystery of our saviour is prefigured';[57] and Ephrem Graecus's statement that 'Isaac carried the wood and was taken up into the mountains to be sacrificed as a blameless lamb. And the Saviour took up the cross, to be sacrificed in Calvary as a lamb on behalf of us.'[58] One of the consequences of the typological approach is an increasing emphasis in the writings of the church fathers on the figure of Isaac. This does not result in Abraham's significance being diminished,

[50] *In Christi Res.* 1 Migne.   [51] *Hom. in Gen.*, PG 54 432.   [52] PP 59 Hall. Cf PP 69 Hall.
[53] Kugel 1997:47.   [54] Paed 1.5.23 Marrou and Hall, cf. *Stroma.* 2.5 Le Boulluec.
[55] *Catena* 1233 Petit, *Adv. Haer.* 4.5.4 Rousseau and Doutreleau.
[56] *Hom. in Gen.* 8.6 Doutreleau. Cf. *Catena* 1252 Petit: 'Thus Christ was carrying his cross. For this was a model of that one.'
[57] Cyril of Alex, *Glaph. in Gen.* PG 69 140A.   [58] *Sermo. in Ab.* 98–99 Mercati.

for he remains the model of faith *par excellence*; rather Isaac's significance dramatically increased. While Abraham remained the model of faith, Isaac became the model of Christ. Thus, for example, Barnabas' brief reference to Genesis 22 is to Isaac, not Abraham, since Jesus 'fulfilled the type' that was established in Isaac.[59] Another example of an increasing emphasis on Isaac is found in the interpretation of Cyril of Alexandria, who explained that it was the promise given to Isaac, not Abraham, that was fulfilled through the cross of Christ.[60]

The typological approach not only provided parallels between Isaac and Christ but also contrasts. The church fathers offered interpretations that stressed the anti-type, or the dissimilarities between Isaac and Christ. Isaac pointed forward to the even more amazing deed in the sacrifice of Christ. These contrasts, such as Melito's comment that 'Christ suffered, [but] Isaac did not suffer' (which will be discussed in the next chapter), demonstrate, first, that the sacrifice of Isaac was not complete, and second, that the Akedah prefigured the future sacrifice of Christ. What is important is that Isaac was not sacrificed and remained thus only the model, waiting to be fulfilled by Christ.

Typology, then, was a reason why the church fathers viewed Isaac as a child. He represented an outline, an immature image of what lay ahead. The child (Isaac) was to be fulfilled by the adult (Christ). The rabbis, on the other hand, maintained that Isaac was an adult. His action was not to be interpreted in the light of any later event but had significance in its own right. Like the church fathers, they also commented on Isaac carrying the wood and the following striking interpretation appears remarkably similar to those mentioned above: '"And Abraham placed the wood of the burnt-offering on Isaac his son." Like a man who carries his cross (צלובו) on his shoulder.'[61] What is even more surprising is that this interpretation is not found in a relatively unknown collection but in one of the best-known rabbinic texts – *Genesis Rabbah* – which is also one of the oldest midrashim.[62] Most unusually, no additional interpretation was offered by the rabbis to elucidate the brief comment. This was undoubtedly deliberate and surely betrays an exegetical encounter. The reference to a cross (צלוב) is as near to an explicit reference to Christianity as we shall find in the rabbinic interpretations during the period under review. This interpretation overcomes the argument put forward by some Christian scholars that the theme of the crucified faithful plays no role in rabbinic legends about

---

[59] *Barn.* 7.3 Prigent and Knight.   [60] Cyril of Alex., *Hom. Pas.* 5 Burns.   [61] GenRab 56.3.
[62] According to Stemberger (1996b: 304) *Genesis Rabbah* was redacted in the first half of the fifth century CE, in Palestine.

martyrs. The case of Akiva may be mentioned because he was martyred by the Romans but, in all the classical rabbinic writings, there is no comparison between Akiva and Isaac and no mention of the Akedah. Scholars such as Martin Hengel argued that 'the cross had become too much a sign of the Passion of Jesus and his followers'[63] for it to have been of any value to the rabbis. The quotation from *Genesis Rabbah*, however, demonstrates that the image of crucifixion could still be incorporated into Jewish exegesis in the fifth century CE.

Nevertheless, some Jewish commentators try to avoid the obvious conclusion that an exegetical encounter between Jews and Christians took place. For instance, Mirkin argues that, far from being influenced by Christian exegesis, the interpretation merely explains why Abraham did not place the wood on the donkey. First, it enabled Abraham to fulfil God's command in every way, and second, that it was standard practice for condemned men to carry their stake to their own execution.[64]

It is also worth considering why the brief interpretation was not expanded on. Concern about Christian reaction or censorship might explain why no further detail was provided; alternatively, much of the material in *Genesis Rabbah* was extremely popular, which might explain why a controversial statement was retained: it was too well known to be easily deleted.[65]

Interestingly, in the two versions of the *Tanhuma* which are believed to have been compiled a few centuries later,[66] when Christianity had established itself as the dominant and dominating religion, the interpretation was either deleted (*Tanhuma Yelamdenu*) or amended (*Tanhuma Buber*) to: 'To whom was Isaac comparable? To one who [after being condemned] was going to be burned with his wood on his shoulders.'[67] The deletion of צלוב, presumably because of its Christian symbolism, indicates Christian influence, as does the lack of additional comment in either *Genesis Rabbah* or its modification in *Tanhuma Buber*. It is not coincidental that between the two-three hundred years between the formation of *Genesis Rabbah* and *Tanhuma*, Justinian's famous code and digest had been published. Designed to bring order and consolidate earlier Roman law, it brought increased restrictions and severity against Judaism. Great care was taken to (self-) censor interpretations that might bring either unwanted internal or external attention. The citation of such a well-known Christian symbol, considered with its later removal, indicates strongly the existence of an exegetical encounter.

---

[63] Hengel 1977:85.   [64] Mirkin 1956–67, II:286.   [65] Jacobs 1995:17.
[66] Cf. Stemberger 1996b:305–6; Bregman 1997:673–4.   [67] TanB *Ve-yera* 46.

What was the purpose behind the rabbinic adoption of Christian interpretation? The rabbis clearly believed that the image of crucifixion was of value in their interpretation of Genesis 22.6. The reference to the 'cross' carried Christian overtones that would have been understood by any Jewish reader or listener. The adoption of this Christian symbol indicates the positive nature of some exegetical encounters. The rabbis were willing to appropriate Christian imagery and apply it to a Jewish context. This feature of Jewish exegesis is rarely acknowledged in the study of Jewish–Christian relations, let alone in the study of rabbinic Judaism. It is too often assumed that influence is one-way and that Christianity was influenced by, and incorporated, interpretations from rabbinic Judaism. However, there is no reason to make this assumption. The rabbinic comparison between Isaac carrying the wood with a man carrying a cross indicates that Judaism may also have internalized ideas from Christianity.

Rather than associating Isaac with death and martyrdom, the purpose was to emphasize Isaac's *willingness* to give up his life and to suffer torture. This is why the rabbis deliberately failed to associate Isaac with martyrs such as Akiva. For example, the following interpretation discusses the martyrdom of a mother and her seven children, and illustrates that neither Abraham nor Isaac were regarded by the rabbis as true martyrs:

The mother says to her seventh and youngest son just before he was to be executed, 'My son, go to the patriarch, Abraham and tell him, "Thus says my mother, 'Do not preen yourself [on your righteousness], saying I built an altar and offered up my son Isaac.' Behold, our mother built seven altars and offered up seven sons in one day. Yours was only a test, but mine was in earnest." '[68]

This passage demonstrates a significant difference between the rabbinic interpretations of Isaac's actions and the interpretations of 4 Maccabees, (discussed in the opening section of this chapter). The rabbis depict Isaac as a mature adult who was willing to give up his life at God's command. Although he was associated with those who suffered, it was Isaac's willingness to suffer that was important. Even when the rabbis refer to the 'ashes of Isaac' they often preceded the discussion with the proviso 'as if it were possible', in other words, as if Isaac had been sacrificed, but had not actually been. The emphasis was not on whether Isaac had actually been sacrificed but on his willingness to be sacrificed, not on martyrdom but on self-offering.

We notice another remarkable similarity between the rabbinic emphasis on Isaac willingly offering himself to his father and the interpretations of

[68] LamRab 1.16.50.

the church fathers. In their view Jesus, like Isaac, was not forced by human hand to carry the cross but carried it freely. For example, Cyril of Alexandria stated:

And the child, Isaac, was loaded with the wood for the sacrifice by the hand of the father until he reached the place of the sacrifice. By carrying his own cross on his shoulders outside the gates (John 19.17–21) Christ suffered, not having been forced by human strength into His suffering, but by His own will, and by the will of God, the Father, according to that said by Him to Pontius Pilate, 'you would have no power above me, unless it had been given to you from above' (John 19.11).[69]

The rabbis also emphasized that Isaac was not forced to offer himself as a sacrifice but willingly gave himself to Abraham. For example, in one interpretation the rabbis portray Isaac speaking to God, as follows:

Sovereign of the Universe, when my father said to me, 'God will provide for Himself a lamb for the burnt offering', I raised no objection to the carrying out of Your words and I willingly let myself be bound on top of the altar and stretched out my neck under the knife.[70]

Other interpretations suggest that because he was concerned that his fear of the knife would invalidate the sacrifice, he told his father to bind him (כפתני) well.[71] Once again, the voluntary nature of Isaac's actions is emphasized.

It is Isaac's willingness to give up his life that provides the basis for these interpretations and appears to be a rabbinic response to the Christian teaching that Christ was willing to give up his life for Israel. The rabbis argued that there existed numerous biblical figures, such as Isaac at the Akedah, who were willing to give up their lives on behalf of Israel. These examples showed that no special significance should be given to the willingness of Christ to give up his life. In the words of the rabbis, 'you find everywhere that the patriarchs and the prophets offered their lives on behalf of Israel'.[72] In other words, the sacrifice of Jesus was not a unique event. Isaac was used to counter Christological claims of uniqueness.

This willingness of Isaac (as well as other biblical heroes) to give up his life is reinforced by the rabbis' suggestion that he was informed in advance of the sacrifice. Abraham tells Isaac that if there is no ram, he will be the offering. Abraham explained, 'God will provide for Himself a lamb . . . And

---

[69] Cyril of Alex, *Glaph. in Gen.*, PG 69 141D–144A: Cf. *Hom. Pas.* 5 Burns.   [70] LamRab Pr. 24.
[71] GenRab 56.8. This is the basis for Milik's emendation of 4Q225 discussed earlier.
[72] MdRI Pisha 1. This passage is especially noteworthy because it has been 'added on' to a section that discusses why Jonah fled from God's command. The passage about Jonah does not relate to the willingness of biblical figures to give up their lives. I am grateful to Prof. Michael Fishbane, who pointed this passage out to me and suggested that it represented a response to Christianity.

if not, you [Isaac] will be the burnt offering, my son.' The word 'lamb' (שה)
when transliterated into Greek means σή (you) and demonstrates that
Isaac had foreknowledge of the impending sacrifice. In other words, this
dual-lingual interpretation (which proves that some rabbis were familiar
with Greek) demonstrates that Abraham told Isaac that 'you (σή) are the
lamb (שה)'.[73] Even though Isaac was informed in advance of the test, he
was still willing to be sacrificed and continued the journey with Abraham.
'One to bind and the other to be bound, one to slaughter and one to be
slaughtered.'

A similar approach can be noted in the writings of Origen, who also
commended Abraham and Isaac for continuing the journey to be sacrificed:
'there is equality and praise for both of them for not going back'.[74] The
rabbis state this as follows: father and son went to Mount Moriah 'with
one perfect (שלימה) heart'. The term שלימה has a liturgical and sacrificial
context. Interestingly, Origen, also describes Isaac as equal to Abraham not
only in terms of walking, but also in the sacrificial function.[75] However,
unlike the church fathers, who laid stress on the fact that Abraham did
not tell his son of the impending sacrifice, the rabbis argued that Isaac's
awareness of what was to happen served to emphasize his full and willing
participation. According to the church fathers, however, Abraham gave no
indication to Isaac of the impending sacrifice. Chrysostom, for example,
mentioned that Abraham concealed the truth and did not reveal to Isaac
what was about to happen.[76]

CONCLUSION

In the early post-biblical interpretations of vv. 6–8, we noticed that Isaac
plays an increasingly important role. He willingly offers himself in sacrifice
and is no longer the child of the biblical story but an adult. Some interpretations portray him as a righteous martyr whose voluntary self-offering
becomes a model for others to follow.

In the interpretations of the church fathers, however, Isaac remains a
youth, as depicted in the biblical story. Although he performs an active
role, he is no longer the adult portrayed in the earlier post-biblical writings.
The church fathers agree that Isaac remained young and had not yet reached
full adulthood; in contrast, the rabbis depict him as a mature adult. This
contrast is significant and represents an example of an exegetical encounter.

[73] PesR 40.6. Cf. GenRab 56.4; TanY *Ve-yera* 23; *Neofiti*.
[74] GenRab 56.4; TanB *Ve-yera* 46; TanY *Ve-yera* 23. Cf. Origen, *Catena* 1253 Petit.
[75] *Neofiti*; Origen, *Hom. in Gen.* 8.6 Doutreleau.   [76] Chry., *Hom. in Gen.*, PG 54 430–1.

The church fathers' emphasis on Isaac's youth is based upon a typological interpretation of the Akedah: Isaac represented Christ. He was a model of the Christ who was going to suffer. Parallels between Isaac and Christ, such as the carrying of the wood and the cross, provide the basis for this interpretation, examples of which can be found throughout the writings of the church fathers.

However, Isaac is also understood as looking forward to Christ, as being fulfilled by Christ. The description of Isaac going to his sacrifice as a youth, in contrast to the Christ going to his sacrifice as an adult, provided the church fathers with a simple and effective image by which to illustrate the fulfilment of the Old Testament by the New. In their interpretations, the sacrifice was completed by Christ, and Isaac the boy was fulfilled by Christ the man. For the church fathers, Isaac was both a model of Christ and an outline to be fulfilled by Christ. As a result of this typological approach, the Akedah was viewed as a type of the redemptive sacrifice of Christ.

The rabbis, for their part, developed the passive, almost peripheral Isaac of the biblical story into a central character whose self-offering was the key to a proper understanding of the Akedah. They describe Isaac as a mature adult who was informed in advance of his impending sacrifice, which reinforces their interpretation that Isaac voluntarily gave up his life. This voluntary self-offering was a rabbinic response to the Christian teaching about the willingness of Christ to give up his life, expounded in the patristic writings. This is another example of an exegetical encounter. The rabbis argued that there were many biblical figures, such as Isaac, who were willing to give up their lives on behalf of Israel, thus implying that the self-sacrifice of Christ was not unique. Isaac, like Jesus, was merely one more figure who was willing to give up his life on behalf of Israel.

The rabbinic description of Isaac carrying the wood, 'like a man carrying a cross', represents a second example of an exegetical encounter, as it parallels the interpretations of the church fathers and, we can assume, appropriated from them. The removal of the term 'cross' from later rabbinic interpretations indicates awareness, and possibly embarrassment, among the rabbis that Jewish tradition had adopted explicitly Christian exegesis.

It is not surprising that these two examples of exegetical encounter are connected with the figure of Isaac, since he is central to both Jewish and Christian interpretations of the Akedah. This will become more apparent in the next chapter.

CHAPTER 5

Verses 9–12: Abraham and Isaac on Moriah

v. 9 When they came to the place which God had told him, Abraham built an altar there, and laid the wood in order, and bound Isaac his son, and laid him upon the altar, upon the wood. v. 10 Then Abraham put forth his hand, and took the knife to slay his son. v. 11 But the angel of the Lord called to him from heaven, and said, 'Abraham, Abraham!' And he said, 'Here am I.' v. 12 He said, 'Do not lay your hand upon the lad, or do anything to him; for now I know that you fear God, seeing that you have not withheld your son, your only son from me.'

ויבאו אל המקום אשר אמר לו האלהים ויבן שם אברהם את המזבח ויערך את העצים
ויעקד את יצחק בנו וישם אתו על המזבח ממעל לעצים: וישלח אברהם את ידו
ויקח את המאכלת לשחט את בנו: ויקרא אליו מלאך יהוה מן השמים ויאמר אברהם
אברהם ויאמר הנני: ויאמר אל תשלה ידך אל הנער ואל תעש לו מואמה כי עתה
ידעתי כי ירא אלהים אתה ולא חשכת את בנך את יחיד ממני

πορευθέντες δὲ ἀμφότεροι ἅμα ἦλθον ἐπὶ τὸν τόπον, ὃν εἶπεν αὐτῷ
ὁ θεός. καὶ ᾠκοδόμησεν ἐκεῖ Αβρααμ θυσιαστήριον καὶ ἐπέθηκεν τὰ
ξύλα καὶ συμποδίσας Ισαακ τὸν υἱὸν αὐτοῦ ἐπέθηκεν αὐτὸν ἐπὶ τὸ
θυσιαστήριον ἐπάνω τωῦ ξύλων. καί ἐξέτεινεν Αβρααμ τὴν χεῖρα
αὐτοῦ λαβεῖν τὴν μάχαιραν σφάξαι τὸν υἱὸν αὐτοῦ. καὶ ἐκάλεσεν
αὐτὸν ἄγγελος κυρίου ἐκ τοῦ οὐρανοῦ καὶ εἶπεν αὐτῷ Αβρααμ,
Αβρααμ ὁ δὲ εἶπεν ἰδοὺ ἐγώ. καὶ εἶπεν μὴ ἐπιβάλῃς τὴν χεῖρά σου
ἐπὶ τὸ παιδάριον μηδὲ ποιήσῃς αὐτῷ μηδέν· νῦν γὰρ ἔγνων ὅτι
φοβῇ τὸν θεὸν σὺ καὶ οὐκ ἐφείσω τοῦ υἱοῦ σου τοῦ ἀγαπητοῦ δἰ
ἐμέ.

EARLY INTERPRETATIONS

Philo makes a number of changes to the biblical story of which two are especially significant and also mentioned by Josephus. The first is that both interpreters are concerned with the negative connotations of the binding of Isaac and, consequently, omit the act of binding altogether from their writings.[1] Philo states that Abraham simply placed Isaac on the altar,[2] while Josephus depicts Isaac as rushing 'to his sacrifice and doom'.[3] These changes avoid having to answer a difficult question about the voluntary nature of Isaac's participation: Why should a self-sacrificing hero need to be bound? They also imply that the act of binding was viewed with some embarrassment because, in the view of both Philo and Josephus, Isaac did not merely passively accept the divine command but actively and joyously welcomed it.

Second, both explain that when Abraham was about to deal the death-blow to his son, God, rather than an angel, ordered him to stop. The purpose of this change is clear: in their view, God could not possibly desire the sacrifice to take place. Josephus, for example, takes care to explain that God 'wished merely to test the soul' and ascertain whether Abraham would be 'obedient'. God was not interested in the sacrifice per se but in the piety of Abraham. Indeed, for Josephus, the main purpose of the Akedah was to emphasize Abraham's piety.[4]

Philo offers a similar interpretation and explains that God returned the gift – Isaac – given to God by Abraham. In other words, God rewarded Abraham for his piety.[5] As far as Abraham was concerned, the action, though not resulting in the intended outcome, was nevertheless 'complete and perfect',[6] and God 'no longer talked to him as God with a man but as a friend with a familiar'.[7]

For his part, Josephus introduces a long speech by Abraham, in contrast to the biblical account, which portrays Abraham as carrying out the sacrifice in silence. Josephus describes how Abraham recalled his prayer for Isaac's birth, his care for Isaac's upbringing and his desire to bequeath his dominion to him. Abraham asks Isaac to 'bear this consecration nobly' and stresses that it is his faith in God that enables him to yield up his son. Rather than Isaac, his initial hope, God will be his protector in his old age.[8]

In Josephus' account, Isaac matches the piety of his father, listening to Abraham's words with 'noble spirit and with joy'. Isaac's role, as we have seen earlier, increases in significance in the eyes of the early exegetes. Josephus offers another example of this by extolling Isaac's heroism and describing how he and not Abraham, as the Bible has it, built the altar.[9] He also portrays Isaac as responding to Abraham's words with a shorter speech of

---

[1] Philo does once fleetingly refer (*Deus Imm.* 4) to the act of binding, offering an allegorical interpretation. However, since this is his only reference, it would seem that the binding was not significant to him.

[2] *De Ab.* 176.   [3] Ant 1.232. Cf. *Bell.* 2.475.   [4] Ant 1.233–4.   [5] *De Ab.* 177.

[6] *De Ab.* 177.   [7] *De Ab.* 273.   [8] Ant 1.228–31.   [9] *Ant.* 1.227.

his own, exclaiming that he would deserve never to have been born at all were he to reject the decision of God and his father. After these few words, Isaac rushes to the altar, an act which Josephus explains demonstrates once again his great courage.[10]

As well as commenting on Isaac's willingness to be sacrificed, early exegetes also discussed Abraham's willingness to sacrifice Isaac. Pseudo-Philo, for instance, explained that God's choice of Israel, as a chosen people, was partly the result of Abraham's enthusiastic response to his command. Abraham's obedience justified God's election of Israel, and Pseudo-Philo linked the Akedah with Israel being God's people:

And I [God] asked for his [Abraham's] son as a burnt offering (*holocaustum*[11]) and he brought him to be placed on the altar. But I gave him back to his father, and, because he did not refuse, his offering was acceptable to me and on account of his blood I chose them.[12]

The willingness of Abraham to sacrifice Isaac also seems to have influenced Paul in the earliest Christian reference to the Akedah in Romans 8.32. Although rather fleetingly, Paul refers to the Akedah when he considers the implications of God giving up his son. Verses 31–5 comprise a series of rhetorical questions leading to the climax of vv. 38–9, 'He who did not spare his own Son, but gave him up for us all, will He not also give us all things with him?'[13]

The phrase 'did not spare his own Son' (τοῦ ἰδίου υἱοῦ οὐκ ἐφείσατο)[14] corresponds to the LXX 'did not spare your beloved son' (οὐκ ἐφείσω τοῦ υἱοῦ σου τοῦ ἀγαπητοῦ). Allusions to Scripture are common in Paul's writings. Biblical themes and stories are imprinted deeply on his mind and provide the imagery with which he not only describes God's deliverance of the people of Israel, but he also justifies his own vocation and status within the nascent Christian community. However, although Paul alludes to Genesis 22, he makes little theological capital of it but simply argues that the death of Jesus was required by God and accepted by Jesus. Paul makes no reference to the willingness of Isaac to give up his life nor does he portray him as a type of Christ; rather, the focus in Paul's writings is entirely on God's gift of his Son.

---

[10] Ant 1.232.

[11] It is for this reason that many people involved in Jewish–Christian dialogue do not use the term 'Holocaust' to describe the destruction of European Jewry between 1933 and 1945 because it is derived from 'burnt offering', indicating sacrificial overtones. The most common alternative is the Hebrew term *Shoah* ('catastrophe'). This is discussed by Isabel Wollaston (1996).

[12] LAB 18.5.   [13] Rom. 8.32.

[14] Gen. 22.2, 12 and 16. Note that Paul's allusion varies slightly from the LXX, which uses ἀγαπητός (οὐκ ἐφείσω τοῦ υἱοῦ σου τοῦ ἀγαπητοῦ). Aquilla has μονογενής and Symmachus has μόνος.

We should also note that Paul does not develop the argument of Romans 8.32 in any detail, nor does he expressly mention the Akedah in any of his other letters.[15] This is mentioned by a number of scholars. For example, Barrett simply states that 'Paul makes no serious use' of the Akedah, and Fitzmyer offers the view that 'as the Pauline allusion is not clear there can be no certainty about it'.[16] It has been suggested by others, however, that the Akedah may have influenced Paul's understanding of Christ's death and that Paul may have been referring to the Akedah when he was explaining how Christ had 'given himself up' (παρέδωκεν).[17] However, there is little evidence to support the argument that the use of this verb should be viewed in terms of the Akedah. If Paul were referring to the Akedah, why is he being so deliberately vague. Why does he fail to *explicitly* mention the Akedah anywhere in his writings, especially on those occasions where a reference may be expected (e.g. Galatians 5.24 and 6.14)?[18]

It is possible, perhaps likely, that Paul deliberately avoided making reference to the Sacrifice of Isaac because he may have been facing interpretations that had been put forward in opposition to his teaching on justification by faith. Although the epistle of James is later than the writings of Paul, James 2.22–4 illustrates this possibility, a view that even Le Déaut acknowledges. Whilst arguing that the Akedah influenced New Testament writings, he admits that Paul consciously avoided referring to Genesis 22.[19] Likewise, Vermes, who argues strongly that 'the Pauline doctrine of Redemption is basically a Christian version of the Akedah', admits that Paul 'did not express himself distinctly' to the Akedah because, Vermes claims, it was 'a well-established doctrinal tradition' in the first century CE. One might ask why it is, if it were so well known, that neither Paul nor other New Testament authors referred to it more frequently and more explicitly.[20]

We should, therefore, conclude that the primary purpose of Romans 8.32 was not to make an implied comparison between God and Abraham, nor was it to imply that atonement was a reward for the actions of Abraham and Isaac. Since neither patriarch was mentioned by Paul, it seems more likely that for Paul the Akedah served as an example of divine, rather than human,

---

[15] Cf. Meile 1980:111–28.   [16] Barrett 1957:99; Fitzmyer 1993:532.

[17] E.g. Gal. 1.4 and 2.20; Eph. 5.2 and 25.

[18] For further discussion, see Daly 1977:67, Le Déaut 1961:204–5 and Chilton and Davies 1978:532.

[19] Le Déaut 1963:572.

[20] Vermes 1961:220 n. 1. It has been argued, e.g. by Daly (1977:68), that Jn 3.16 ('For God so loved the world that he gave His only Son (τὸν υἱὸν μονογενῆ ἔδωκεν), that whoever believes in him should not perish but have eternal life') was influenced by early Jewish interpretations of the Akedah. This verse certainly uses beloved son imagery and contains similarities with Rom. 8.32. Whereas Paul uses both the negative ('did not spare') and the positive ('gave'), John offers only the positive ('gave'). Although it is possible that Jn 3.16 is influenced by the Akedah, its focus is on God giving up his most precious gift, and the reference to the Akedah is, at best, an allusion.

faithfulness, for God had already indicated his great love by offering the costliest gift possible: his own Son. In other words, the Akedah illustrates for Paul not the faithfulness of Abraham or Isaac, but rather the faithfulness of God.[21] It is worth remembering that ch. 8 of Romans examines the action of God in terms of divine fatherhood.

Paul's ambiguous reference to the Akedah may be further clarified when viewed in the context of Paul's understanding of Isaac. He was the 'seed', the son of the promise in faith[22] because, first, the promise of a son preceded the covenant by 430 years[23] and, second, because righteousness was attributed to Abraham before he was circumcised.[24] Paul did not view Isaac as a figure of Jesus like, for example, Adam,[25] because Isaac was not a figure of faith. Rather, his importance lay in his being the son of the figure of faith, Abraham. As a result, Paul shows little inclination to develop a detailed exegesis of Genesis 22 and does not make any Christological comparison. Thus, we are left only with an echo, rather than with an explicit reference to either Isaac or the Akedah in the writings of Paul.[26]

INTERPRETATIONS OF THE PALESTINIAN RABBIS AND THE GREEK CHURCH FATHERS

As might be expected, the interpretations of vv. 9–12 offer further examples of typology from the church fathers and of Isaac's full and voluntary participation from the rabbis. For the rabbis, v. 10 especially provided an opportunity to expound on the willingness of Isaac to be sacrificed, which, as we noted in the previous chapter, provided the basis for many of the rabbinic interpretations of the Akedah. For instance, one of the earliest Targums, the Fragmentary Targum, states:

'Abraham stretched out his hand and took the knife to kill Isaac, his son.' Isaac answered and said to Abraham his father: Bind my hands properly that I may not struggle in the time of my pain and disturb you and render your offering unfit and be cast into the pit of destruction in the world to come. The eyes of Abraham were turned to the eyes of Isaac, but the eyes of Isaac were turned to the angels of heaven. Isaac saw them but Abraham did not see them. In that hour the angels of heaven went out and said to each other: Let us go and see the only two just men in the world. The one slays, and the other is being slain. The slayer does not hesitate, and the one being slain stretches out his neck.[27]

---

[21] Dunn 1988:501.
[22] Gen. 21.12 quoted in Rom. 9.7, and identified with Christ in Gal. 3.16 and with all believers in Gal. 4.28.
[23] Gal. 3.17.   [24] Rom. 4.9–11.   [25] Rom. 5.14.
[26] Cf. Moberley 2000:133.   [27] Frg. *Tg.* Gen. 22.10.

This interpretation contains three important elements, each of which is commonly found in the rabbinic writings and demonstrates both Isaac's proactive contribution and his importance to the rabbis' understanding of the Akedah. First, Isaac asks Abraham to bind him;[28] second, Isaac, not Abraham, sees the heavenly angels;[29] and third, the angels, who were watching events unfold on Moriah, were astounded by the equal enthusiasm of both father and son to fulfil God's command.[30]

In this way, the rabbis extended the biblical story of sacrifice to one of self-sacrifice, and the voluntary nature of Isaac's actions became the focus of rabbinic interpretations. The Akedah no longer consisted of the sacrifice of a son by a father but became the self-offering of a hero. Isaac was not depicted as the passive victim of the biblical story, rather, in the words of the rabbis, he had 'cast himself before his father'.[31]

The rabbinic emphasis on Isaac's self-offering offers a number of examples of exegetical encounter and reinforces one of the main conclusions of this book: the most significant exegetical encounters are most commonly found in those interpretations that deal with the figure of Isaac. We have already seen in the last chapter that discussions among the church fathers and the rabbis concerning Isaac's age and his carrying the wood for the burnt offering represent two examples. The interpretation of the Fragmentary Targum quoted above provides further evidence. By depicting Isaac as being informed in advance of his impending sacrifice, as well as describing how he asked his father to bind him, the Targum reinforces the portrait of him as a heroic figure, willing to give up his life for Israel.

The emphasis on Isaac's self-offering led the rabbis to associate the Akedah primarily with Isaac rather than with Abraham (who remained the central figure for the church fathers). As a result, the biblical story became known in the Jewish tradition as 'The Binding of Isaac' (עקדת יצחק) rather than, for example, 'The Test of Abraham'. It is also worth noting in the passage from the Fragmentary Targum that the rabbis state that Isaac, rather than Abraham, saw the heavenly angels, perhaps indicating his superiority in comparison with Abraham. It is, therefore, not surprising that, on those occasions when the rabbis discussed the Akedah with reference to the three patriarchs, they primarily associated it with Isaac alone. The following comment on the love of the three patriarchs for God illustrates this. The rabbis interpret Deuteronomy 6.5, 'you shall love the Lord your God with all your heart, with all your soul and with all your might', thus:

[28] E.g. GenRab 56.8; TanB *Ve-yera* 46; TanY *Ve-yera* 23; PesR 40.6.
[29] E.g. GenRab 65.10; TanB *Toldot* 13.
[30] E.g. GenRab 56.4 and 5; TanY *Ve-yera* 23; TanB *Ve-yera* 46 .   [31] E.g. LevRab 2.10.

'With all your heart', like our father Abraham, as it is said, 'But you Israel . . . the offspring of Abraham who loves Me' (Isaiah 41.8). And 'with all your soul', like Isaac who bound himself upon the altar as it is said, 'And Abraham stretched out his hand and took the knife to slay his son.' And 'with all your might (מאדך), thank (מאד) Him as did Jacob, as it is said, 'I am not worthy of all the mercies and of all the truth which You have shown your servant. (Genesis 32.11)'.[32]

Thus Isaac's love for God is epitomized by his actions at the Akedah. The rabbis suggested that, because Isaac was a fully grown adult, in contrast to his father who was an old man, he must have metaphorically 'bound himself' for, if he had so desired, he could have prevented his elderly father from binding him. This answers the question set by the rabbis: 'is it possible to bind a man aged 37 years?'[33] Isaac's request to his father to bind him implied, first, that he welcomed the sacrifice and, second, that he was not forced into it.

For their part, the church fathers applied this description not to Isaac but to Jesus and explained that Jesus willingly offered himself to be sacrificed. Isaac was a child, guided by his father and eager to fulfil the divine command, while Jesus was a grown man who obeyed his Father, willingly gave up his life and was not forced by human strength into the sacrifice. For example, Cyril of Alexandria makes the following contrast:

the child being led to the sacrifice by his father indicates through symbol and outline that neither human strength nor the greed of the conspirators led our Lord Jesus Christ to the cross, but [the desire of] the Father.[34]

Thus both the church fathers and the rabbis emphasized the importance of voluntary self-offering. It was their interpretation of the significance of the self-offering, rather than whether or not it took place, that was important and that accounted for differences in their interpretations. For the church fathers, the child Isaac was an outline of the adult Christ and, therefore, the self-offering of Isaac merely foreshadowed the saving action of Christ. For the rabbis, the self-offering of the adult Isaac was sufficient to provide benefit, *zecut avot*, to Isaac's children (the Jews) for future generations.

We also notice the same distinction in rabbinic and patristic interpretations of the role of the angels. In our examination of the interpretations of vv. 1–2, we showed that both the early interpreters and the rabbis viewed the angels as initiating the test, whereas the church fathers made no mention of their role. However, the fathers did consider the significance of the angels

---

[32] *Sifre* 32; *Mid. Tan. on Deut.* 6.5.   [33] GenRab 56.8.
[34] *Hom. Pasc.* 5 Burns. Cf. Cyril of Alex, *Glaph. in Gen.*, PG 69 141D–144A.

in their interpretations of what took place on Moriah. Like the rabbis, they portrayed the angels as watching the events unfold, and agreed with them that the angels were astounded by the actions of Abraham and Isaac. This shared interpretation is illustrated by a comment of Ephrem Graecus: 'The angels were amazed and the powers and all the authorities, thrones, rulers and all the armies. The heavens took notice, the sun and moon, and the choruses of stars at this unexpected sight.'[35] This is remarkably similar to a comment in the Isaiah Targum, which describes the angels as 'quaking' and 'shaking' with amazement.[36]

The church fathers' interest in the angels is partly explained by their contention that the angel who called out to Abraham to stop the sacrifice is identified with Christ. According to Origen, 'just as among us men "He was found in appearance as a man" (Philippians 2.7) so also among angels He was found in appearance as an angel'.[37] Gregory of Nyssa makes reference to Isaiah 9.6, associating Christ with the angel of great counsel who appeared to Abraham on Moriah.[38]

As we saw earlier, the rabbis portrayed the angels as being amazed by the actions of Abraham and Isaac, both of whom were viewed with an equal level of admiration. The church fathers offered similar descriptions of amazement. John Chrysostom asked, 'What amazes and astounds me more – the courageous attitude of the patriarch or the obedience of the son?'[39] Similarly, Gregory of Nyssa commented:

At which of the two should I be more amazed? The one who throws his hand upon his son for the love of God or the one who obeys his father unto death? They strive for honour with each other: one lifting himself above nature; the other reckoning that disobedience towards his father was more difficult than death.[40]

Although the rabbis shared with the church fathers an image of angelic amazement, their main concern was Isaac's experience on Mount Moriah. In their view, so willing was Isaac to give up his life that they described Isaac's actions in particular and the Akedah in general in terms such as 'the blood of the binding of Isaac' or 'the ashes of Isaac'.[41] This is startling because

---

[35] Eph Grae, *Sermo. in Ab.* 144 Mercati.
[36] *Tg. Isa.* 33.7 (Codex Reuchlinianus).   [37] *Hom. in Gen.* 8.8 Doutreleau.
[38] *De Deitate*, PG 46 572D–573A. Isa. 9.6 ('For unto us a child is born, unto us a son is given; and the governement shall be upon his shoulder; and his name shall be called Wonderful, Counsellor, Mighty God, Everlasting Father, Prince of Peace') was commonly associated with Christ from as early as Justin; cf. *Dia.* 126 Goodspeed.
[39] Chry, *Hom. in Gen.*, PG 54 431.   [40] *De Deitate*, PG 46 572B.
[41] E.g. GenRab 49.11; 94.5; LevRab 36.5; *Num. Rab.* 17:2; MdRI Pisha 7 and 11.

the biblical account explicitly states that the angel stopped Abraham from harming his son and commanded him 'not to do anything' to Isaac.[42] For example, the *Mekhilta de Rabbi Ishmael* says:

'And when I see the blood (וראיתי את הדם), I will pass over you' (Exodus 13.12 and 25) – I see the blood of the Binding of Isaac (רואה אני דם עקדתו של יצחק). For it is said, 'And Abraham called the name of that place, the Lord will see' (יהוה יראה). Likewise it says in another passage, 'And as He was about to destroy the Lord beheld (ראה) and repented Him' (1 Chronicles 21.15). What did He behold? He beheld the blood of the Binding of Isaac (מה ראה, ראה דם עקדתו של יצחק), as it is said, 'God will for Himself see to the lamb.' (אלהים יראה לו השה לעלה)[43]

This interpretation clearly suggests that Isaac's blood was shed – an opinion repeated in the *Mekhilta de Rabbi Shimon ben Yochai*, which states that Isaac 'gave one fourth of his blood on the altar'.[44] Similarly, the *Tanhuma* refers to a quarter of Isaac's blood being shed.[45] How should such interpretations be understood? Some scholars play down the significance of these rabbinic interpretations that depict Abraham shedding the blood of his son. Lauterbach, for example, suggested that the rabbis were simply referring to 'the readiness of Isaac to give his blood as a sacrifice'.[46] Hayward has suggested that they should be understood in terms of *zecut avot* because God viewed the Akedah as worthy of reward, rather than in terms of sacrifice.[47]

Nevertheless, we should not ignore the obvious meaning – that Isaac's blood was shed. We should also explore the association between the shedding of blood and sacrifice, and especially sacrifice in the Temple. The rabbis draw attention to this by depicting both Abraham and Isaac expressing concern that Isaac should be fit for sacrifice.[48] For example, one interpretation explains that when Abraham cut wood for the sacrifice he deliberately chose fig and palm trees for the burnt offering because they were halakhically suitable for sacrifice in the Temple.[49]

The use of the terms 'the blood of the binding of Isaac' and 'the ashes of Isaac' imply that either blood was shed or that Isaac was actually sacrificed. The adoption by the rabbis of 'the ashes of Isaac' (since ashes would be all that remained of a burnt offering) serves to link the Akedah to fasting, atonement[50] (to be discussed in more detail in the next chapter) and the Temple. Blood and ashes were an intrinsic aspect of atoning ritual since

---

[42] GenRab 56.7.   [43] *MdRI* Pisha 7 and 11.   [44] MdRSbY *Ve-yera* 6.   [45] TanY *Ve-yera* 23.
[46] Lauterbach 1933–5, I:57.   [47] Hayward 1990:297–9.
[48] E.g. GenRab 56.8; TanY *Ve-yera* 23; TanB *Ve-yera* 46.   [49] *Tg. Ps. Jon.* to v. 3; cf. BT *Tam.* 29b.
[50] E.g. GenRab 49.11; BT *Ta'an.* 16a; *Tg.* 1 Chron. 21.15.

biblical times[51] and there is a tradition that states that the Temple was rebuilt where Isaac's ashes were found.[52]

Did the rabbis go as far as to suggest that Isaac died? Strikingly, the answer is 'yes' for Isaac is described in terms reminiscent of Jesus in the eighth-century CE *Pirkei de Rabbi Eliezer*,[53] which stated that Isaac died and, soon after, experienced resurrection:

> When the sword touched his neck the soul of Isaac took flight and departed but when he heard the voice from between the two cherubim saying . . . 'do not lay a hand' his soul returned to his body and [Abraham] set him free, and he stood on his feet. And Isaac knew the resurrection of the dead as taught by the Torah, that all the dead in the future would be revived. At that moment he opened [his mouth] and said, 'Blessed are You, O Lord, who revives the dead.'[54]

Like the rabbinic reference to carrying a cross in *Genesis Rabbah*, the reference to the death and resurrection of Isaac is likely to have been influenced by Christianity. However, *Pirkei de Rabbi Eliezer* is dated later than our timescale. Is there evidence for this interpretation in the first six centuries? Some scholars, such as Spiegel, have suggested that suggestions about Isaac's death and resurrection existed much earlier than the eighth century. He argued that the term 'the ashes of Isaac' should be understood literally and that 'the Haggadah about the ashes of Isaac who was consumed by fire like an animal sacrifice . . . is ancient indeed'.[55]

Spiegel's argument would be strengthened if interpretations from the first six centuries CE stated this explicitly. However, during this time the rabbis associated the Akedah not with the death of Isaac, but with redemption. The Akedah illustrated God's miraculous life-saving power, and on those occasions when Isaac was cited in connection with the resurrection of the dead, his death is not cited:

> Through the merit of Isaac, who offered himself upon the altar the Holy One, Blessed be He, shall raise the dead. For it is written, 'From heaven the Lord looked upon the earth to hear the groaning of the captive, to deliver the children of the dead' (Psalm 102.20).[56]

This interpretation makes it clear that Isaac was associated with the resurrection of the dead (and commonly linked to the second benediction of the Amidah, 'Blessed are you, Lord, who resurrects the dead', as we shall discuss in the next chapter). The association between Isaac and resurrection exists as a result of the merit of his action (*zecut avot*). It was his action, his

---

[51] E.g. Jon. 4.6; Isa. 58.5; Lam. 3.16.   [52] BT *Zeb.* 62a.
[53] Stemberger (1996b:329).   [54] PRE 31.   [55] Spiegel 1967:44.   [56] PRK Sup. 1.20.

willingness to offer himself up unto death, rather than death itself, which was important to the rabbis.

However, one might argue that the rabbis referred to Isaac's death when they described his heavenly vision in the Fragmentary Targum. This interpretation implies that he did die because it was an ancient and well-known tradition that no person could see God and survive.[57] For example, does the following interpretation suggest that Isaac's vision of the angels resulted in his death?

When his father bound him and he took up the knife to slaughter him, the Holy One, Blessed be He, was revealed [to him] above the angels. He opened the firmament, and Isaac lifted up his eyes and saw the chambers of the chariot and he trembled and shook . . . He trembled when he saw the Holy One, Blessed be He, the chambers of the chariot, and the angels.[58]

However, another interpretation clarifies the meaning of the trembling of Isaac:

When our father Abraham bound his son on the altar, he [Isaac] looked up and gazed at the Shekhina. Said the Holy One, Blessed be He, If I slay him now I will make Abraham, my friend, suffer. Therefore I decree that his eyes be dimmed.[59]

This reconciliation of the interpretations indicates that, although the rabbis acknowledged that Isaac either suffered some injury, such as impaired vision, or shed blood on Moriah, he did not die.

Consequently, we can conclude that the *Pirkei de Rabbi Eliezer* represents the first occasion when the rabbis suggest that Isaac died and underwent resurrection. In other words, this interpretation is likely to be an eighth-century CE development (indicating that an exegetical encounter with Christianity continued after the first six centuries).

It is worth recalling one interpretation discussed earlier, which commented on the martyrdom of the seven sons and described the Akedah simply as a 'test' rather than a 'deed'.[60]

Nevertheless, we must not ignore the rabbinic references to Isaac's blood and ashes. They are significant because they imply first, that Isaac willingly participated in the sacrifice, and second, that he suffered from his experience. This reinforces what has already been identified as one of the main rabbinic interpretations of the Akedah: the self-offering of Isaac. It

---

[57] Based on Ex. 33.20.   [58] TanB *Toldot* 22. Cf TanY *Toldot* 13.

[59] GenRab 65.10. Cf. *Tg. Ps. Jon.* to Gen 27.1, which suggests that Isaac's vision of the throne of glory was responsible for his weak eyes.

[60] LamRab 1.16.50. The former term implies that the testing was incomplete and the latter that it was completed.

is worth remembering that the terms 'the blood of the binding of *Isaac*' and 'the ashes of *Isaac*' refer to Isaac. Thus, first and foremost, the rabbis emphasize that Isaac was totally committed to fulfilling God's command, and that under the most severe of circumstances he showed great willingness to be sacrificed. Indeed, he was so eager to obey his father and God's command that even after blood starting flowing he did not attempt to stop the sacrifice.[61]

The rabbinic interpretations, which emphasize the centrality of Isaac, contrast with those of the church fathers, which stress the role of Abraham. Both the church fathers and the rabbis agreed that the sacrifice was extremely close to completion when the angel of the Lord intervened, but disagreed over the significance of the near-sacrifice. For the rabbis, Isaac was the focus; for the church fathers, it was Abraham. For example, Gregory of Nyssa stated that Abraham

reaches the prophesied land with him, builds an altar to God and the child arranges the wood for his father. The fire is ready and not yet is the deed stopped. This is so none of the faint-hearted could say that even if he had withstood the test thus far, Abraham would not have continued in the same way if he had come closer to the suffering because he could get no closer.[62]

Gregory explains that attention should be directed towards Abraham, who withstood the test because he was on the verge of sacrificing his passive son when the angel called. In the words of Athanasius, 'the patriarch was tried through Isaac'.[63] Thus the Akedah remained a test of Abraham. Although Isaac became a more significant figure in the interpretations of the church fathers, Abraham remained the pivotal character.

The centrality of the figure of Abraham was partly influenced by the emphasis of the New Testament,[64] but also represented a reaction against the rabbinic stress on Isaac. The existence of exegetical influence becomes more apparent still when we consider the rabbinic references to the suffering of Isaac, for he was called a 'child of suffering'.[65] A similar interpretation suggested that God associated himself with those who suffered, epitomized by Isaac.[66]

It is no coincidence that many of the interpretations of the church fathers were concerned with emphasizing that Isaac did not suffer. Their interpretations betray an awareness of the rabbinic interpretations for, as I mentioned earlier, the biblical text provides no indication that Isaac suffered or shed blood. Consequently, there was no reason why they should consider

---

[61] *Tan. Y. Ve-yera* 23.   [62] Greg of Nys, *De Deitate* PG 46 572B.   [63] Athan, *Epist.* 6 Migne.
[64] See comments on v. 3 above.   [65] LevRab 36.5.   [66] GenRab 94.5.

whether Isaac suffered or not unless they were aware of contemporary Jewish exegesis. Patristic interpretations, such as the following passage from Melito, illustrate an exegetical encounter between Jews and Christians:

> But Christ suffered, whereas Isaac did not suffer for he was the model of the Christ who was going to suffer. But Isaac was silent bound like a ram, not opening his mouth nor uttering a sound.[67]

Although his interpretation was also partly influenced by imagery from Isaiah 53, Melito demonstrates knowledge of contemporary rabbinic interpretations that viewed Isaac as suffering. We saw earlier that Melito's writings showed awareness of Jewish interpretations, and in this quotation he described the Akedah by its rabbinic title, the Binding of Isaac, using the verb 'bind' (συμποδίζω). This usage is extremely rare in the writings of the church fathers, although it is also found in the Bodmer poem.

For Melito, the Akedah provided a link between Christ (in terms of the Word) and the ram and between Jesus (in terms of the body) and Isaac. Lieu, in her important study of Jews and Christians in the second century CE, cites Melito's emphasis on the binding as an example of the 'fluidity and interaction which . . . encompasses both Christian and Jewish traditions'.[68] Melito's reference to the Suffering Servant in Isaiah illustrates not only a desire to show that Christ fulfilled Scripture, but also enabled him to respond to rabbinic interpretations that describe Isaac as voicing his opinion. Melito flatly contradicts this and states that Isaac was silent. His comment provides another example of familiarity with Jewish categories of thought and of an exegetical encounter.

Melito's emphasis on Isaac not suffering can also be found in many of the patristic writings. Clement of Alexandria, a second-century church father from Alexandria, discusses the significance of the sacrifice of Isaac not being completed in the following typological interpretation:

> He [Jesus] is Isaac . . . who is a type of the Lord, a child as a son; for he was the son of Abraham as Christ the Son of God, and a sacrifice as the Lord but he was not immolated as the Lord. Isaac only bore the wood of the sacrifice, as the Lord the wood of the cross . . . Isaac did everything but suffer, as was right, yielding the precedence in suffering to the Word. Furthermore, there is an intimation of the divinity of the Lord in his not being slain. For Jesus rose again after his burial, having suffered no harm, like Isaac released from sacrifice.[69]

Clement explains that Isaac was a type for Christ because he was returned to Abraham unharmed. Clement also contrasts the humanity of Isaac with the

---

[67] Frg. 9 Hall.   [68] Lieu 1996:225. Cf. Wilken 1976:64–7.   [69] Paed 1.5.23 Marrou and Harl.

divinity of Christ, since Christ was the only individual actually to undergo death and resurrection. The Akedah should be viewed as a pale shadow of the sacrifice to come because Isaac was not sacrificed but returned afterwards to normal life; Christ, on the other hand, was sacrificed and returned to life only after death.

Cyril of Alexandria also explained the significance of Isaac not being sacrificed. Cyril was concerned to demonstrate that Christ was unique and that no biblical character, including Isaac, could approach the status of Christ, who was the first and only person to die and yet defeat death:

But Isaac, having been placed on the wood, is stolen away from death and suffering. And the God-given ram goes into the sacrifice . . . But existing as God, unsuffering and immortal, [Christ] carried himself out from under death and suffering . . . The words said in Psalms refer to Him, 'sacrifices and offerings you have not desired, but a body you have prepared for me; in burnt offerings and sin offerings you have taken no pleasure. Then I said, "Behold, I have come. In the head of the book it has been written about me. I wished to do your will" (Hebrews 10.5–7).[70]

Cyril's interpretation is important for two reasons. First, in contrast to the rabbinic description of Isaac as a 'child of suffering', Cyril notes that only Christ suffered. Indeed, unlike Isaac who was saved by the ram, Christ had the power to carry himself out from under death. Thus the Akedah was a pale shadow of the new teaching just as Isaac was a pale shadow of Christ. As a result, no sacrifice took place and Isaac was 'stolen away'.

Second, Cyril's interpretation contrasts markedly with the rabbinic emphasis on 'the blood of the binding of Isaac'. Cyril quotes Hebrews 10.5–7 because these verses were taken from a passage that contrasts the 'pale shadow of the law' with 'faith in Christ'. Hebrews emphasizes that all previous sacrifices were only a pale shadow of the sacrifice to come. The Akedah represented these previous sacrifices according to Cyril. Consequently, the rabbinic interpretation that Isaac's blood had been spilt was irrelevant because it was unacceptable to God ('in burnt offering . . . you have taken no pleasure') and because Christ had yet not arrived ('Behold, I have come').

Although Cyril's interpretations, as well as those of Clement and Melito, appear to respond to rabbinic interpretations of Isaac, they do not refer explicitly to Jewish interpretations. However, Athanasius provides us with irrefutable evidence of this exegetical encounter and makes explicit what we have found implicitly in the writings of Cyril, Clement and Melito.

---

[70] *Glaph. in Gen.*, PG 69 144A.

Athanasius illustrates the intense desire of the church fathers to emphasize the fact that Isaac did not suffer. In his *Festal Letter* announcing the date of Easter to his Egyptian churches, Athanasius warns Christians against celebrating Passover with Jews because the biblical figures had already been fulfilled and the true lamb had been sacrificed. The Jews continued to keep Passover because they did not understand that it was a type of the paschal mystery of Christ. As for the Akedah, Athanasius recalls that it is through the expectation and vision of Christ that Abraham experienced the festive joy:

And when he was tried, by faith he sacrificed Isaac, and offered up his only-begotten son – he who had received the promises. When Abraham offered his son, he was worshipping the Son of God; when he was prevented from sacrificing Isaac it was Christ that he saw in that ram offered as a substitute in immolation to God . . . the patriarch [Abraham] was really put to the test through Isaac. However, the one who was sacrificed was not Isaac but he who was foretold in Isaiah: 'he shall be led as a lamb to the slaughter, and as a sheep before her shearers he shall be speechless' (Isaiah 53.7[71]); but he took away the sins of the world. Abraham was commanded not to lay his hand on the little boy, lest the Jews, on the pretext of the sacrifice of Isaac, should reject the prophetic declarations concerning our Saviour, especially those of Psalm 40.7: 'You wanted neither sacrifice nor oblation, you prepared for me a body'[72] and should refer all such things as these to the son of Abraham. For the sacrifice was not properly the setting to rights (διόρθωσις)[73] of Isaac but of Abraham who also offered, and by that was tried. Thus, God accepted the will of the offerer but prevented that which was offered from being sacrificed. For the death of Isaac did not procure freedom for the world but that of our Saviour alone.[74]

Athanasius makes it clear not only that the Akedah in general was a subject of controversy between Christians and Jews, but also that the figure of Isaac was of specific concern. In his view, Isaac is not only a model for Christ, but is also a prophecy of the one who was to come. Athanasius provides us with evidence of patristic awareness of the importance of Isaac in rabbinic inter-pretations. His comments demonstrate a desire to emphasize the figure of Abraham, whose action is in some sense prophetic. In contrast to the other church fathers, who discuss the significance of Abraham without explicit reference to Jewish interpretations, Athanasius refers directly to rabbinic interpretations and confirms that patristic emphasis on Abraham repre-sents an example of exegetical encounter. The quotation from Athanasius indicates his response against contemporary Jewish interpretations.

[71] Cf. Melito Frg. 9 Hall.   [72] Cf. Heb. 10.5–7 and Cyril's citation of the same verse.
[73] Cf. Heb. 9.10.   [74] Athan., *Epist.* 6 Migne.

A number of other aspects of this passage illustrate the patristic emphasis on Abraham. The quotation from Psalm 40.7, traditionally considered as a messianic text, with reference to Hebrews 10.5–7 indicates that the 'body' is not applied to Isaac but to Abraham. The Syriac word that translates διόρθωσις means 'to make straight' or 'make right' and is also applied to Abraham because he was tested.

Athanasius' interpretation therefore indicates, from a Christian perspective, the basis upon which an exegetical encounter took place:

- For Jews, Isaac's blood was shed and he suffered for the benefit of Israel. During the first few centuries he was associated with the resurrection of the dead and from the eighth century at the latest, the rabbis suggested that he died and was resurrected.
- For Christians, there was no sacrifice and Isaac did not suffer. The Akedah looked forward to Jesus Christ whose suffering, death and resurrection benefited Israel and the whole world.

Athanasius' comments shed light on the interpretations of other church fathers, which offer the same emphasis without explicitly referring to rabbinic interpretations. As a result, the dichotomy between the sacrificed Christ and that of the unharmed Isaac must be viewed as another example of an exegetical encounter between the rabbis and the church fathers.

To conclude this chapter we will briefly explore the significance of the Passover festival, because Athanasius and Melito, both of whom have provided us with examples of an exegetical encounter with rabbinic interpretations, also mention Passover. Their interpretations were written (and/or spoken) at Easter, which is celebrated around the same time as Passover. In the next chapter I will explore the better known association between the Akedah and Rosh ha-Shana, but it is worth pointing out that the rabbis also linked the Akedah with Passover. This may explain why Easter was chosen by Athanasius and Melito as an appropriate time to discuss the significance of Genesis 22 and their response to rabbinic interpretations.

Like Rosh ha-Shana, Passover was also viewed as a new year: 'this month [of Nissan] shall be unto you the beginning of months' (Exodus 12.2). The festival not only commemorated past redemption from Egypt, but also represented the future redemption.[75] The rabbis suggested that Isaac was born in the month of Nissan and was also bound in the same month. They associate Isaac with the Passover lamb, and, in an interpretation of Exodus 12.5 'your lamb (שה) shall be without blemish, a male of the first year', the rabbis

---

[75] ExRab 15.11.

explain that the reason the lamb was chosen was as a result of the Akedah. They therefore link the Akedah with redemption and Passover and, for example, mentioned its role in an interpretation of the parting of the Red Sea.[76]

The link between the Akedah and redemption is also relevant as illustrated in the following interpretation, when Moses successfully pleads with God to be merciful to the people after the episode of the Golden Calf:

'Remember Abraham, Isaac and Israel' (Exodus 32.13). Why are the three patriarchs mentioned here? Our rabbis say: Moses said, If they are guilty to be burnt, remember Abraham who gave himself to be burnt in the fiery furnace . . . If they are guilty to be slain, remember Isaac their father who stretched out his neck on the altar to be slain for your name's sake. May his immolation take the place of the immolation of his children; and if it is banishment that they deserve, then remember their father Jacob who was banished from his father's house to Haran. Let all those acts [of the patriarchs] now atone for their act [in making the calf].[77]

This interpretation not only associates the Akedah and Passover with the redemption from Egypt, but also associates it with atonement. In other words, it is not only a reminder of the liberation from Egypt, but also points to deliverance from sin. As a result, the rabbis associated atonement (i.e. redemption from sin) with the Akedah. As we will see in the next chapter, once atonement had become primarily associated with Rosh ha-Shana and the Days of Penitence, so the Akedah followed and its connections with Passover were weakened.

It is difficult, and perhaps not relevant to an examination of exegetical encounters, to discover whether the Akedah was associated initially with Passover or with Rosh ha-Shana. Both festivals were linked with Abraham and Isaac, both celebrated the New Year and both were associated with atonement and redemption from sin. The significance of atonement will be explored in more detail in the next chapter. Nevertheless, the earlier connection between the Akedah and Passover may shed light on why Melito and Athanasius offered their interpretations around Easter.

CONCLUSION

Although Philo and Josephus emphasize the importance of Isaac, both maintain the biblical emphasis on the faith and piety of Abraham. It is true that Isaac played a more active role in their interpretations of vv. 9–12 than

---

[76] Cf. *Mekhilta Bes.* 4. See above pp. 283–43.   [77] ExRab 44.5.

the biblical account would suggest, but they continue to stress the actions of Abraham. For Pseudo-Philo, the willingness of Abraham to give up his son explains why Jews were chosen by God. The emphasis was again on Abraham – God chose Israel 'because he [Abraham] did not refuse'.

Paul was also primarily interested in the willingness of a father to sacrifice his son and, during a discussion of the implications of God having sent his only Son, referred indirectly to the Akedah. Paul's reference should not be viewed as significant or as a key with which to understand his writings because he makes no other allusions to the Akedah. For Paul, Isaac's significance was dependent upon being a son of the faithful Abraham rather than upon his actions at the Akedah.

Verses 9–12 enabled the rabbis to continue the emphasis of their interpretations of vv. 6–8 and to demonstrate the complete willingness and full participation of Isaac in the Akedah. As a result, Isaac became the main character in rabbinic exegesis and the story became known as *The Binding of Isaac*. The centrality of Isaac becomes particularly apparent in those interpretations that contain references to the shedding of his blood as well as references to his ashes. I suggested that the purpose behind these interpretations was threefold:

- to stress the willingness of Isaac, even after suffering injury, to give up his life;
- to portray Isaac as one who suffered;
- to associate Isaac in particular and the Akedah in general with atonement (to be discussed in the next chapter).

The rabbis suggest that Isaac's blood actually was shed and that he did suffer. The importance of these interpretations lies not in the subject of blood and ashes, but in the willingness of Isaac to give himself up for his father and to God. The similarity to Christian teaching about Christ is striking. In the first six centuries the rabbis stressed Isaac's self-offering and willingness to die. It was Isaac's association with the hoped-for resurrection of the dead that led, shortly after this period, to an expanded interpretation, which again demonstrates Christian influence, and described Isaac's death and resurrection.

The church fathers put forward the opposite view. First, Isaac did not suffer, only Christ suffered and for this reason Isaac was not sacrificed. Isaac needed to be ransomed to escape death whereas Christ died to overcome death. Second, as Cyril of Alexandria points out, all earlier sacrifices were only a pale shadow of the future sacrifice of Christ. Even had Isaac shed blood, the sacrifice would, like the previous sacrifices, have been unacceptable to God. Third, in contrast to the rabbis, the church fathers maintained an emphasis on Abraham, for it was through Isaac that Abraham was tested.

Taken together, the interpretations of the church fathers and the rabbis on vv. 9–12 offer more evidence for an exegetical encounter as most clearly indicated by the interpretations of Athanasius in his *Festal Letter*. The fact that the church fathers were keen to emphasize that Isaac did not suffer suggests an awareness of the rabbinic interpretations for, as far as the biblical story is concerned, there was no need for such emphasis. Isaac is at the heart of the exegetical encounter.

CHAPTER 6

Verses 13–14: The sacrifice of the ram

v. 13 And Abraham lifted up his eyes and looked, and behold, behind him was a ram, caught in the thicket by his horns; and Abraham went and took the ram, and offered it up as a burnt offering instead of his son. v. 14 So Abraham called the name of that place the Lord will provide; as it is said to this day, 'On the mount of the Lord it shall be provided.'

וישא אברהם את עיניו וירא והנה איל אחר נאחז בסבך בקרניו וילך אברהם ויקח את האיל ויעלהו לעלה תחת בנו: ויקרא אברהם שם המקום ההוא יהוה יראה אשר יאמר היום בהר יהוה יראה

καὶ ἀναβλέψας Αβρααμ τοῖς ὀφθαλμοῖς αὐτοῦ εἶδεν, καὶ ἰδοὺ κριὸς εἷς κατεχόμενος ἐν φυτῷ σαβεκ τῶν κεράτων· καὶ ἐπορεύθη Αβρααμ καὶ ἔλαβεν τὸν κριὸν καὶ ἀνήνεγκεν αὐτὸν εἰς ὁλοκάρπ-ωσιν ἀντὶ Ισαακ τοῦ υἱοῦ αὐτοῦ. καὶ ἐκάλεσεν Αβρααμ τὸ ὄνομα τοῦ τόπου ἐκείνου κύριος εἶδεν, ἵνα εἴπωσιν σήμερον ἐν τῷ ὄρει κύριος ὤφθη.

EARLY INTERPRETATIONS

Josephus completes his narrative of the Akedah with a description of God's pleasure at the extent of Abraham's piety and obedience and promise to him of a 'great dominion'. At the end of God's speech, a ram appears 'from obscurity' and is sacrificed. Abraham and Isaac embrace each other and both return to Sarah.[1] A number of translations read 'behind' (אחר) as 'one' (אחד)[2], although others have retained the reading אחר. Interestingly, Philo avoids mentioning the sacrifice of the ram and does not even mention the ram's appearance in his main commentary De Abrahamo (although he does

---

[1] Ant 1.236. Cf. Ant 7.333.
[2] Examples of the former include Tg. Ps.-Jon. (והא דיכרא חד), Neofiti (והא דכר חד) and the Samaritan Pentateuch (איל אחד). Examples of the latter include, e.g., Onk (והא בתר דכרא אחיד באילנא), Sym (et apparuit aries post hoc) and the Vulgate (viditque post tergum arietem).

briefly refer to the ram elsewhere).[3] His omission of the sacrifice of the ram implies a sense of embarrassment. Perhaps Philo was concerned to end his account of the story with praise for its heroes, for 'the record of it as such stands graven not only in the sacred books but in the minds of the readers'.[4]

The near sacrifice of Isaac led Philo to make a comparison between Isaac and the *tamid* lamb, an atonement offering that was sacrificed twice daily in the Temple.[5] Isaac was a paradigm of the *tamid* not by virtue of its association with atonement, but because Isaac was blameless, like a lamb without blemish.[6] The same description is applied in 1 Peter 20 to Christ who is described as 'a lamb without blemish or spot'.

Interestingly, neither Philo nor Josephus interpret the Akedah in terms of atonement. For example, although Josephus emphasizes Isaac's willingness to be sacrificed and links Mount Moriah with the site of the Temple, he does not focus on any expiatory consequences of the Akedah; he does not state that Isaac died for others or that his merits were passed on to others. This is especially significant considering the influence on his work of the *Iphigenia*, mentioned above,[7] in which Euripides concludes that Iphigenia's death had expiatory value. Yet, as far as Josephus is concerned, even such blessings as did arise did so as a result of the piety of Abraham, not Isaac.[8]

However, the concept of atonement was developed in some detail by the author of 4 Maccabees, who argued that the suffering and death of the righteous martyrs had redemptive efficacy for Israel and secured God's pardon for his people. Nevertheless, although the Akedah is mentioned on a number of occasions, it is not possible to say that any of these institute an explicit link with atonement. Isaac appears to have been portrayed not as an example of vicarious atonement, but as a model for martyrs. For example, Eleazer is described as withstanding the torture as follows:

by means of reason he became youthful again in spirit and, by reason like that of Isaac prevailed over many-headed torture. O blessed old age, revered gray head, life loyal to the Law and perfected by the faithful seal of death.[9]

While the author refers to Isaac's willingness to die, there is no reference to his death nor to vicarious atonement resulting from his actions. Although Isaac is willing to sacrifice his life, it is Eleazer, not Isaac, who suffers a martyr's death. Isaac is depicted as a model of courage, willingness and

---

[3] *De Fuga* 132.   [4] *De Ab.* 177.
[5] Philo comments (*De Ab.* 198) that 'following the law of the burnt offering he would have dismembered his son and offered him limb by limb'.
[6] Cf. *De Sac.* 110.   [7] See vv. 6 to 8.   [8] *Ant* 1.234–5.
[9] 4 Mac. 7.14–15. Cf. Van Henten 1997:241–3.

endurance – yet his actions are no more atoning than those of David, Aaron or the other biblical characters mentioned in 4 Maccabees.

Some scholars have turned to the writings of Pseudo-Philo in support of the argument that during this period the early interpreters viewed the Akedah as atoning for the sins of Israel. According to Perrot, 'the sacrifice of Isaac is a true sacrifice and lies behind Temple sacrifices for the forgiveness of sins'.[10] Le Déaut, slightly more circumspectly, agrees that the author regarded the Akedah as a form of expiation of sin.[11] However, Chilton and Davies challenge this conclusion and argue that Isaac's reward is nothing more than inheritance in the next world.[12] For example, in the following passage, Pseudo-Philo lays stress upon the actions of Isaac and their consequences but does not introduce a notion of expiation. Isaac states:

'Now, my blessedness will surpass that of all men because there will be nothing like this – about me future generations will be instructed and through me the peoples will understand that the Lord has made the soul of a man worthy to be a sacrifice'. And when he had offered the son on the altar and had bound his feet so as to kill him, the Almighty hastened to send his voice from on high with the words: 'Do not kill your son – do not destroy the fruit of your body. For now I have made you appear to those who know you not and I have closed the mouths of those who are always speaking evil of you. I shall always remember you, and your name and his will abide from one generation to the next.'[13]

It is clear that Isaac's eventual willingness was sufficient in its own right to result in his special status – even though he appeared to question God's command. However, there is little to suggest that the Akedah was atoning. It is true that in Pseudo-Philo's view the Akedah would continue to have an effect in the future and that God was expected to maintain his concern for Israel. Nevertheless, God responds to the Akedah with a pledge of continued deliverance, not a pledge of forgiveness for sins.

An association with deliverance seems to lie behind the commemoration of the Akedah in *Jubilees*, a book that places considerable emphasis on the chronology and the timing of festivals, suggesting (among other things) that the patriarchs were ritually observant. *Jubilees* locates the Akedah in the month of Nisan and describes Mastema as coming before God on the twelfth day of the first month (Nisan) before accusing Abraham.[14] Although *Jubilees* does not mention Passover by name, it seems to have

---

[10] Harrington, Perrot and Bogaert 1976:172.
[11] Le Déaut 1963:190, a position supported by Swetnam (1981:54).
[12] Chilton and Davies (1978:525–8). Cf. Jacobson (1996, II:868).   [13] LAB 32.1–4.
[14] Cf. Daly 1977:55, Endres 1987:51 and Horbury and McNeil 1981:13–15. However, Davies and Chilton (1978:519) deny that a significant link exists 'between Isaac and any Passover theme'.

this festival in mind because Abraham departed with Isaac and his two servants on the twelfth of Nisan and arrived at the mountain three days later. The arrival thus took place on the fourteenth of Nisan, the same day as the beginning of Passover. In addition, the detailed description of Passover in *Jubilees* uses the same chronological terms as those found in the retelling of the Akedah.[15] For example, the festival that commemorates the Akedah lasts seven days, as does Passover.[16] Thus, the book of *Jubilees* describes the Akedah as a Passover story, relating the event to the deliverance from Egypt, and possibly also to future deliverance. It is worth noting that this association between the Akedah and Passover reinforces the view of the early interpreters, which linked the Akedah with God's redemptive action.

INTERPRETATIONS OF THE PALESTINIAN RABBIS AND THE GREEK CHURCH FATHERS

Unsurprisingly, the church fathers drew a parallel between the sacrifice of the ram and the sacrifice of Christ. The ram was the true anticipation of the Redeemer. Melito, for example, comments:

> On behalf of Isaac the righteous one, a ram appeared for slaughter
> So that Isaac might be released from bonds
> The ram, slain, ransomed (ἐλυτρώσατο) Isaac
> So also the Lord, slain, saved us
> And bound (δεθεὶς), released us
> And sacrificed, ransomed us (ἐλυτρώσατο).[17]

Melito suggests that the sacrifice of the ram in substitution for Isaac provided an analogy with the sacrifice of Christ as a ransom for humankind. Thus the deliverance of Isaac by the slaughter of the ram foreshadows the deliverance of humankind by the death of Christ. In contrast to rabbinic exegesis, which emphasizes the atoning aspects of the Akedah (see below), Melito argues that because Isaac needed 'ransoming' there could be no redemption through the Akedah. Isaac required the saving act of the sacrifice of the ram because his action on Moriah was not, on its own, sufficient to achieve redemption; only the ram, being the model of Christ, was able to redeem him. In contrast to the rabbis, Melito's interpretation reduces the significance of Isaac.

Comparisons between the ram and Christ were common in the writings of the church fathers, and both Isaac and the ram were understood as figures

[15] *Jub.* 49.1–23.   [16] *Jub.* 19.18–19.   [17] Frg. 10 Hall.

for Christ. Origen, for example, proposes a dual analogy with Christ, in which the ram represents the flesh that suffered, while Isaac represents Christ in Spirit, which remained incorruptible.[18] In spirit, Christ/Isaac offered himself to his father; in flesh, Christ the ram was offered on the cross and the altar. Athanasius also considered the significance of the ram and states that Abraham 'saw Christ in the ram which was offered up instead of Isaac as a sacrifice to God'.[19] Likewise, Cyril of Alexandria describes Isaac as representing the Word, while the ram represents the human Christ.[20] This enables Cyril to emphasize that Isaac was not sacrificed and that 'the knife was not borne against Isaac' but against the ram/Christ.[21]

Gregory of Nyssa, who was undoubtedly influenced by Origen and perhaps also by Melito,[22] offered a detailed typological exegesis in a liturgical homily preached at an Easter vigil. For Gregory, the value of the Akedah lay in its representation of Christ taking up the sins of the world through his sacrifice. The focus, therefore, was on Isaac and on the ram, which resulted in a double typology of Christ:

The father of Isaac did not spare that beloved one, and the only-begotten became an offering and a sacrifice, and the lamb was slain in his place. One can see in the story all the mystery of the true religion. The lamb is hung from wood, caught by the horns, and the only-begotten carries upon himself the wood for the whole offering. You see how He who bears all things by the word of power, the same one both bears the burden of our wood and is taken up by the wood, ready to carry as God and being carried as lamb, as the Holy Spirit distributes the great mystery figuratively between both the beloved son and the sheep indicated with him; so that by the sheep is displayed the mystery of the death, and by the only begotten the life uninterrupted by death.[23]

Thus, for Gregory, the ram offered in the place of Isaac corresponds to Christ offered for the world. Isaac carrying the wood and the lamb being sacrificed are respectively Christ who bore the sins of the world (the wood) and Christ the crucified. The surviving only-begotten son (Isaac) represents the undivided life of the Son of God and the lamb represents death. In their interpretations of the ram, we can see once again that the church fathers are keen to emphasize that Isaac did not suffer, die or was resurrected.

Verses 13–14 provide the rabbis with another opportunity to discuss to what extent Isaac suffered on Mount Moriah. They also associate the Akedah with the sacrifices carried out in the Temple, describing it as a

---

[18] *Hom. in Gen.* 8.9 Doutreleau.   [19] Athan, *Epist.* 6 Migne.
[20] Cyril of Alex., *Hom. Pas.* 5 Burns. Cf. *Glaph. in Gen.*, PG 69 144A.
[21] Cyril of Alex., *Hom. Pas.* 5 Burns.   [22] Cf. Drobner 1982:55.
[23] Greg. of Nys., *In Sanc. Pas.*, PG 46 601 C–D.

precursor to the Temple sacrifices, and especially sacrifices of atonement. For example, Yose ben Yose, the fifth-century poet, interprets the Akedah in terms of the Temple service.[24] In addition, the sacrificial ram mentioned in Leviticus 16.3 is depicted as recalling Isaac[25] and the ram on Moriah is compared to a sin offering.[26] In an anonymous *piyyut* Isaac asks his father to say a blessing just before the sacrifice is to take place.[27]

The daily *tamid* offering is also linked with the Akedah through an interpretation of Leviticus 1.10–11:

'And he shall kill the bullock before the Lord' (Leviticus 1.5) while of the ram it says, 'And he shall slaughter it on the side of the altar northward (צפונה)' (Leviticus 1.10). When Abraham our father bound Isaac his son, The Holy One, blessed be He, instituted the sacrifice of two lambs, one in the morning and one in the evening. What is the purpose of this? It is in order that when Israel offers the daily offering upon the altar and reads the scriptural text 'northward before the Lord,' the Holy One, Blessed be He, may remember the Binding of Isaac. Elijah says, I call heaven and earth to witness whether a heathen or an Israelite, a man or a woman, a manservant or a maidservant reads this verse, 'northward before the Lord' the Holy One, Blessed be He, remembers the Binding of Isaac, as it is said, 'northward before the Lord'.[28]

The word 'northward' (צפונה) is understood in terms of 'preservation' (צפון), and the rabbis suggest that the Akedah is preserved in God's memory whenever the *tamid* sacrifices are carried out. Such is the importance of the Akedah that whether Jew or gentile repeats the verse, God remembers the Akedah. The *tamid* offering serves to remind God of the Akedah and to petition him to show compassion. The Mishnah prescribes that the *tamid* offering should be bound hand and foot using the same verb as that which describes the binding of Isaac (and, consequently, reinforcing its association with Isaac).[29]

Interestingly, this interpretation seems to have influenced Romanos, who adds the same detailed comment concerning Abraham's act of binding: 'And he [Abraham] bound the feet and hands of the son whom he had engendered'.[30] Another indication of an exegetical encounter in the *Kontakion* of Romanos is his explanation of the necessity to bind Isaac, for he describes Abraham as saying 'first I shall bind and then kill him, so that his movement may not prevent my quick strike . . .' There is no mention elsewhere in the writings of the Greek church fathers of the need to prevent Isaac

[24] Horbury and McNeil 1981:169–71.   [25] LevRab 2.11.   [26] GenRab 56.9.
[27] Anonymous *piyyut* reconstructed from Genizah manuscripts by Sokoloff and Yahalom (1999: 124–31).
[28] LevRab 2.11.   [29] M *Tam.* 4.1: 'They do not tie the lamb but they bind it.'
[30] Rom, *In Ab.* 19 Grosdidier de Matons.

from moving, but the same interpretation is found in rabbinic interpretations that describe Isaac as asking Abraham to bind him in case he moved involuntarily and so make the sacrifice unfit.[31]

Let us now examine the rabbinic interpretations of the ram. The rabbis associated the ram wholly with Isaac. For example, when the rabbis interpreted the words 'And he sacrificed it instead of his son', they portrayed Abraham as requesting God to 'regard the blood of this ram as though it were the blood of Isaac, my son, and its *emurim*[32] as though they were the *emurim* of Isaac, my son'.[33] Thus, in contrast to the church fathers who described the ram as ransoming Isaac, the rabbis described the ram as representing Isaac. The ram's importance is dependent upon its association with Isaac. Consequently, Abraham is depicted as asking God to accept the sacrifice as if it were Isaac.

This interpretation is based upon the Mishnaic concept of exchange known as תחת ('instead of')[34] – the same word is used v. 13 – which validated the substitution of one item for another. It is worth noting that the exchange of Isaac for the ram is similarly depicted in an interpretation of Gregory of Nazianzen. Gregory explained that the exchange was carried out because God would not accept Isaac as a sacrifice and that, as a result of Isaac's rejection, Abraham was commanded to exchange the offering.[35] For the rabbis, on the other hand, the offering by Abraham of his son, and the self-offering by Isaac, were accepted by God – there was no mention of rejection.

As well as exhibiting a similar approach, the adoption of the concept of exchange in the interpretation also illustrates a significant difference between the church fathers and the rabbis. The former reduces the significance of Isaac's contribution and, in the case of Gregory, actually deprecates his role. This is to be contrasted with the rabbinic emphasis on the centrality of Isaac, whose offering was wholly acceptable to God. The son was only exchanged because the test was already completed. In the words of

---

[31] See vv. 6 to 8.

[32] Defined by Jastrow (1903, I: 50) as 'whatever is consecrated as offering for festivals'.

[33] GenRab 56.9. Cf. JT *Ta'an* 65d; TanB *Ve-yera* 46; TanY *Ve-yera* 23. In TanY *Shelah* 14 the rabbis discuss the meaning of 'instead of' (בנו תחת) and describe the ashes of the ram as the ashes of Isaac: 'The text is in no way defective. What is the purpose of בנו תחת? Abraham said, "Sovereign of the Universe, behold I am slaughtering the ram, so You shall regard it as if my son is slaughtered before You". He took up its blood and said, "Regard it as though the blood of Isaac were sprinkled before You". He took up the ram and flayed it and said to Him, "Regard it as if the skin of Isaac were flayed before You on the altar". He burned it and said, "Regard it as though the ashes of Isaac were heaped up before You on the altar".'

[34] M *Tem.* 5.5: 'Behold this [animal] is instead of (תחת) this, this is in place of this'.

[35] *Orat.* 45; *In Sanc. Pas*, PG 36 653B.

the rabbis, 'although the deed was not carried out He accepted it as though it had been completed'.[36] For the church fathers, the son was exchanged because Isaac was not acceptable. The moment when the test would be completed had not yet arrived. In the words of Melito, 'Christ suffered, whereas Isaac did not suffer for he was the model of the Christ who was going to suffer'.[37]

The rabbis even went beyond the concept of exchange, and another interpretation depicts Abraham as asking God to regard the sacrifice of the ram 'as though I had sacrificed my son Isaac first and then this ram instead of him'.[38] As a result, the ram was no longer a substitute for Isaac but had been transformed into Isaac himself – Isaac became the sacrificial ram, as it were, and was considered as if he had been sacrificed. This is developed further by later rabbinic interpretations that state that the ram had grown up in Heaven and its name was Isaac.[39]

The association between Isaac and the ram is reinforced by a rabbinic interpretation according to which the lamb was included among those newly born animals suitable for sacrifice (Leviticus 22.27) because of the 'the merit of Isaac'.[40] The ram's purpose is fulfilled in Isaac and can only be understood in terms of Isaac. This represents the logical sequence of the interchange of the lamb for Isaac, which is expressed by one interpretation of Leviticus 22.7 that 'The lamb was chosen second [after the ox] in order to recall the merits of the upright one who bound himself on the altar and stretched out his neck for your name's sake'.[41]

As a result, the ram, like Isaac, was associated with *zecut avot*, and the rabbis commented that when, in the future, Israel remembered the ram the people would benefit. The benefits were twofold: redemptive and atoning. One instrument of redemption was the blowing of the ram's horn, which the rabbis interpreted eschatologically:

'Abraham lifted up his eyes, and looked, and behold, behind him (אחר) there was a ram'. What does 'behind' (אחר) mean? Said Rabbi Judan, 'After all that happened' (אחר) Israel still falls into the clutches of sin and is led astray by troubles; yet they will ultimately be redeemed by the ram's horn, as it says, 'And the Lord will blow the horn . . .' (Zechariah 9.14).[42] Rabbi Haninah ben Rabbi Isaac said, 'Throughout the year Israel are in sin's clutches and led astray by their troubles, but on New Year they will take the shofar and blow on it and eventually they will be redeemed by the ram's horn as it says, "And the Lord will blow the horn and so on" . . . Because

[36] GenRab 55.5. Cf. Philo, *De Ab.* 177. [37] Frg. 9 Hall. [38] GenRab 56.9.
[39] MHG on Gen. 22.9. Cf. Mann 1940:68 [Heb.]. [40] LevRab 21.11. [41] Frg. *Tg.* Lev. 22.7.
[42] Note the quotation from Zech. 9.14, which is a commonly cited verse in both Jewish and Christian exegesis. See vv. 4 to 5.

our father Abraham saw the ram extricate himself from one thicket (סבך) and go and become entangled (מסתבך) in another, the Holy One, Blessed be He, said to him, 'So will your children be entangled (להסתבך) in countries changing from Babylon to Media, from Media to Greece and from Greece to Edom; yet they will eventually be redeemed by the ram's horn'.[43]

The rabbis interpreted the biblical phrase 'and behold he saw a ram behind, caught by its horns in a thicket' to mean that, even after all God had done for Israel, the people still sinned; nevertheless, God would still redeem Israel by the ram's horn. They also suggested that אחר referred to the end of the year, when Israel would be redeemed. Finally, just as the ram became entangled in one thicket after another, so would the people be entangled in four kingdoms – Babylon, Persia, Greece and Edom – before they were to be redeemed by God. It is worth noting that the rabbis understood redemption to mean not only deliverance from exile and persecution, but also deliverance from sin.

Both aspects of redemption were also discussed in rabbinic interpretations that examined the phrase 'the Lord will see' (יהוה יראה). The following text is an interesting example:

Abraham worshipped and prayed to the Name of the Word of the Lord, and said: 'O Lord, You are He that sees and is unseen! I pray: all is revealed before You. It is known before You that there is no division in my heart at the time when you told me to offer Isaac, my son, and to make him dust and ashes before You. But I departed immediately in the morning and did your word with joy and fulfilled it. Now I pray for mercy before You, O Lord our God, that when the children of Isaac come to a time of distress, You may remember on their behalf the binding of Isaac, their father, and loose and forgive them their sins and deliver them from all distress, so that the generations which follow him may say: In the mountain of the Temple of the Lord, Abraham offered Isaac, his son, and in this mountain – of the Temple – the glory of the Shekhina of the Lord was revealed to him.'[44]

It is worth noting that Abraham appeals on behalf of Isaac's children, perhaps because of the emphasis on the suffering of Isaac. The references to Isaac's blood and ashes are also mentioned in petitions to God to show forgiveness to Israel. For example, in a Genizah fragment Isaac states, 'May it be Your will that a quarter measure of my blood provide atonement for Israel'.[45] Thus Isaac's experience on Moriah becomes central to Abraham's plea to God and is integrated into early Jewish liturgy. We can be confident, regardless of the late dating of the first Jewish prayer books, that the Akedah played a significant role in early Jewish liturgy. It was mentioned at least as

---

[43] GenRab 56.9.　　[44] Frg. *Tg.* Gen. 22.14.　　[45] Mann 1940:67 [Heb.].

early as the second century CE because the Mishnah (*Ta'anit* 2.4) appeals to God to show compassion to Israel on account of the Akedah.

Three elements of the rabbinic interpretations are especially important to understanding the place of the Akedah in Jewish liturgy. First, Abraham suppressed his pity in order to do God's will; second, Abraham appealed to God to show compassion to Isaac's children; and third, as a result of the merit of the Akedah (זכות עקדה), God was asked to defend and/or redeem Israel.

The reason why references to the Akedah are a common feature of Jewish liturgy can be explained by its association with *zecut avot*, which enabled Israel to appeal to God to show compassion. For example, an important reference to the Akedah is found in the supplication 'And He is merciful' which occurs after the Amidah on Mondays and Thursdays. This is one of a number of supplications or *selichot* that were probably first compiled for fast days but were also read on other occasions.[46] It beseeches God to 'remember and give heed to the Covenant between the Pieces (with Abraham) and let the binding (upon the altar) of his only son appear before You'.[47]

Jewish liturgy retained the rabbinic tendency to associate the Akedah primarily with Isaac, aiming to fulfil the maxim that 'since Isaac was redeemed it is as if all Israel were redeemed'.[48] For example, the earliest prayer book, the ninth-century *siddur* of Sa'adia, refers to the Akedah as follows:

You are the Lord who chose Abram and brought him out of Ur of the Chaldees, and named him Abraham. You made a covenant with Isaac and swore to him on Mount Moriah.[49]

It is worth emphasizing that Sa'adia states that God's oath was sworn to Isaac, not Abraham as is recounted in the biblical story (which is doubtless one reason why editors of later prayer books changed the rendering[50]). Sa'adia's composition appears deliberate and is paralleled by *Targum Pseudo-Jonathan* and the *Fragmentary Targum*, both of which refer to the covenant made with Isaac on Mount Moriah.[51] We should also note that an emphasis on Isaac is found in the seder of Amram, which referred to Isaac as God's only son (יחידך).[52]

The liturgical references to Isaac in particular and the Akedah in general were matched by pleas for mercy, such as the following plea: 'O Merciful

---

[46] Reif 1993: 85–8.   [47] Singer 1962:62; Hedegard 1951:78–9 [Heb.].
[48] JT *Ta'an.* 2.4, 65d.   [49] Davidson *et al.* 1970:6.
[50] E.g. Singer 1962:9. Cf. LevRab 29.9, which describes the seventh month (בחודש השביעי) as the month of oath (ירחא דשבועתא), because God swore an oath to Abraham (כי שבעתי) on Moriah.
[51] *Tg. Ps.-Jon.* and Frg. *Tg.* Lev. 26.42.   [52] Hedegard 1951:9 [Heb.].

One, remember for our sake the covenant of Isaac, the bound', to which the congregation replies, 'For his sake, let Him forgive.'[53] These pleas illustrate the association between the Akedah and Rosh ha-Shana.[54]

The name Rosh ha-Shana is not found in the Bible – it is merely designated as 'in the seventh month, on the first day of the month' (Leviticus 23.24). By mishnaic times its importance had grown, as illustrated by a whole chapter of the Mishnah being devoted to it. The association between the Akedah and Rosh ha-Shana was established in the first few centuries of the common era, as demonstrated by the following plea:

When the children of Isaac are in the thrall of transgression and evil deeds, remember for their sake the Binding of Isaac, their father, and be filled with mercy for them. Have mercy on them, and turn for their sake the measure of judgement to the measure of mercy. When? 'In the seventh month . . .'

However, the Akedah was originally evoked in times of general distress and not only at Rosh ha-Shana.[55] For example, the earliest liturgical reference to the Akedah in the Mishnah relates to prayers on any fast day: 'may He who answered Abraham our father in mount Moriah answer you and hearken to the voice of your crying this day'.[56] The *selicha* in the earliest prayer books adds, 'and may He who answered Isaac his son when he was bound on the altar answer us . . .'[57] It is also worth noting that none of the Targums mention the Rosh ha-Shana–Akedah association. Even the reading of Genesis 22 was not associated with Rosh ha-Shana in Mishnaic times because Leviticus 23 provided the scriptural reading.[58] By the fifth century CE, the reading of Genesis 22 was a key element of the Jewish lectionary cycle, and its reading on Rosh ha-Shana was firmly established, although there are still signs of previous controversy.[59]

Another example of the Akedah being associated with divine compassion at all times (rather than just on Rosh ha-Shana) is to be found in an interpretation that explains that the Akedah is endowed with the same expiatory qualities as any sacrifice: '"My beloved is unto me as a cluster of henna" (Song of Songs 1.14). The cluster refers to Isaac, who was bound on the altar like a cluster of henna because he atones for the iniquities of Israel.'[60] In this interpretation the Akedah is represented by a cluster of henna because it symbolizes atonement.

---

[53] Rosenfeld 1956:391.   [54] PRK 23:9.
[55] E.g. JT *Ta'an.* 2:4, 65d; GenRab 56.10.   [56] M *Ta'an.* 2.1–4.
[57] The litany 'May He who answered . . .' is also mentioned in JT *Ber.* 4.3, 8a and JT *Ta'an.* 2.2, 65c, but neither is identical to the version found in the earliest prayer books.
[58] Tos *Meg.* 3.5.   [59] Tos *Meg.* 3.5. BT *Meg.* 31a   [60] SOSRab 1.14.

Of course, atonement is central to Rosh ha-Shana, and the rabbis state that the ram's horn is blown on Rosh ha-Shana to remind God of Abraham and Isaac's willingness to obey the divine command. One interpretation, which discusses the significance of the ram being caught by its horns, states that when Jews ask for forgiveness from God on Rosh ha-Shana, they should blow the ram's horn (*shofar*) and God would forgive them.[61] However, we should note that in biblical times the blowing of the ram's horn was not solely associated with the Akedah but with numerous events, such as the theophany on Sinai, the proclamation of the Jubilee year, signalling a time of war, and Temple music.

Nevertheless, during the period under review, the Akedah became an essential feature of the liturgy during the Ten Days of Awe – beginning with Rosh ha-Shana and ending with Yom Kippur. The Ten Days represent a period of divine judgement. For example, the following *piyyut* was composed by Eleazar ha-Kallir of the sixth century CE:

When God desired to heal the transgression of Israel, He taught them how to offer up prayer to Him, that prayer which had availed their fathers, 'ancient mountains', and bade them call upon him with their voice, to deliver them from the snare. The righteousness of those ancestors He bade them enunciate in their supplication; their acts during their lives He directed to be recounted, at 'the acceptable season, the day of salvation' (Isaiah 49.8) on which the ram was entangled by his horns and the covenant of oath established. We declare God's power by the ten recognitions of His sovereignty founded upon the ten trials through which Abraham passed. The appointed number of memorial voices, the *zichronot* and the *shofarot* we sound on the cornet is also ten in commemoration of Isaac, who blessed his son (Jacob) and made him 'lord' with ten blessings. And the Eternal then regarded the beloved child of Abraham, who had come from Naharaim, even Isaac, who was bound on Mount Moriah, his hands behind him fastened. May his ashes procure mercy for the remnant of Israel who early and late approach God in prayer.[62]

The beginning of the *piyyut* affirms the standard rabbinic view that prayer replaced sacrifice after the destruction of the Temple[63] and explains that the recounting of the *zecut avot* was particularly significant at 'the acceptable season' (Rosh ha-Shana), when the people would appeal to God to show mercy. The *piyyut* states, first, that the Akedah took place on the 'day of salvation' (equated with Rosh ha-Shana), and second, commends the retelling of the Akedah as of particular benefit.[64]

---

[61] BT RHS 16a. Cf. TanB *Ve-yera* 46; TanY *Ve-yera* 23.   [62] De Sola 1901, III:120–1.
[63] E.g., BT *Ber.* 26b, which states that prayer replaced the daily sacrifices.
[64] E.g., TanY *Ve-yera* 23.

The rabbinic emphasis on the atoning benefits of the Akedah is, unsurprisingly, paralleled by the interpretations of the church fathers, who also discussed it in terms of atonement. For example, Pseudo-Ephrem Graecus wrote:

> The sacrifice here is the wood of a tree; soon it will be the wood of a cross. The name of this wood, *sabach*,[65] is the forgiveness of this one. The name of the wood of the cross is similarly forgiveness for sinners. [This name comes] from what befell Isaac and from the matters of my son. A ram is bound in this one, Christ is nailed in that one. This one is slaughtered on behalf of Isaac having been endangered, that one is crucified on behalf of the world.[66]

It is worth pointing out, however, that in early Christian liturgy, in contrast to the Jewish, there are only a few references to Genesis 22. The fact that the Akedah is not given special emphasis is interesting, bearing in mind the significance of sacrifice, especially in the Eucharistic liturgy. It is true that the Akedah is mentioned during the offertory prayers, associated with epiclesis (a petition for the descent of the Holy Spirit upon the bread and wine), alongside Abel, Noah, Moses and Aaron, and Samuel. In line with the interpretations of the church fathers, the liturgical stress lies on Abraham, not Isaac.[67] The same emphasis is found in other early Eastern liturgies such as those of the Maronites,[68] as well as in the liturgy of James.[69]

On the other hand, the reading of Genesis 22 was an important element of the Christian lectionary cycle and was mentioned by Egeria during her visit to Jerusalem in the late fourth century CE. The Easter cycle was the major feature of the liturgical year. It began eight weeks before Easter and continued for a further seven weeks afterwards, concluding with Pentecost. Genesis 22 was commonly read on the Thursday before Easter in Cappadocia, Jerusalem, Constantinople, Nestorian Syria and the West. Considering that readings were often quite different from church to church, this consensus is quite remarkable.[70] We should also remember, as mentioned in the previous chapter, that the homilies of Melito (*Peri*

---

[65] Melito (Frg. 11 Hall) was one of the first church fathers to comment on σαβεκ: 'For the Lord was a lamb like the ram which Abraham caught in a sabach tree.' He suggests that σαβεκ represents the cross and associates the ram entangled in the tree with Christ fastened to the cross and is followed by church fathers such as Eusebius (*Catena* 1277 Petit), who interprets שבק as 'forgiveness' (cf. שבק, in Aramaic, which means 'forgiveness'). Cf. Salvesen 1991:45, Ter Haar Romeny 1997:323–31. Note, however, that both Diodorus and Gennadius explain that σαβεκ is the name of the plant. See Petit 1986:199–202.

[66] Ps Eph Grae, *In Ab*. Mercati (1915:103).

[67] Quoted from the liturgy of Basil. Brightman 1896:320; Swainson 1884:79.

[68] Quoted by Lietzmann 1979:71.   [69] Brightman 1896:41; Swainson 1884:218.

[70] Hall 1971:139–40; Botte 1951:93–4.

Pascha), as well as the interpretations of Gregory of Nyssa (*In Sanctum Pascha*) and Athanasius (*Epistle 6*), each of which discuss the Sacrifice of Isaac, were all composed at Easter. As a result, it is clear that, although Genesis 22 was not mentioned as much as in Jewish liturgy, it still played a significant role in Christianity.

CONCLUSION

It is striking that none of the early interpreters commented in any detail on the ram that was sacrificed in the place of Isaac. Philo omits mentioning the ram altogether, and Josephus only briefly refers to it. In addition, I have argued that the early interpreters did not view the Akedah in terms of the expiation of sin. Neither Josephus nor Philo consider whether the Akedah had expiatory consequences, although we noted that 4 Maccabees maintains that the suffering and death of the righteous martyrs had redemptive efficacy and secured God's pardon. However, 4 Maccabees makes no reference to Isaac's death or to vicarious atonement resulting from his actions. It is true that Isaac was willing to sacrifice his life, but it was Eleazer, not Isaac, who suffered a martyr's death. Isaac is simply depicted as a model of courage and endurance.

Pseudo-Philo offers a similar interpretation, for while he gives Isaac a special status, he does not suggest that the Akedah resulted in atonement. Although he states that the Akedah would, in the future, result in God's deliverance of Israel, he does not imply that it prompted God to forgive sins. This view is reinforced by *Jubilees*, which associates the Akedah with Passover and links events on Moriah with God's redemptive, rather than atoning, action.

Both the church fathers and the rabbis, however, discuss the concept of atonement in their interpretations. For example, the fathers were particularly keen to comment on the appearance and sacrifice of the ram and drew a parallel with the sacrifice of Christ. The ram was significant because it resulted in the deliverance of Isaac, which foreshadowed the deliverance of humankind by the death of Christ. The ram was the true anticipation of the Redeemer because it 'ransomed' Isaac, who required the saving act of its sacrifice because he could not save himself. Christ, in contrast, overcame death.

The result of these interpretations was to minimize the significance of Isaac, and the church fathers' interpretations of these verses, in direct contrast to those of the rabbis, repeated a number of features that we noted in interpretations of earlier verses: most importantly, an emphasis on Abraham, on the fact that only Christ, not Isaac, suffered. Thus Isaac's action was incomplete and the benefits of the Akedah were insufficient to deliver atonement.

In their writings, the rabbis continued to maintain an emphasis on Isaac by associating the ram with Isaac and interpreting it in terms of Isaac, thus continuing their emphasis on him. The ram's significance was wholly dependent upon Isaac, and a number of interpretations discussed the importance of the ram as a substitute for Isaac, an approach we also noticed in the interpretations of Gregory of Nazianzen. One rabbinic interpretation described the ram as having been transformed into Isaac himself. The identification of Isaac with the ram resulted in the ram being associated with *zecut avot*, the benefits of which were both redemptive and atoning.

Significantly, a number of rabbinic interpretations associated the Akedah with the sacrifices carried out in the Temple, especially atoning sacrifices such as the *tamid* offering, which prompted God to show compassion. In this context, I pointed to an interpretation of Romanos as an example of an exegetical encounter because he applied the rabbinic description of the binding of the *tamid* offering to the binding of Isaac.

The association between the Akedah and the *tamid* offers one explanation of why the Akedah became an important feature of Jewish liturgy from an early period: both were viewed in terms of atonement. Taken together, the views of the rabbis and the church fathers demonstrate an exegetical encounter. From the Christian perspective, the Akedah cannot be viewed as atoning because Isaac needed to be ransomed and required the saving act of the sacrifice. From the Jewish perspective, the Akedah was atoning because it prompted God to show compassion to his people. Its association with *zecut avot* provided further support for Israel's petition to God to be merciful.

The large number of references to the Akedah in Jewish liturgy repeated many significant features of the rabbinic interpretations that we have already seen above – in particular, an emphasis on Isaac and an appeal to God to show compassion to Israel. In Christian liturgy, however, there are only a few references to the Akedah, and these are also consistent with the interpretations of the church fathers demonstrating an emphasis on the action of Abraham. Both Judaism and Christianity arranged that Genesis 22 should be read at significant times of the year, ensuring that it retained an important position in the annual cycle.

CHAPTER 7

The artistic exegetical encounter

So far we have examined Genesis 22 from oral and written perspectives, but the purpose of this chapter is to consider the story from the perspective of the artist. Artistic interpretation has often been ignored in studies of biblical interpretation. Biblical commentaries, for example, rarely pay attention to figurative representation except on their front cover. This is partly because the question as to whether the artist has played a role in interpreting biblical stories is raised by the Bible itself. The well-known command in Exodus 20 has been interpreted to mean that Jews and Christians would automatically have opposed every form of figurative visual representation:

You shall not make for yourself a graven image, or any likeness of anything that is in the heaven above, or that is in the earth beneath, or that is in the water under the earth; you shall not bow down to them or serve them; for I the Lord your God am a jealous God (Exodus. 20.3 ff.).

These verses were discussed by Josephus, who was known for being hostile to images.[1] Roman writers of the first century such as Tacitus and Pliny also remarked about the absence of statues and images in Jewish cities and synagogues. However, before it is too readily assumed that these writings demonstrate a lack of artistic representations, even Josephus reported that there existed groups, such as the Hasmonean family in the first century BCE, who produced figurative art.

As far as the rabbis were concerned, there were, as so often, differing views. On the one hand, Rabban Gamaliel II, head of Yavneh, was criticized for going into a bath-house that boasted a statue of Aphrodite,[2] and the Mishnah stated that 'No one may make ornaments for an idol: necklaces or ear-rings or finger-rings', although Rabbi Eliezer offered a minority opinion arguing that 'if for payment, it is permitted'.[3] On the other hand, many rabbinic passages make reference to the widespread existence of Jewish figurative art, justified perhaps on the grounds that idolatry

[1] *Jos., Bell.* 2.195; Ant 17.151.   [2] *M. Av. Zarah* 3.4   [3] *M. Av. Zarah* 1.8.

had been eradicated and was no longer considered a danger to the people.[4] A gentile also gave expression to this view in a discussion with Rabbi Akiva, 'You know in your heart as I know in mine that there is nothing real in idolatry'.[5]

Unsurprisingly, therefore, the rabbinic writings witness to opposing views. However, it is clear that Jewish artistic interpretation did exist, and the following quotation from the Targum confirms that biblical representations, including the hand of God, were considered fit subjects for a floor, which was continually being trodden upon. The Targum mentions that figurative art in synagogues was approved as long as it was used not for idolatrous purposes, but only for decoration:

You shall not set up a figured stone in your land, to bow down to it, but a mosaic pavement of designs and forms you may set in the floor of your places of worship, so long as you do not do obeisance to it.[6]

Figurative art also played a role in the everyday life of the early church, although biblical commentators have once again tended to ignore or minimize comments in the writings of the church fathers about the acceptability of figurative art.[7] Like the rabbis, the church fathers were concerned about the idolatrous nature of art in places of worship. For example, at the Council of Elvira in approximately 300 CE, the thirty-sixth canon stated that there should be no pictures in a church in case the object of worship was depicted on the walls. Nevertheless, the early church was not as hostile to art as has been almost universally assumed. Tertullian, like Rabban Gamaliel II, states that figurative representation was not forbidden because it was not idolatrous.[8]

The existence of artistic interpretation of Scripture indicates that biblical interpretation does not just consist of homily, commentary, poetry and liturgy. The visual form must also be considered. Interpreters of Scripture were not only preachers, teachers and liturgists, but they were also artists. Biblical interpretation is like an electric cable or plug, made up of several individual wires, which together are capable of conducting spiritual

---

[4] *Sifre* on Deut. 32.17 states, '"And they sacrificed to demons, gods they had never known" (Deut. 32.17) – whom the nations do not know; "New gods that came but lately" (Deut. 32.17) – every time one of the gentiles saw it, he said, "It is a Jewish image." Similarly, the verse, "As my hand has found the kingdoms of the idols and their graven images from Jerusalem and Samaria" (Isa. 10.10) teaches us that Jerusalem and Samaria supply all the people of the world with moulds.' Cf. BT *Yoma* 69b; *San.* 64a; *SOS. Rab.* 8.8

[5] BT *Av. Zarah* 55a.

[6] *Tg. Ps. Jon.* (to Lev. 26.11). Rabbinic acceptance of figurative art is found in JT *Av. Zarah* 3.2, 3, 42d.

[7] Murray 1977: 313–45.   [8] Tertullian, *Adv. Mar.* 2.22.

and creative energy of great intensity. When they are brought together, a connection is made; when left independent, they remain isolated. Combined, they provide light; left alone, their contribution is limited.

Only two wires are normally traced and discussed — the oral and written forms. As a result, artistic interpretations are relegated to play the role of poor cousin and when studied, depictions are viewed with the lens of the writer, not from the perspective of the artist.

This chapter will demonstrate that, while artistic exegetes share many of the same interpretations as their literary brethren, they sometimes stress different aspects of the biblical story and provide new and even conflicting interpretations. The artistic contribution provides its own insight into biblical interpretation. Artistic interpreters offer their own interpretations of Genesis 22, which, it should be stressed, congregants see in synagogues and churches and reflect thereon.

Figurative art fulfilled an important function in everyday life in both Judaism and Christianity in late antiquity, and the Sacrifice of Isaac was one of a small number of popular biblical images found in Jewish and Christian art in late antiquity. These included *Noah, Daniel in the Lion's Den, The Twelve Tribes of Israel* and *King David*. Each character suggested the promise of deliverance. In Christian art it is also found with the *Raising of Lazarus* and *The Good Shepherd*. It appears in many forms including frescoes, sarcophagi and mosaics. Images have also been found on glass, jewellery, amulets, seals and even ivory. This chapter will focus on representations depicted on mosaics and frescoes, in synagogues and churches, in chapels and catacombs as they are representative of artistic portrayals of the Akedah.

It is clear that Genesis 22 was a popular subject for the artists because there are a number of references to its portrayal. Augustine discussed this subject:

The deed is so famous that it recurs to the mind of itself without any study or reflection, and is in fact repeated by so many tongues, and portrayed in so many places, that no-one can pretend to shut his eyes or his ears from it.[9]

Gregory of Nyssa, for instance, also commented:

I have seen many times the likeness of this suffering in painting and not without tears have I come upon this sight, when art clearly led the story before the sight.[10]

Gregory's remark that 'art clearly led the story' is suggestive and implies that artistic biblical interpretation may well have influenced literary forms

---

[9] Augustine, *Faust.* 22.73.   [10] Greg. of Nys., *De Deitate* PG46. 573.

of biblical interpretation. As we shall shortly see, there is no reason to assume that artists slavishly followed the interpretations of their literary and liturgical brethren. In fact, there are a number of occasions when it seems that artistic exegetes created representations of the Akedah, which retained an influence over later interpreters.

CHRISTIAN ARTISTIC EXEGESIS

For many years, scholars of early Christian art, like those of Jewish art, have been excessively influenced by trends in the *written* tradition. As a result, images were understood primarily in terms of the crucifixion of Christ. Scholarly debates centred on whether the artistic representations should be understood in terms of typology or in terms of deliverance. Some scholars suggested that, because patristic writings do not offer a detailed typological understanding of the relationship between the figures of Isaac and Jesus until after the conversion of Constantine (312 CE), typological representations could not appear in art before then. They therefore placed an emphasis on deliverance[11] and pointed out, for example, that Isaac was never portrayed as bound on the altar until the mid-fourth century. Recently Jensen, who has offered a critique of the existing scholarship, has questioned the validity of arguments based on a few existing pre-Constantinian images and challenged the accuracy of their dating. Jensen also suggested that typology could be discovered in early Christian literature such as in the writings of Melito, Tertullian and Origen.[12]

The weakness with all these arguments is that they are based upon literary tradition. They do not begin from the image but from the written word. Studies of art sometimes seem concerned to show that the written word has influenced the image. This is illustrated by Jensen who suggests that 'homilies and liturgies were the most important sources from which early Christian imagery derives meaning for its audience'.[13] Is it possible that artistic interpretation influenced the written word? It is necessary to begin by examining artistic interpretation in its own right, with reference to the biblical story. Mercea Eliade proposed this approach in his pioneering study of the phenomenon of religion when he suggested that a phenomenon should be studied first 'in its own frame of reference, with freedom afterwards to integrate the results of this procedure in a wider perspective'.[14] Only afterwards should attention be directed towards the context, including the written interpretation. After this process has been completed it will

---

[11] Van Woerden 1961: 214–55.   [12] Jensen 1994: 105.   [13] Jensen 1994: 106.   [14] Eliade 1960: 13.

Plate 1. Catacomb of Callixtus

be possible to consider to what extent artistic biblical interpretation sheds light on the existence of the exegetical encounter.

In funereal art the images illustrate examples of divine intervention and express the desire that God may show the same favour to the deceased. Funereal art, found on sarcophagi and catacomb paintings, proclaims the hope that the deceased may find happiness beyond the grave.

The earliest catacomb frescoes illustrate the theme of deliverance. For instance, the Callixtus catacomb in Rome (Plate 1) is dated from the first half of the third century CE. Abraham and the child Isaac are offering thanks for their deliverance. In the foreground, to their right stands the ram, erect and proud. Quite clearly, the three main characters are Abraham, Isaac and the ram. Behind the ram are an olive tree and the wood for the sacrifice.

Another (late) third-century fresco located in the Catacomb of Priscilla, Rome (Plate 2) illustrates the same theme. It shows the boy Isaac carrying wood and Abraham[15] pointing to the fire on an altar or to a tree. Nearby (presumably) stands the ram. Abraham is looking up to the heavens, perhaps hearing the word of God.

[15] Van Woerden 1961: 222.

Plate 2. Catacomb of Priscilla

Plate 3. Catacomb of Peter and Marcellinus

Two other fourth-century frescoes have very similar images. In the late third- or early fourth-century fresco in the Catacomb of Peter and Marcellinus (Plate 3) Abraham holds a knife in his raised right hand and at his feet is the child Isaac – naked, kneeling and bound for the sacrifice. The ram appears on the far side of the altar, which is alight and the image is above a scene of the paralytic carrying his bed. Cubiculum C in the Via

Plate 4. Cubiculum C in the Via Latina

Latina (Plate 4), from the late fourth century, reproduces this image almost exactly. The altar has wood burning upon it; to the left is the ram, which appears to be looking for Abraham who has a sword in his hand. Abraham is looking at something (an angel? the voice of God?) while Isaac is kneeling with his hands behind his back. Below is a representation of a servant with a donkey, possibly at the foot of the mountain.

All the examples of catacomb art emphasize the aspect of deliverance and do not indicate typology. This artistic interpretation either parallels, or perhaps even precedes, the early Christian prayer for the dead (*commendatio animae*), which contained a cycle of deliverance. The earliest reference to this prayer is from the seventh century, although it is believed to have originated much earlier. Originally, Jonah, Noah, Isaac, the three young men in the furnace, Daniel and Susannah were mentioned in the prayer. Later the list was expanded.[16]

In addition to frescoes, we commonly find images of the Sacrifice of Isaac in early Christian sarcophagi. The Mas d'Aire Sarcophagus from the third century is the earliest. It shows the child Isaac, bound and kneeling. Abraham grasps his hair from behind and raises the knife to strike. Abraham's eyes are not on Isaac but on the ram, which is standing at his side (almost nuzzling him). The ram appears eager to be sacrificed. Sarcophagi provide a variety of altars – sometimes Isaac is bound upon an altar, sometimes next to the altar and sometimes, as at Mas d'Aire, there is no altar. Sarcophagi also fail to portray the ram caught by its horns or caught in a bush. Thus, the evidence suggests that the Christologically interpreted ram was not of importance to the artists. None of the sarcophagi show Isaac carrying wood as a model of Christ carrying the cross. The concern of the artist is significantly different to that of the literary exegete as there is little interest in typology.

Many of the sarcophagi that are dated in the fourth and fifth centuries provide evidence of post-biblical interpretation that cannot be found in contemporary Christian literature. For instance, a number depict two or three assistants or onlookers, which implies that the Sacrifice of Isaac did not take place in secret. This may also indicate that artistic interpretations contain traditions that would have otherwise been lost. For example, in a Luc-de-Bearn sixth-century sarcophagus, a man and woman are watching the sacrifice. The woman, who has her hand to her mouth to indicate dismay, may be Sarah. The appearance of Sarah at the sacrifice is mentioned in the poems of St Ephrem of Syria and other Syriac writings, but rarely in the Greek or Latin fathers. She is also portrayed in the chapels of the El Bagawat (Egypt) necropolis, which are dated from the fourth century CE.

In El Bagawat the story is depicted several times. It is found in the chapel of Exodus where Abraham stands next to an altar, which is already alight. On the other side of the altar stands Isaac with his arms crossed while his mother Sarah stands at his side under a tree and lifts her arms to the sky in an act of prayer. The ram stands under a tree and the hand of God is seen to the right of the name Abraham. In the fifth-century Chapel of Peace we find the Sacrifice of Isaac, as one in a number of images (Plate 5); these include

---

[16] This prayer was extended to include Enoch, Elijah, Abraham, Job, Lot, Moses, David, Peter, Paul and Thecla.

Plate 5. Chapel of Peace (Fakhry 1951)

the symbols of peace, justice and prayer, alongside Adam and Eve, the ark
with Noah and his family, Jacob, Daniel and the lions, the annunciation
and Paul and Thecla (described in the apocryphal *Acts of Paul* as a convert
and companion of Paul).

In the image of the Sacrifice of Isaac a hand (of an angel?) is throwing
two knives in the air and another is held by Abraham. Isaac, a child, is
unbound and his arms are outstretched, perhaps in supplication. Archaeologists have suggested that mother and son are holding incense.[17] Sarah
has a halo around her head and Abraham, Isaac and Sarah are all identified. A tree/plant with flowers is drawn on the right hand side, probably to balance the tree on the left. As a result of the inclusion of Sarah
in the representation of the Sacrifice of Isaac, the artists of El Bagawat
expand the biblical story and portray its significance for the whole family. They do not follow the biblical account, which depicts the story in

[17] Fakhry 1951: 73.

Plate 6. San Vitale

terms of a father–son relationship, but offer their own interpretation, in a manner reminiscent of Gregory of Nyssa's phrase 'art leading the story by sight'.

Two of the most famous church mosaics in late antiquity in Ravenna – San Vitale and San Apollinare in Classe – include representations of Genesis 22, and both associate it with the offerings of Abel and Melchizedek, thus linking the biblical narrative to the liturgy of the Eucharist. For example, in San Vitale we find a portrayal (Plate 6) of the mosaics of Cain and Melchizedek sharing a church altar near which are placed the bread and wine. Nearby appear the three angels announcing the promise of a son while Abraham offers them a calf and Sarah stands in the doorway of a tent. To the right is a representation of the Sacrifice of Isaac.

Isaac is kneeling on the altar and Abraham's sword is raised but the hand of God appears to prevent the sacrifice. At Abraham's feet is the ram looking at Abraham, striking a typical Christological pose. These mosaics flank the real church altar where the Eucharist was celebrated. The biblical figures are linked by the following prayer:

Be pleased to look upon these offerings with a gracious and favourable countenance, accept them even as you were pleased to accept the offerings of your just servant Abel, the sacrifice of Abraham, our patriarch and that of Melchizedek, your high priest – a holy sacrifice, a spotless victim.

This prayer and its reference to the Sacrifice of Isaac came into use by the fourth century CE, and it is clear that artistic interpretation paralleled the liturgical development, such as the reference to Genesis 22 during

Plate 7. Dura-Europos (interior wall decorations) (Kraeling 1956)

the offertory prayers. Thus in early Christian art, the Sacrifice of Isaac focussed on deliverance and the Eucharist as represented by images of the communion and divine deliverance. Images are found in funereal art because the story was understood in relation to death and resurrection. The ram is significant in artistic interpretation, not because of any Christological significance, but because of its allusion to deliverance. The Isaac-Christ typology is rarely found in artistic interpretation during this period, and when it is found it is associated with the liturgy.

JEWISH ARTISTIC EXEGESIS

One of the most famous Jewish representations of the Akedah was found when the third-century CE Dura-Europos synagogue was uncovered in 1932. Externally, Dura-Europos was modest in the extreme, being located in a private house and could not compare architecturally with Sardis. However, its uniqueness lay in its interior, for its wall decorations were second to none (Plate 7). The city itself was founded by Seleucus I in approximately 300 BCE and remained a Seleucid outpost until mid-second century BCE when it was captured by the Parthians. For the next three centuries it flourished as a centre for east-west trade. In the second century CE it was captured by the Romans until it was destroyed by the Persians in 256 CE and never resettled.

Dura-Europos contained sixteen temples catering to the needs of an eclectic pantheon of Roman, Greek and Persian gods. It also contained a modest Christian chapel. In the synagogue there are more than thirty

Plate 8. Dura-Europos (Ezekiel Cycle) (Kraeling 1956)

scenes covering the four walls of a 40 foot room. Several images surround the Torah shrine (on the base level):
• Esther
• Elijah restoring life to the son of the widow of Zarephath (1 Kings 17).
• Samuel anointing David (1 Samuel 16)
• Moses as a baby floating in the Nile and rescued by the daughter of Pharaoh (Exodus 2).
The Ezekiel Cycle (Plate 8) is a good illustration of the elaborateness of the paintings. It is based on Ezekiel 37 and the description of the resurrection of the dead. God is symbolized by the hand and Ezekiel is depicted three times as he receives divine commission. At the prophet's feet lie numerous body parts instead of the bones mentioned in the biblical text and beside him the mountain has split in two with an olive tree on each peak. To the right is a fallen house, illustrating an earthquake during which the resurrection would occur and to the right of one mountain stands Ezekiel, whose right hand is raised to the hand of God stretched out to him. His left hand points to the three lifeless bodies besides which stands a female figure who probably represents the *pneuma* providing the *ruah* to revive the dead. Further right stands Ezekiel again pointing to the three *psychai* who renew the lifeless bodies.

Plate 9. Dura-Europos (Image of Akedah) (Kraeling 1956)

In addition to the richness of the painting, two features are depicted elsewhere: the hand of God and the gesture of Ezekiel's right hand. In this gesture, the palm is turned outward and the second and third fingers are held extended, while the thumb, the fourth and fifth fingers are doubled back against the palm. The most familiar analogy is the Christian gesture of benediction, found commonly in Byzantine art. Some associate this gesture with general pagan practice, suggesting that it is a cultic gesture that brings immortality to his followers (implying that Ezekiel works a comparable miracle by bringing life to the corpses).[18]

The image of the Akedah (Plate 9) is found over the opening for the ark, the Torah shrine. This was the most prominent feature of the synagogue and was always built on the Jerusalem orientated wall, indicating the direction in which Jews should direct their prayers. Images surrounding the ark would literally be in front of the eyes of Jewish congregants and the choice of imagery in this location carried extra significance.

The ark of the scrolls, which housed the Torah, stood inside the shrine and several images and inscriptions refer to it. The significance of the ark became so well known that John Chrysostom accused Jews of exaggerated veneration for their ark. Its significance in Dura-Europos was exaggerated

[18] Kraeling 1956: 194; Goodenough 1953–68, X: 184.

even more because the Torah shrine belonged to a phase of synagogue decoration that was distinct from and earlier than other synagogue paintings. Unlike the other images, which were replaced during repainting, it was retained and not touched, indicating its importance.

The image portrays the menorah, the palm branch (*lulav*) and citron (*etrog*) on the left hand side, and in the centre the Temple, and to the right the Akedah. The symbols of Sukkot and the Temple suggest a vision of a future feast of Tabernacles to be celebrated in Jerusalem by all nations as described in Zechariah 14. It is not clear whether the portrait of the Temple anticipates the future Temple, which was to be built on the site of the destroyed Temple, or simply the Temple of the past. The synagogue building had been dedicated 170 years after the destruction of the Second Temple but restoration was still a realistic dream as Julian the Apostate would make clear 120 years later.

If congregants examined the characters in detail, they would see a primitively drawn Abraham, knife in hand, standing resolutely with his back to the onlooker, and the little bundle of Isaac lying on the altar, also with his back to the onlooker. This is emphasized by the shock of black hair on both figures, rather than the portrait of any facial features. Isaac is clearly a child and appears unbound. In the distance a tiny figure, also with a shock of black hair, stands before a tent with an opening on the top. This figure has been variously interpreted as Abraham's servant,[19] Ishmael,[20] Abraham himself in his house[21] and Sarah.[22] However, arguments are readily available to render each proposal unlikely. For instance, the figure appears to be wearing a man's clothing and is therefore unlikely to be Sarah; he is not wearing the same clothes as Abraham (and therefore unlikely to be Abraham); the traditions concerning hostility between Isaac and Ishmael were influenced by the rise of Islam (seventh century), which makes Ishmael less likely. It is possible that the character is another depiction of Isaac as the tent is touching the altar upon which Isaac lays, the figure is the same size as Isaac and both have black hair. It is also worth remembering that, according to the biblical narrative, Sarah died after the Akedah and that the first time Isaac was comforted was when Rebecca was brought to him and taken into his mother's tent (Genesis 24.67). The open hand of God appears beside the tent, which is the earliest surviving image.[23]

---

[19] Kraeling 1956: 343.   [20] Prigent 1990: 116.
[21] Du Mesnil du Buisson 1939: 24–7.   [22] Goodenough 1953–68, IV: 189.
[23] The hand symbolizing the *bat kol* is found in many literary works including both rabbinic and non-rabbinic writings. E.g., Jos., *Ant.* 1.13; 4.233; Philo, *De Ab.* 32, 176; *Tan. Va-Yera* 23; *PRE* 31.

The artistic exegete has made a number of changes to the biblical story, such as Isaac being unbound, the third character and the presence of the hand of God. However, the representation of the Akedah at Dura-Europos is closer to the biblical story than many other representations. For instance, following the biblical account, the ram is pictured behind Abraham (Genesis 22.13) and Isaac is lying on the altar (Genesis 22.9).

In the lower foreground the rather large ram waits patiently, tethered to a tree. The Hebrew text is probably the source for this illustration for, unlike the LXX, it describes the ram as 'behind' Abraham. It is centrally located, which emphasizes its importance to the artist. Although the rabbis suggested that the ram had been created on the sixth day of creation and was waiting since for its moment of destiny,[24] they did not give a great deal of attention to it nor did they describe it being tethered to a tree. There appears no Jewish literary source for this artistic interpretation. However, the fourth-century Coptic Bible describes a 'ram tied to a tree',[25] which may indicate the existence of a Jewish artistic interpretation retaining a tradition no longer found in Jewish literature. This suggestion is supported by artistic evidence elsewhere, both Jewish and Christian, that depicts the ram tied to a tree (see below). The possibility of Christian influence suggests that artistic biblical interpretation may demonstrate a close relationship between Judaism and Christianity.

Another important discovery was made in 1929 during an excavation in the eastern Jezreel valley, just south of Galilee, which unearthed a mosaic floor of a sixth-century synagogue called Beith Alpha. A sequence of three scenes, bordered like a carpet, make their way to the Torah located in a wall orientated towards Jerusalem (Plate 10). These scenes are:
1. The Akedah
2. The zodiac with Helios and his four horses
3. The ark

At the entrance, a mosaic lion and a bull flank bilingual inscriptions, which in Greek acknowledge the artists and in Aramaic thank the donors. These inscriptions date the synagogue to the reign of Justin (518–527).

The narrative plane (Plate 11) moves from left to right, from the donkey to the ram to Isaac; from the accompanying youths to Abraham. The

[24] Cf. *M. Avot* 5.6; *PRE* 31. Note similarity with 1 Pet. 20, 'You know that from your empty way of life inherited from your ancestors, you were ransomed – not by perishable things like silver or gold, but by precious blood like that of an unblemished and spotless lamb, namely Christ. He was foreknown before the foundation of the world but was manifested in these last times for your sake.'

[25] Although the Targums mention a tree (e.g., *Tg. Ps. Jon.* 22.13), they describe the ram as being caught, rather than tied. Ciasca 1885: 22.

Plate 10. Beith Alpha (mosaic floor) (Sukenik 1932)

Plate 11. Beith Alpha (Image of Akedah) (Sukenik 1932)

Hebrew, naturally, moves from right to left identifying Isaac, the ram and the command issuing from the hand of God. Abraham throws Isaac into the fire on the altar while the hand of God, as at Dura-Europos, prevents the sacrifice. A large ram is tied to a tree and is standing erect. The ram, following the biblical story, is caught by one horn but, unlike the biblical account, is tied to a tree.

Once again the artist emphasizes the importance of the ram, which is even bigger than the tree. In contrast to Jewish literary tradition in the first six centuries, which rarely refers to the ram, the artistic biblical interpreters give it a central role. It is interesting that later rabbinic writings, such as the eighth-century CE *Pirkei de Rabbi Eliezer*, discuss the ram in detail. This literary development might be viewed as having been influenced by these earlier depictions. Since this literary development occurred much later than the artistic representations, it could be argued that the literary interpretation was based upon the artistic. This would indicate a reversal of previous assumptions that the image supported the written word. In this case, the written word supported the image, and art, once again, is shown to lead the story.

Returning to the mosaic, two servants, one of whom has a whip in his hand, hold the ass which has a bell around its neck. Above, the hand of God presents some interesting features, for it extends from a dark area, which looks like the end of a sleeve and is described by archaeologists as a 'cloud'.[26] Perhaps the most remarkable figure is the child Isaac, floating

[26] Sukenik 1932: 40.

beyond Abraham's fingertips. Does Abraham hold him close, or at arm's length in preparation for the loss? Isaac is suspended and his arms are crossed but not bound, swinging precariously between the flames of the sacrifice and his obedient father. The trial is still Abraham's – but not unequivocally for we focus on the helpless, dangling figure of the son. The flames, which almost touch Isaac, are reminiscent of the rabbinic phrase, 'ashes of Isaac', perhaps indicating a link between the interpretations.

In addition, the ambiguity of the mosaic raises the question of Isaac's willingness. As mentioned earlier, the rabbis emphasize Isaac's voluntary obedience by describing his maturity and giving his age as twenty-six, twenty-seven or thirty-seven years old.[27] The Jewish artistic portrayal of Isaac, however, as a child, suggests that he had little active role in the sacrifice. It is even possible to view him as a reluctant participant. Once again, artistic interpretation possesses its own emphasis, significantly different from the literary interpretation.

A recent and immensely important archaeological portrayal of the Akedah was discovered in 1993 in an early fifth-century synagogue in the city of Sepphoris, capital of the Galilee. Judah ha Nasi lived in Sepphoris in the early part of the third century, bringing with him institutions of Jewish leadership, and the city enjoyed a renaissance. Sepphoris had eighteen synagogues at the time of Judah ha Nasi and remained the capital of the Galilee until the end of the third century CE, when the Sanhedrin and Patriarchate moved to Tiberias. A general overview shows that it was a Jewish city similar to the pagan cities of the region – there were no clear separate neighbourhoods on the basis of religious, social or economic criteria.

The mosaic floor is the most important part of the synagogue that has survived, covering the building's entire floor and consisting of fourteen panels. The central band depicts the zodiac. Each of the twelve signs, which surround the sun, is identified with the name of the month in Hebrew. Most have images of young men, the majority clothed but some naked; the four seasons are depicted in the corners accompanied by agricultural objects characteristic of each season.

The Akedah is depicted in two panels and the first (Plate 12) has a Greek inscription, 'be remembered for good, Boethos (son) of Aemilius with his children. He made this panel. A blessing upon them. Amen.' The word 'amen', written in Hebrew, ends the benediction. The archaeologists Weiss

---

[27] *Gen. Rab.* 56.8.

Plate 12. Sepphoris (Panel 1 – Abraham and servant, Weiss)

and Netzer suggest that the panel shows the two servants who remain at the bottom of the mountain with the ass. One holds a spear while his other hand is raised slightly in a gesture we have already seen made by Ezekiel in Dura Europos. The other servant sits under a tree, at the foot of the mountain holding the ass.[28]

There is no other instance of a servant making the special sign and an alternative explanation is required. Rather than a servant, perhaps the figure is Abraham instructing the servant to remain behind. The shoes of

[28] Weiss and Netzer 1996: 30–1.

Plate 13. Sepphoris (Panel 2 – shoes only, Weiss)

Abraham appear to be exactly the same as those portrayed in the right hand panel (Plate 13) This panel is badly damaged and depicts the head of an animal tethered to the tree by its left horn; below are two upturned pairs of shoes – a small pair for Isaac and a large pair for Abraham. In another small section of the panel Weiss and Netzer suggest there exists the blade of a vertically held knife with traces of a robe to its right.

The small pair of shoes again indicates that, for the Jewish artistic exegetes, Isaac was not the adult of rabbinic literary interpretation, but that he was a boy. The idea of removing shoes is probably derived from other biblical passages such as Moses at the burning bush (Exodus 3.5) and Joshua in the presence of the Lord's Host (Joshua 5.15). The portrait indicates that, when Abraham and Isaac reached the sacred spot, they removed their shoes out of respect for the sanctity of the site.

Once again the artist offers an interpretation that conflicts with the written. In *Genesis Rabbah*, Abraham is compared favourably to Moses. One of the reasons why he was deemed superior was because he was not asked by God to remove his shoes at Mount Moriah.[29] The artistic interpreter

---

[29] *Gen. Rab.* 55.6.

provides evidence for an alternative tradition, perhaps in a debate about the significance of the removal or non-removal of shoes.

These three Jewish portraits of the Akedah indicate that it was part of an extensive tradition of synagogue decoration. It is highly unlikely that its existence in three synagogues was mere chance. Synagogue artists – as well as the congregations – viewed the Akedah as a significant story. Its location in or near the Torah shrine and its depiction alongside the Temple associated Genesis 22 with redemption and God's promise to Abraham and his children. It is important to observe that Isaac is always portrayed as a child, which indicates that artistic interpreters do not necessarily follow literary interpretations. In art, the exegetes emphasize the helplessness of the child and not the voluntary self-offering found in literary exegesis. They also expand the role of the ram. Whereas in the biblical story the ram appears to have been on Mount Moriah by chance, the artistic representation emphasizes the significance of the ram through its size and prominent position. Artistic interpretation offers its own insight into the Akedah and demonstrates that an examination of literary interpretations on their own, although illustrative of the diversity of literary tradition, does not tell the whole story.

CONCLUSION

The diversity of Jewish and Christian representations of the Akedah is striking. Artists who created images based on the biblical story should be understood as exegetes in their own right, who offer their own interpretations, some of which conflict with the better-known interpretations found in the writings of the church fathers or the rabbis.

There are a number of significant similarities between the representations of Jewish and Christian artists, indicating common approaches to biblical interpretation. Interestingly, some representations, produced by both Jewish and Christian artists, vary significantly from the biblical text: For example, the ram being tied to a tree, rather than being caught by its horns in a bush. Consequently, artistic exegesis reinforces the main conclusion of this study of Jewish and Christian biblical interpretation: the existence of an exegetical encounter. It seems that artists were involved in their own exegetical encounter.

There is a rich diversity of Jewish and Christian artistic interpretations of the Akedah. For many hundreds of years some scholars and religious leaders have criticized these artistic representations, seeing in their diversity the possibility of danger and error. Jean D'Espagne, a seventeenth-century

French Protestant theologian, was annoyed that in the contemporary Bible 'Isaac is here painted on his knees before an altar and Abraham behind him holding a knife in his hand, which is lifted up to give the blow. But this picture is false and doth bely the holy History.'[30] Martin Luther also complained that 'the picture commonly painted about Abraham about to kill his son is incorrect'.[31] In fact, from the very beginning the portrayal of the Akedah exhibits not errors but *interpretations* of the biblical text. Sometimes these interpretations mirror liturgical or literary developments. On other occasions they are not found elsewhere.

Artistic interpretation is bound to the biblical text but has developed its own rules of interpretation. A study of artistic interpretation is critical to any study of biblical interpretation. In the words of the church father Gregory of Nyssa, and valid for Jewish as well as Christian art, there are occasions when 'art clearly led the story'.[32] For this, students of biblical interpretation should be truly grateful.

---

[30] D'Espagne 1655: 148–9.   [31] Pelikan 1964: 110.   [32] Greg. of Nys., *De Deitate*, PG 46 573.

Conclusion

Bound by the Bible has shed light on the exegetical relationship between Judaism and Christianity in the first six centuries CE and has demonstrated that the encounter was closer than had previously been suggested. By developing a series of criteria, which recognize the occurrence of an exegetical encounter, a relationship based on familiarity has been depicted. Numerous examples have been uncovered, not in isolation but multiply attested, which makes an exegetical encounter a significant factor in Jewish and Christian interpretations. While each example on its own may be explained as coincidental, or as a result of the exegetes separately arriving at the same conclusion, multiple attestation strongly implies an exegetical encounter.

The exegetical approach overcomes some of the weaknesses of previous studies of Jewish–Christian relations, such as dependence on the existence of parallels or on the dating of significant texts. The choice of Genesis 22 provides a biblical text that is of much interest to both Jews and Christians and that is similar in both the Greek and Hebrew versions.

During the course of this study three categories of interpretation have been identified: first, shared interpretations, which indicate a common approach to the biblical text; second, interpretations that indicate a possible exegetical encounter; third, interpretations that indicate a probable exegetical encounter.

Bound by the Bible has highlighted the following examples of shared interpretations:

- Both the rabbis and church fathers are concerned to respond to the charge that God desired human sacrifice (vv. 1–2).
- Both the rabbis and church fathers explain that the Akedah enabled Abraham to be exalted throughout the world (vv. 1–2).
- Both the rabbis and church fathers explain that God's words 'Take your son, your only one, whom you love, Isaac . . .' were intended to make Isaac more beloved to Abraham (vv. 1–2).

- Both the rabbis and church fathers create a dialogue between Abraham and God in their interpretation of God's command (vv. 1–2).
- Both the rabbis and church fathers suggest that Abraham set out immediately upon receiving the command to sacrifice Isaac (v. 3).
- Both the rabbis and church fathers state that Abraham did not challenge God (v. 3).
- Both the rabbis and church fathers explain that Abraham was not concerned about being derided as a childkiller or as a madman (v. 3).
- Both the rabbis and church fathers state that Abraham kept silent when he received the command to sacrifice Isaac (v. 3).
- Both the rabbis and the church fathers comment on the miracle of the milk returning to Sarah's breasts (v. 3).
- Both the rabbis and church fathers assume that Abraham did not tell Sarah about the divine command because he thought she would try to prevent the sacrifice (v. 3).
- Both the rabbis and church fathers associate Genesis 22 with the death of Sarah (v. 3).
- Both the rabbis and church fathers explain that the purpose of the three-day journey was to ensure, first, that Abraham was tormented during the journey, and second, that he was no longer in a state of shock when he arrived at Moriah (vv. 4–5).
- Both the rabbis and church fathers describe the servants as being stubborn, like an ass, and blind (vv. 4–5).
- Both the rabbis and church fathers explain that Abraham did not lie but spoke prophetically to the servants (vv. 4–5).
- Both the rabbis and church fathers suggest that the angels were watching events unfold on Moriah and were astounded by the equal enthusiasm of Abraham and Isaac to fulfil God's command (vv. 6–8).
- Both the rabbis and church fathers emphasize the importance of the principle of voluntary self-offering (vv. 13–14).
- Both the rabbis and church fathers interpret the Akedah in terms of atonement (vv. 13–14).

As well as identifying a significant number of shared interpretations, this study has also highlighted examples of possible and probable exegetical encounters. The examples of a possible encounter include the following.

The exaltation of Abraham

Both the rabbis and Basil of Seleucia explain that the purpose of Genesis 22 is to exalt Abraham, and both use nautical imagery in their analysis.

Abraham is described by Basil as a skilled helmsman who steers a ship safely in stormy seas so that his actions may became known throughout the world. The rabbis, using similar imagery, explain that God tested (נסה) Abraham so that his actions would become known (lit. a 'banner' or 'sail' – נס) throughout the world and suggesting that the Akedah should be seen like the ensign of a ship (vv. 1–2).

A Christian version of 'merit of the fathers' (zecut avot)

Irenaeus offers a meritorial interpretation of the Akedah, which may represent a Christian equivalent of the rabbinic concept of *zecut avot*. In the view of Irenaeus, Abraham's action resulted in God 'offering His only-born and beloved Son'. In other words, God rewarded Abraham and gave up his Son because Abraham was willing to sacrifice Isaac. This understanding of Irenaeus' interpretation is reinforced by an Armenian version, which emphasizes Abraham's reward by demonstrating correspondence between merit (Abraham's willingness to sacrifice Isaac) and reward (God's willingness to give up his Son) (v. 3).

The obedience of Abraham

Both Jewish and Christian exegetes adopt the imagery of an advocate and use the same technical word, *synagoria* (συνηγορία סניגוריא) in a discussion of the obedience of Abraham. It is worth noting that סניגוריא is removed in the parallel interpretations edited after the redaction of the Jerusalem Talmud (v. 3).

The third day

The church fathers do not refer to the third day as an example of Christian fulfilment of Scripture, ignoring an obvious parallel with the resurrection of Christ. Origen is one example of the patristic omission of a reference to its Christological significance. For their part, the rabbis offer a series of scriptural quotations, the purpose of which is to emphasize the life-giving consequence of different biblical stories, all of which are linked by a three-day period. The rabbis stress the combination of biblical references to the three-day period rather than the single three-day trek to Moriah. Abraham's journey is understood as one more example of a life-giving miracle, which prevents the verse from being promoted by Christian exegetes as a proof-text (vv. 4–5).

The site of the Akedah

Eusebius' interpretation concerning the site of the Akedah contains a synthesis of the rabbis' dual emphasis on sanctity and sacrifice. Unlike other Christian interpreters, Eusebius did not repeat the traditional association between Moriah and Jerusalem (and/or the Temple) and was the first church father to identify the site of the Akedah as the site of the crucifixion. His interpretation also sheds light on sixth-century CE travel accounts that describe Abraham's altar as standing against the slope of Golgotha. A remarkably similar interpretation is found in *Targum Pseudo-Jonathan* (vv. 4–5).

The destruction of the Temple

The rabbis consider whether the destruction of the Temple signals the end of the covenant between the Jewish people and God, a well-known subject of controversy between Jews and Christians. The explanation that God would keep his promise to Israel is reinforced by a quotation from Zechariah 9.9. The interpretation responds both to internal needs (i.e. to encourage Jews) and to external needs (i.e. to respond to gentile derision). The fact that a well-known Christian proof-text is quoted in support of the rabbinic position suggests that the interpretation may have been partly directed at Christianity (vv. 4–5).

Cyril of Alexandria's polemic

Cyril refers explicitly to a Jewish criticism of Christianity, which describes Jesus as 'a small and random figure'. This criticism is not found elsewhere in Jewish or Christian writings, which suggests that it was not part of the *Adversus Iudaeos* literature. The Jewish claim that Jesus was an incidental figure may represent a Jewish polemic against Christianity (vv. 4–5).

Most importantly, we have identified the following examples of a probable exegetical encounter.

Specific examples

The rabbinic description of Isaac carrying a cross
The reference to a cross (צלוב) is as near to an explicit reference to Christianity as we find in the rabbinic interpretations during the period under

review. Strikingly, no additional interpretation is offered by the rabbis to elucidate the brief comment, which is undoubtedly deliberate and itself betrays exegetical influence (vv. 6–8).

Melito's adoption of Jewish categories of thought

Melito's awareness of rabbinic interpretations and his interest in Isaac result in a number of parallels between Isaac and Jesus: Isaac carrying the wood to the place of slaughter is understood as a reference to Christ carrying the cross; both remain silent, indicating their acceptance of the will of God; Isaac, like Jesus, knows what was to befall him; both Isaac and Jesus were bound; and, finally, neither was sorrowful at the impending sacrifice. Melito's awareness of Jewish categories of thought is also illustrated by his adoption of the Jewish description 'binding' (συμποδιζόμενον), which demonstrates rabbinic influence (vv. 6–8 and 9–12).

Romanos' description of Isaac being tied by hand and foot

The Mishnah's statement that the *tamid* offering should be 'bound hand and foot' (מעקד) influenced Romanos, who added the same detail: 'And he [Abraham] bound the feet and hands of the son whom he had engendered, as he said, "first I shall bind and then kill him, so that his movement (ὅρμημα) may not prevent my quick strike . . ."' Another sign of an exegetical encounter is his use of ὅρμημα to explain the necessity of binding Isaac. The prevention of movement on the part of Isaac is not repeated elsewhere in the writings of the Greek church fathers but is paralleled by rabbinic interpretations that describe Isaac as asking Abraham to bind him in case he moved involuntarily and made the sacrifice unfit (vv. 13–14).

Chrysostom's concern with what happened before the Akedah

The rabbis are concerned that the biblical story appeared *in vacuo* and pay keen attention to what preceded the Akedah, a subject of interest to only one church father, John Chrysostom. The rabbis offer a number of interpretations of 'after these things' and, similarly, Chrysostom considers the opening phrase in some detail. Chrysostom and the rabbis ask the same question: What was it that occurred before the Akedah that could elucidate its purpose? Both agree that, since the Akedah was recounted shortly after God's promise to Abraham, its purpose was to instruct people 'in the same love as the patriarch and in showing obedience to the Lord's commands' (vv. 1–2).

General examples

The priesthood of Abraham

Both Jewish and Christian interpreters agree that Abraham was superior to Moses. The rabbis suggest that Abraham had received divine authority to be a priest, which had never been and would never be rescinded. However, the church fathers suggest that Abraham's priesthood was transferred via Melchizedek to Christ. Underlying the issue of priesthood is that of authority. For the rabbis, authority lies with Abraham, whereas for the church fathers it lies with Jesus, a view most clearly expressed by Origen who argues that the eternal priesthood of Christ is foreshadowed by the priesthood of Abraham and Isaac. The rabbis compare Abraham favourably with Moses to show that Abraham was suitable both for priesthood and also for kingship implying that no other person could be chosen. Abraham, and by extension the Jews, retains this authority forever. In other words, this authority cannot be taken away or appropriated by another figure (v. 3).

Isaac's age

The church fathers suggest that, although Isaac played an important role, he was, according to some interpreters, a young man and, according to others, a child. In their view Isaac had not yet reached full adulthood. Their emphasis on Isaac's youth is partly based upon a typological interpretation of Isaac as a model of Christ: Isaac the boy was 'completed' by Christ the man. Eusebius most clearly expresses this view when he describes Isaac as the lamb and Christ as the ram. Isaac's age provides the church fathers with a simple and effective image by which to illustrate the fulfilment of Scripture: the sacrifice of Isaac is completed by Christ and the Akedah is a model of Christ's future redemptive sacrifice. The rabbinic position is quite different, and the age of Isaac is variously understood as twenty-six, thirty-six or thirty-seven years. It is significant that, whilst the precise age varies, the rabbis consistently portray Isaac as an adult. None of the rabbinic interpretations, in direct contrast to those of the church fathers, hint that Isaac might have still been a child, and perhaps influenced by the early interpretations Isaac remains a fully developed and mature adult (vv. 6–8).

Isaac's willingness to be sacrificed

The rabbis explain that Isaac was willing to give up his life at God's command. Like the church fathers who explain that Jesus was not forced by human hand to carry the cross but carried it freely and willingly gave himself up to his Father, so the rabbis emphasize that Isaac freely carried the wood, was not forced to offer himself as a sacrifice but willingly gave himself to his father. For example, Isaac asks Abraham to bind him, he carries his own cross and, although he was informed in advance of the sacrifice, he continued with the journey. Indeed, Isaac is reported to have said to God, 'I raised no objection to the carrying out of your words and I willingly let myself be bound on top of the altar and stretched out my neck under the knife.' Thus the rabbis extend the biblical story of sacrifice to one of self-sacrifice, and the voluntary nature of Isaac's actions becomes the focus of their interpretations. The Akedah no longer consists of the sacrifice of a son by a father but becomes the story of the self-offering of a hero. Isaac is not depicted as the passive victim of the biblical story; rather, in the words of the rabbis, he 'cast himself before his father'. Although the church fathers agree that Isaac accepted his father's desire to sacrifice him, they do not view his action as proactive but as passive. The rabbinic interpretation may represent a response to the Christian teaching that Christ was willing to give up his life for Israel, as the rabbis argue that numerous biblical figures, such as Isaac, were willing to give up their lives on behalf of Israel. Thus no special significance should be given to the willingness of Christ to give up his life for 'you find everywhere that the patriarchs and the prophets offered their lives on behalf of Israel' (vv. 6–8).

Rabbinic emphasis on Isaac versus patristic emphasis on Abraham
An emphasis on Isaac's self-offering leads the rabbis to associate the Akedah primarily with Isaac rather than with Abraham and, as a result, the biblical story became known as The Binding of Isaac (עקדת יצחק). This view is reinforced in Jewish liturgy and, for example, the earliest prayer book refers to God's covenant with Isaac on Mount Moriah, a view paralleled by *Targum Pseudo-Jonathan* and the *Fragmentary Targum*. It is worth noting that the rabbinic interpretations of the ram are also dependent on Isaac, and the rabbis depict Abraham as requesting God to 'regard the blood of this ram as though it were the blood of Isaac'. They depict Abraham as asking God to accept the sacrifice as if he had sacrificed Isaac first and the ram afterwards. In contrast, the church fathers stress the role of Abraham and, in the words of Athanasius, explain that 'the patriarch was tried through Isaac', so that the Akedah remains a test of Abraham. Although Isaac becomes a more significant figure in the interpretations of the church fathers in comparison with the biblical story, Abraham remains the pivotal character.

The centrality of Abraham is partly influenced by the New Testament emphasis but also represents a reaction to the rabbinic stress on Isaac (vv. 6–8, 9–12 and 13–14).

Did Isaac suffer?

The rabbinic terms 'ashes of Isaac' and 'blood of Isaac' indicate that Isaac suffered from his experience. The Akedah therefore represents a severe test of Isaac's self-offering, for so eager was he to obey his father and God's command that even after blood starting flowing he did not attempt to stop the sacrifice. However, the church fathers, particularly Melito and Cyril of Alexandria, are vehement in their assertions that Isaac did not suffer. Their interpretations betray an awareness of the rabbinic interpretations, for the biblical text provides no indication that Isaac suffered or shed blood, and there is no obvious reason why they should consider the question of his suffering unless there is an exegetical encounter. In contrast to the rabbinic depiction of Isaac as epitomizing suffering (בעל יסורין), Cyril makes it clear that only Christ suffered, because the ram ransomed Isaac, who was 'stolen away'. Christ, however, was sacrificed although he had the power to carry himself out from under death. Thus, according to the church fathers, the Akedah was a pale shadow of the future sacrifice just as Isaac was a pale shadow of Christ. Indeed, even if Isaac had shed blood, all previous sacrifices, including the Akedah, were irrelevant because they were unacceptable to God. In the words of Athanasius, 'the death of Isaac did not procure freedom to the world but that of our Saviour alone' (vv. 9–12).

LAST WORD

Bound by the Bible has demonstrated a close exegetical relationship between Jewish and Christian biblical interpretation. Genesis 22, central to both religions, stimulated a rich diversity of interpretation over the first six centuries CE. It is the central thesis of this book that neither Jewish nor Christian interpretations can be understood properly without reference to the other.

The existence of exegetical encounters has implications for the study of rabbinics and patristics. It is no longer acceptable to study these subjects in a vacuum, without an awareness of the factors influencing their development. In order to understand properly Jewish or Christian exegesis in late antiquity it is essential to understand each other's interpretations and the influence of one upon the other.

For various reasons the significance of the exegetical encounter has not been taken seriously. The traditional Christian teaching of contempt for

Judaism, resulting from the *Adversus Iudaeos* literature, has understandably reduced the desire among the majority of rabbinic scholars to take patristics seriously. For their part, patristics scholars rarely demonstrate a genuine interest in and a good understanding of rabbinic Judaism. I hope that *Bound by the Bible* has shown how valuable and even essential it is to explore the interpretations of Judaism and Christianity together. The exegetical encounter, which took place so long ago, can point the way forward today.

Epilogue

Jewish and Christian interest in the Binding of Isaac has remained as strong in modern times as it did in the first six centuries CE. The biblical story continues to attract significant attention in theological writings as well as in the arts and literature.[1] Modern writers have somewhat different concerns from those in late antiquity but, like the rabbis and church fathers, they ask similar questions of the biblical narrative and their writings demonstrate a continuing exegetical encounter. Clearly it is not possible to refer to many of the modern works that deal with Genesis 22, but the writings briefly discussed below are, in my view, among the most significant as well as representative. They are also to a certain extent inter-related, which reinforces the main thesis of *Bound by the Bible*: that Jews and Christians share not only a common biblical text but also a common exegetical tradition.

Arguably, modern theological interpretations of the Akedah begin with the writings of one the most prominent post-enlightenment Christian theologians, Søren Kierkegaard and his book *Fear and Trembling*, a title chosen to describe Kierkegaard's discomfort with Genesis 22. His approach to the Sacrifice of Isaac significantly differs from that of the church fathers and the rabbis. Reflecting the dilemma of the post-enlightenment, he grapples with different philosophical and ethical issues. One century earlier, Immanuel Kant admitted he was unable to accept that God would command a man to kill his son – an act that he deemed unethical – and concluded that Abraham should have replied to God as follows: 'That I must not kill my good son is quite certain, but that you who appear to me as God are indeed God, of this I can never become certain . . .'[2] In other words, Abraham should have rejected the command because it was opposed to the moral law.

Kierkegaard, however, rejected Kant in his discussion of the teleological suspension of the ethical. In his commentary on the Akedah he describes

---

[1] Cf. Moberley 1988:303.   [2] Rabel 1963:334–5.

Abraham as the 'knight of faith' because he was willing to carry out God's will. Kierkegaard acknowledged that Abraham's willingness to kill Isaac was incommensurable with the ethical. Dissatisfied with the traditional interpretations explaining the reasons for Abraham's obedience to God's command, which in his view amounted to a poor substitute for faith, Kierkegaard concluded that Abraham believed with certainty that all things were possible with God. Kierkegaard points out that, if the purpose of the Akedah were simply to give up the son in joyless resignation, to receive him joyfully would have been awkward and difficult. Abraham would have loved God but would not have exhibited faith. In contrast, Abraham's faith was a surrender of his own judgement of right and wrong in favour of unconditional acceptance of God's will.

Kierkegaard has influenced generations of Jewish as well as Christian writers. For example, Jewish scholar Eliezer Berkovits refers to Kierkegaard when he addresses the challenge to faith posed by the Holocaust. Abraham makes not a leap of faith, he argues, but shows trust in God and in the continuing covenantal relationship between God and Israel. In his view, the 'very essence of trust consists not in "leaping" but in standing firm'.[3] Berkovits grapples with the contradiction between God's promise of a son and God's command to sacrifice the son. He suggests that the Akedah is a story of monumental faithfulness because Abraham retains his faith in the covenant with God, which mirrors those Jews who retained their faith in God when they were forced to live in ghettoes and concentration camps.

Another writer who relates the Akedah to the Holocaust is Elie Wiesel. He describes Isaac as the 'first survivor'. Wiesel is acutely aware that, like the mother in 4 Maccabees, there exists a gulf between the biblical narrative and the experience of the Holocaust.

We have known Jews who, like Abraham witnessed the death of their children; who like Isaac lived the Akedah in their flesh; and some who went mad when they saw their father disappearing on the altar, in a blazing fire whose flames reached the highest heavens.[4]

For Wiesel, the story of Isaac did not end on Moriah, and consequently the Akedah has something to teach Jews who survived the Holocaust. He links Jewish survival to Isaac because Isaac, 'the survivor', remained defiant and defied death.

The Akedah has also been given attention by those who escaped the Holocaust and made their way to the Land of Israel such as Amir Gilboa,

---

[3] Berkovits 1976:124.   [4] Wiesel 1976:95.

who was the sole survivor from his family. Gilboa immigrated to Israel before World War II and carried feelings of guilt for the deaths of those he left behind for the rest of his life. His poem *Yitzhak* portrays Isaac as a child who naively protests against the impending sacrifice only to learn that Abraham has been sacrificed. The poem expresses the impotence of the father who is too weak to withstand God's command. As a result, the son destroys the father's tradition.

Some Israeli novelists and poets view the Akedah as a metaphor for the sacrifice by fathers of their children to ensure the survival of Israel. According to one scholar of modern Hebrew literature, the biblical story is interpreted in terms of a dissonance in the father–son relationship such as the failure of a father to protect his children. In stories and poems that deal with the wars following Israel's independence, fathers are depicted not only as sending out sons to fight but also as sacrificing them on the altar of Zionism. Eli Alon, for instance, complains that 'the sons pay for their father's deeds'[5] and protests that Israelis are forced into the sacrificial role of an eternal Isaac. The love of God, a central religious motif, is lost.[6]

Yehudah Amichai also touched on this subject in his poem *The True Hero of the Akedah*, composed shortly after the 1982 Lebanon War. Amichai's condemnation of the disregard of suffering in the context of war is reminiscent of World War I poetry and especially of Wilfred Owen, who described himself as a 'conscientious objector with a very seared conscience'.[7] Owen, in his famous poem *The Parable of the Old Man and the Young*, describes how the angel was too late to save Isaac. Commenting on the moment when the angel called out to Abraham to stop the sacrifice, Owen writes, 'But the old man would not so, but slew his son – and half the seed of Europe, one by one'.[8] Amichai portrays Isaac and the angel as indifferent witnesses to the suffering of the ram, which is identified as the true hero of the biblical story because it is the only figure in the biblical narrative that died. All the others – Abraham, God, the angel and Isaac – had gone home.

Criticism of Abraham is also common in the writings of feminist writers. For example, Hartsoe depicts Sarah as understanding the will of God better than Abraham because she knew that God did not desire a small boy as burnt offering. Sarah, rather than Abraham, understands sin, forgiveness

[5] Quoted in Abramson 1990:109.   [6] Cf. Kartun-Blum 1988: 294ff.
[7] Owen 1963:27.   [8] Owen 1963:42.

and love.[9] Others, such as Trible and Ostriker argue that the absence of Sarah is extremely significant. Ostriker argues that the Akedah demonstrates a struggle between the mother-goddess and the father-god and that biblical patriarchy was concerned with silencing women.[10] Delaney also tackles the issue of male violence and delivers a forceful sociological critique of the story. Her study examines the 1990 trial of a Californian man who murdered his son. The father justified his actions on the basis of Genesis 22 because, like Abraham, he claimed he was told to sacrifice his son. Delaney attacks patriarchal society and, in her view, the associated hierarchical structure of authority.

The shocking actions of Abraham also continued to stimulate Jewish and Christian artists. There are many hundreds of artistic interpretations of the biblical story, and among the best known are those by Caravaggio, Rembrandt and more recently Chagall. Caravaggio portrays Abraham as an old man about to slit his son's throat when an angel with his right hand prevents the sacrifice and with his left points to the ram. Abraham looks bemused whilst Isaac looks terrified. Rembrandt captures the moment when the angel pins Abraham's arm, preventing the father from sacrificing his son. Abraham is surprised and drops his knife. As for Chagall, the deliverance of Abraham and Isaac is depicted alongside the crucifixion.

Both ancient and modern interpreters share a fascination with the Akedah. When Jews and Christians study interpretations of Genesis 22, rabbinic, patristic or modern, they discover a shared emphasis on the importance of the biblical text and a willingness among the exegetes to be open to, and to engage with, each other's teachings. Some Jewish interpretations respond to and adopt Christian interpretation, and likewise, some Christian interpretations respond to and adopt Jewish interpretations. In order to understand their own tradition of biblical interpretation, Jews and Christians need to be aware of the exegetical encounter. A realization that rabbinic Judaism was concerned with and influenced by Christian biblical interpretation (and vice versa) will contribute to a reacquaintance by Jews and Christians to each other's interpretations.

Jews and Christians need to be reminded that the history of their relationship is not simply one of condemnation and contempt. There is an additional story to be told of the Jewish–Christian encounter. Rather than simply breeding contempt, familiarity has also generated admiration and

---

[9] Hartsoe 1981: 13ff.   [10] Ostriker 1993: 37–41.

respect. On an exegetical level, at least, Jews and Christians took into account the interpretations that each developed, sometimes appropriating the others' interpretations and incorporating them into their own exegetical tradition. Perhaps the moment has arrived when Jews and Christians will begin to truly realize the significance of a shared exegetical tradition and the extent to which they are bound by the Bible.

Bibliography

PRIMARY SOURCES: TEXTS AND TRANSLATIONS

THE BIBLE

Targum Versions

1. Onkelos

Sperber, A. (ed.) (1959). *The Bible in Aramaic, I: The Pentateuch According to Targum Onkelos*. Leiden, Brill.

2. Pseudo-Jonathan

Clarke, E. G. *et al.* (eds.) (1984). *Targum Pseudo-Jonathan of the Pentateuch: Text and Concordance*. New Jersey, Ktav.

3. Palestinian Targum

Díez Macho, A. (ed.) (1968–78). *Neophyti, I: Targum Palestinense ms. de la Biblioteca Vaticana, Edicion Principe*. Textos y Estudios 'Cardenal Cisneros' del Instituto 'Arias Montano', Madrid, consejo superior de Investigaciones Cientíﬁcas.

Klein, M. (ed.) (1980). *The Fragment Targums of the Pentateuch According to their Extant Sources*. Analecta Biblica 80, Rome, Biblical Institute Press.

 (1986). *Genizah MSS of Palestinian Targum to the Pentateuch*. Cincinnati, Hebrew Union College.

4. Christian

Goshen-Gottstein, M. (ed.) (1973). *The Bible in the Syropalestinian Version* Jerusalem, Magnes Press.

Coptic version

Ciasca, A. (ed.) (1885). *Sacrorum bibliorum: Fragmenta copto-sahidica*. Rome, Musei Borgiani.

Greek version

Harl, M. (1994). *La Bible d'Alexandrie: La Genèse.* Paris, Cerf.
Wevers, J. *et al.* (ed.) (1931–93). *Septuaginta: Vetus Testamentum Graecum auctoritate academiae scientiarum gottingensis.* Göttingen, Deutsche Bibelgesellschaft.

Hebrew version

Eilliger, K. and W. Rudolph (eds.) (1967–77). *Biblia Hebraica Stuttgartensia* Stuttgart, Deutsche Bibelgesellschaft.

Latin version

Weber, R. (ed.) (1969). *Biblia Sacra iuxta Vulgatam versionem.* Stuttgart, Deutsche Bibelgesellschaft.

New Testament

Nestle E., B. Aland and K. Aland (eds.) (1993). *Novum Testamentum Graece.* Stuttgart, Deutsche Bibelgesellschaft.

TRANSLATIONS AND COMMENTARIES

Chilton, B. (ed.) (1987). *The Aramaic Bible: The Isaiah Targum.* Edinburgh, T&T Clark.
Grossfeld, B. (ed.) (1988). *The Aramaic Bible: Targum Onqelos to Genesis* Edinburgh, T&T Clark.
Le Boulluec, A. and D. Pralon (eds.) (1988). *La Bible d'Alexandrie, II: L'Exode.* Paris, Cerf.
Le Déaut, R. (ed.) (1978–81). *Targum du Pentateuch: Traduction des deux recensions palestiniennes complètes avec introduction, parallèles, notes et index.* SC 245, 256, 271, 282, Paris, Cerf.
Maher, M. (ed.) (1992). *The Aramaic Bible: Targum Pseudo-Jonathan: Genesis.* Edinburgh, T&T Clark.
McNamara, M. (ed.) (1992). *The Aramaic Bible: Targum Neofiti I Genesis.* Edinburgh, T&T Clark.

HELLENISTIC GREEK WORKS

Colson, F. H. and G. H. Whitaker (eds.) (1949–62). *Philo with an English Translation.* LCL, London, Heinemann.
Marcus, R. (ed.) (1953). *Philo Supplement I: Questions and Answers on Genesis and Exodus.* LCL, London, Heinemann.
Thackeray, H. St J. (ed.) (1950–65). *Josephus with an English Translation.* LCL, London, Heinemann.

APOCRYPHAL AND PSEUDEPIGRAPHAL WORKS

Abel, F.-M. (ed.) (1948). *Les Livres des Maccabées.* Paris, J. Gabalda.
Charlesworth, J. H. (ed.) (1985). *The Old Testament Pseudepigrapha.* New York, Doubleday.
Harrington, D., C. Perrot and P.-M. Bogaert (eds.) (1976). *Pseudo-Philon: Les Antiquités Bibliques.* SC 229, 230, Paris, Cerf.
Jacobson, H. (1996). *A Commentary on Pseudo-Philo's* Liber Antiquitatum Biblicarum. Leiden, Brill.
Milik, M. (ed.) (1994). *Qumran Cave 4.* Discoveries from the Judean Desert, 13, Oxford, Oxford University Press.
Sparks, H. F. D. (ed.) (1984). *The Apocryphal Old Testament.* Oxford, Oxford University Press.

RABBINIC WRITINGS

The Talmudic literature

1. Mishnah (M)

Albeck, C. (ed.) (1952–8). *Shisha sidre mishnah.* Jerusalem, Mosad Bialik.
Danby, H. (ed.) (1933). *The Mishnah.* Oxford, Oxford University Press.

2. Tosefta (Tos)

Lieberman, S. (ed.) (1955–88). *The Tosefta.* New York, Bet ha-midrash le-rabanim ba-'Amerikah.
Neusner, J. *et al.* (eds.) (1977–86). *The Tosefta.* New Haven, Ktav.

3. Jerusalem Talmud (JT)

Benrend, B. (ed.) (1866). *Talmud yerushalmi: kemo she-nidpas be venetsi'ah bi-shenat 5282.* Krotoschin.
Neusner, J. *et al.* (eds.) (1982–94). *The Talmud of the Land of Israel.* Chicago, Chicago University Press.
Wewers, G. A. *et al.* (trans.) (1980–). *Übersetzung des Talmud Yerushalmi.* Tübingen, Mohr.

4. Babylonian Talmud (BT)

Epstein, I. (ed.) (1935–82). *The Babylonian Talmud.* London, Soncino.

The Midrashic literature

1. Mekhilta de Rabbi Ishmael (MdRI)

Lauterbach, J. Z. (ed.) (1933–5). *Mekilta de Rabbi Ishmael.* Philadelphia, Jewish Publication Society.

2. Mekhilta de Rabbi Shimon be Yochai (MdSbY)

Epstein, J. N. and E. Z. Melamed (eds.) (1955). *Mekhilta d'Rabbi Simon b. Jochai.* Jerusalem, Mekize Nirdamim.

3. Sifra (on Leviticus)

Finkelstein, L. (ed.) (1956). *Sifra or Torat Kohanim According to Codex Assemani LXVI.* New York, Jewish Theological Seminary of America.
Neusner, J. (ed.) (1988) *Sifra: An Analytical Translation* Atlanta.

4. Sifre (on Numbers)

Horovitz, H. S. (ed.) (1966). *Siphre D'be Rab: Fasciculus primus: Siphre ad Numeros adjecto Siphre zutta.* Jerusalem, Bet ha-midrash le-rahanim ba-'Amerikah.
Neusner, J. (ed.) (1986). *Sifré to Numbers: An American Translation and Explanation.* Atlanta, Scholars Press.

5. Sifre (on Deuteronomy)

Finkelstein, L. (ed.) (1939). *Siphre ad Deuteronomium H. S. Horovitzii schedis usis cum variis lectionibus et adnotationibus.* Berlin, Bet ha-midrash le rahanim ba-'Amerikah.
Hammer, R. (ed.) (1986). *Sifre: A Tannaitic Commentary on the Book of Deuteronomy.* New Haven, Yale University Press.

6. Midrash Tannaim (on Deuteronomy)

Hoffman, D. (ed.) (1908–9). *Midrasch Tannaim zum Deuteronomium.* Berlin, Hevrat mekitse nirdamim.

7. Midrash Rabbah

Freedman, H. and M. Simon (eds.) (1961). *Midrash Rabbah: Translated into English.* London, Soncino.
Mirkin, M. A. (ed.) (1956–67). *Midrash Rabbah.* Tel-Aviv, Yavneh.
Theodor, J. (ed.) (1912). *Bereschit Rabba mit kritischem Apparat und Kommentar,* Vol. 1. Berlin, n.p.

8. Pesikta de Rab Kahana (PRK)

Braude, W. G. and I. J. Kapstein (eds.) (1975). *Pesikta de-Rab Kahana.* Philadelphia, Jewish Publication Society.
Mandelbaum, B. (ed.) (1962). *Pesikta de Rav Kahana: According to an Oxford Manuscript with Variants.* New York, n.p.

9. Pesikta Rabbati (PesR)

Friedmann, M. (ed.) (1980). *Pesikta Rabbati: Midrasch für den Fest-Cyclus und die ausgezeichneten Sabbathe.* Vilna, ha madpis Y. Qayzer.
Braude, W. G. (ed.) (1968). *Pesikta Rabbati: Discourses for Feasts, Fasts and Special Sabbaths.* New Haven, Yale University Press.

10. Tanhuma-Yelamdenu (TanY)

Berman, S. A. (ed.) (1996). *Midrash Tanhuma-Yelammedenu [Genesis-Exodus].* New York, Ktav.
Zondel ben Joseph, E. (ed.) (1875). *Midrash Tanhuma.* Warsaw, N. D. Visberg.

11. Tanhuma-Buber (TanB)

Buber, S. (ed.) (1885). *Midrasch Tanhuma.* Wilna, ha-Almanah veha-Ahim Rom.
Townsend, J. T. (ed.) (1989–95). *Midrash Tanhuma [Genesis-Leviticus].* New York, Ktav.

12. *Midrash Zuta*

Buber, S. (ed.) (1894). *Midrasch Suta: Haggadische Abhandlungen über Schir ha-Schirim, Ruth, Ecah und Koheleth, nebst Jalkut zum Buche Echah.* Berlin, n.p.

13. Tanna de-bê Eliyahu (Tan Eli)

Friedman, M. (ed.) (1960). *Seder Eliahu Rabba und Seder Eliahu zuta Tanna d'be Eliahu.* Jerusalem, Bamberger and Wahrman
Braude, W. G. and I. J. Kapstein (eds.) (1981). *Tanna debe Eliyyahu: The Lore of the School of Elijah.* Philadelphia, Jewish Publication Society.

14. Pirkei de Rabbi Eliezer (PRE)

Friedlander, G. (ed.) (1916). *Pirke de Rabbi Eliezer.* New York, n.p.

15. Midrash ha-gadol

Margulies, M. (ed.) (1947). *Midrash ha-gadol 'al hamishah humshe Toran: sefer Bere'shit.* Jerusalem, Mosad ha-Rav kook.

APOSTOLIC AND GREEK FATHERS

Athanasius

Migne, J. P. (ed.) (1857–66). *Epistolae Heortasticae VI. PG 26.*

Barnabas

Lake, K. (ed.) (1912) *Apostolic Fathers (I) with an English Translation.* LCL, London, Heinemann.
Prigent, P. and R. A. Knight (eds.) (1971). *L'épître de Barnabé.* SC 172, Paris, Cerf.

Basil of Seleucia

Migne, J. P. (ed.) (1857–66). *Oration VII. PG* 85.

Catena

Evans, E. (ed.) (1956). *Tertullian's Treatise on the Incarnation.* London, SPCK.
Petit, F. (ed.) (1986). *Collectio Coisliniana.* Louvain, Peeters.
    (1995). *La chaîne sur la Genèse (édition intégrale).* Louvain, Peeters.

Chrysostom

Harkins, P. W. (ed.) (1979). *Saint John Chrysostom: Discourses against Judaizing Christians.* Washington, Catholic University Press of America.
Hill, R. C. (ed.) (1986–92). *Homilies on Genesis.* Washington, Catholic University Press of America.
Malingrey, A.–M. (ed.) (1980). *Sur le sacerdoce dialogue et homélie/Jean Chrysostome; introduction, texte critique, traduction et notes.* SC 272, Paris, Cerf.
Migne, J. P. (ed.) (1857–66). *Adversus Iudaeos. PG* 48.
Migne, J. P. (ed.) (1857–66). *Homiliarum in Genesim (XLVII). PG* 54.

Clement of Alexandria

Marrou, H.-I. and M. Harl (ed.) (1960). *Le Pedagogue I.* SC 70, Paris, Cerf.
Le Boulluec, A. (ed.) (1981). *Les Stromates V.* SC 278/9, Paris, Cerf.

Clement of Rome

Lake, Kirsopp (ed.) (1912). *Apostolic Fathers (I) with an English Translation.* LCL, London, Heinemann.

Cyril of Alexandria

Burns, W. H. (ed.) (1991). *Lettres Festales.* SC 372, Paris, Cerf.
Migne, J. P. (ed.) (1857–66). *De adoratione et cultu in spiritu et veritate. PG* 68.
    (1857–66). *Glaphyrorum in Genesim. PG* 69.
    (1857–66). *Homilae Paschales. PG* 77.
    (1857–66). *In Malchiam prophetam commentarius. PG* 72.

Ephrem Graecus

Mercati, S. I. (ed.) (1915). *S. Ephraem Syri Opera*. Rome, Pontifical Biblical Institute.

Gregory of Nazianzen

Bernardi, J. (ed.) (1978). *Discours/Grégoire de Nazianze*. 1–3. SC 247, Paris, Cerf.
Migne, J. P. (ed.) (1858–66). *Oratio XLV: In Sanctum Pascha. PG* 36.

Gregory of Nyssa

Migne, J. P. (ed.) (1857–66). *De Deitate Filii et Spiritus Sancti. PG* 46.
    (1857–66). *In Christi Resurrectionem Oratio 1. PG* 46.

Irenaeus of Lyons

Rousseau, A. and L. Doutreleau (eds.) (1965–82). *Contre les hérésies: Livre IV.* SC
    100, Paris, Cerf.

Justin Martyr

Goodspeed, E. J. (ed.) (1914). *Die ältesten Apologeten*. Göttingen, Vandenhoeck &
    Ruprecht.
Williams, A. L. (ed.) (1935). *Justin Martyr, the Dialogue with Trypho: Translated,
    Introduction and Notes*. London, SPCK.

Melito of Sardis

Hall, S. G. (ed.) (1979). *Melito of Sardis: On Pascha and Fragments*. Oxford, Claren-
    don Press.

Origen

Borret, M. (ed.) (1967–). *Contre Celse/Origène*. SC 136, Paris, Cerf.
    (1981). *Homélies sur le Lévitique*. SC 287, Paris, Cerf.
Brésard, L. and H. Crouzel (eds.) (1991–2). *Commentaire sur le cantique des can-
    tiques/Origène*. SC 375–6, Paris, Cerf.
De Lange, N. (ed.) (1983). *La lettre à Africanus*. SC 302, Paris, Cerf.
Doutreleau, L. (ed.) (1976). *Homélies sur la Genèse*. SC 7, Paris, Cerf.
Jaubert, A. (ed.) (1960). *Homélies sur Josué*. SC 71, Paris, Cerf.
Migne, J. P. (ed.) (1857–66). *Exegetica in Psalmos. PG* 12.

Pseudo-Ephrem Graecus

Mercati, S. I. (ed.) (1915). *S. Ephraem Syri Opera*. Rome, Pontifical Biblical Institute.

Pseudo-Gregory of Nyssa

Mercati, S. I. (ed.) (1915). *S. Ephraem Syri Opera*. Rome, Pontifical Biblical Institute.

Polycarp

Lake, K. (ed.) (1913). *Apostolic Fathers (II) with an English Translation*. LCL, London, Heinemann.

Romanos

Grosdidier de Matons, J. (ed.) (1964). *Romanos de Mélode: Hymnes*. SC 99, Paris, Cerf.
Moskhos, M. (1974). 'Romanos' Hymn on the Sacrifice of Abraham: A Discussion of the Sources and a Translation'. *Byzantion* 44: 310–28.
Carpenter, M. (1972). *Kontakia of Romanos: Byzantine Melodist*. Columbia, University of Missouri Press.

Socratis Hermiae Sozomeni

Migne, J. P. (ed.) (1857–66). *Historia Ecclesiastica*. PG 67.

Tertullian

Rendall, G. H. and T. R. Glover (eds.) (1931). *Tertullian, Apology, De spectaculis, with an English Translation by T. R. Glover. Minicius Felix with an English Translation by Gerald H. Rendall*. LCL. London, W. Heinemann.

REFERENCES

Abramson, G. (1990). 'The Reinterpretation of the Akedah in Modern Hebrew Poetry'. *Journal of Jewish Studies* 41: 101–14.
Agus, A. R. E. (1988). *The Binding of Isaac and Messiah*. Albany, NY, State University of New York.
Alexander, P. S. (1988). 'Jewish Aramaic Translations of the Hebrew Scriptures'. *Mikra: Text, Translation, Reading and Interpretation of the Hebrew Bible in Ancient Judaism and Early Christianity*. M. J. Mulder (ed.). Philadelphia, Fortress Press: 217–54.
Allen, W. (1981). 'The Sacrifice of Isaac'. *The Big Book of Jewish Humour*. W. Novak and M. Waldoks (eds.). New York, Harper and Row.
Armstrong, G. T. (1979). 'The Cross in the Old Testament According to Athanasius, Cyril of Jerusalem and the Cappadocian Fathers'. *Theologia Crucis: Festschrift Erich Dinkler*. C. Andresen and G. Klein (eds.). Tübingen, Mohr: 17–38.
Ashby, G. W. (1972). *Theodoret of Cyrrhus as Exegete of the Old Testament*. Grahamstown, South Africa, Rhodes University Publications.

Attridge, H. W. (1976). *The Interpretation of Biblical History in the* Antiquitates Judaicae *of Flavius Josephus*. Missoula, Scholars Press.

  (1989). *The Epistle to the Hebrews: A Commentary on the Epistle to the Hebrews*. Philadelphia, Fortress Press.

Attridge, H. W. and G. Hata (eds.) (1992). *Eusebius, Christianity, and Judaism*. Studia Post-Biblica, Leiden, Brill.

Avi-Yonah, M. (1973). 'Goodenough's Evaluation of the Dura Paintings: A Critique'. *The Dura-Europos Synagogue: A Re-evaluation (1932–72)*. J. Gutmann (ed.). Chambersburg, PA, American Academy of Religion: 117–35.

Aziza, C. (1977). *Tertullien et le judaïsme*. Paris, Les Belles Lettres.

Baer, Y. (1961). 'Israel, the Christian Church and the Roman Empire from the time of Septimus Severus to the Edict of Toleration of A. D. 313'. *Scripta Hierosoymitana* 7: 79–149.

Barnes, T. D. (1971/1985). *Tertullian: A Historical and Literary Study* (Revised and updated, 1985). Oxford, Clarendon Press.

  (1981). *Constantine and Eusebius*. London, Harvard University Press.

Barrett, C. K. (1957). *A Commentary on the Epistle to the Romans*. London, Black.

Barth, L. M. (1990). 'Introducing the Akedah: A Comparison of Two Midrashic Presentations'. *A Tribute to Geza Vermes*. P. R. Davies and R. T. White (eds.). Sheffield, JSOT Press: 125–38.

  (1994). 'Textual Transformations: Rabbinic Exegesis of Genesis 22:14.' *Bits of Honey: Essays for Samson H. Levey*. S. F. Chyet and D. H. Ellenson (eds.). Atlanta, Scholars Press: 3–23.

Baskin, J. (1983). *Pharoah's Counsellors: Job, Jethro and Baalam in Rabbinic and Patristic Traditions*. Chico, CA, Scholars Press.

  (1985). 'Rabbinic-Patristic Exegetical Contacts in Late Antiquity: A Bibliographical Reappraisal'. *Approaches to Ancient Judaism, v: Studies in Judaism and its Greco-Roman Context*. W. S. Green (ed.). Atlanta, Scholars Press: 53–80.

Batten, L. W. (1913). *Ezra and Nehemiah: A Critical and Exegetical Commentary*. Edinburgh, T&T Clark.

Berkovits, E. (1976). *Crisis and Faith*. New York, Sanhedrin Press.

Berman, L. (1997). *The Akedah: The Binding of Isaac*. Northvale, NJ, Aronson.

Bickerman, E. J. (1945). 'The Date of Fourth Maccabees'. *Louis Ginzberg Jubilee Volume: On the Occasion of his 70th Birthday*. S. Lieberman, S. Zeitlin, S. Spiegel and A. Marx (eds.). New York, American Academy for Jewish Research: 105–12.

Birnbaum, P. (ed.) (1951). *High Holiday Prayer Book*. New York, Hebrew Publishing Company.

Bloch, R. (1955). 'Note méthodologique pour l'étude de la littérature rabbinique'. *Recherches de Science Religieuse* 43: 194–227.

Blowers, P. M. (1988). 'Origen, the Rabbis and the Bible: Towards a Picture of Judaism and Christianity in Third Century Caesaria'. *Origen of Alexandria: His World and his Legacy*. C. Kannengiesser and W. Petersen (eds.). Notre Dame, University of Notre Dame Press: 96–116.

Blumenkranz, B. (1946). *Die Judenpredigt Augustins: Ein Beitrag zur Geschichte der jüdisch-christlichen Beziehungen in den ersten Jahrhundert*. Basel, von Helbing & Lichtenhahn.

(1977). *Juifs et chrétiens: Patristique et Moyen Age*. London, Variorum Reprints.

Botte, B. (1951). 'Abraham dans la Liturgie'. *Cahiers Sioniens* 5: 88–95.

Bowe, B. (2002). 'From Guarded Turf to Common Ground: Biblical Terrain and Contemporary Dialogue among Jews and Christians'. *Jews and Christians in Coversation*. E. Kessler, J. Banki and J. Pawlikowski (eds.). Cambridge, Orchard Academic Press: 15–24.

Bowker, J. (1969). *The Targums and Rabbinic Literature: An Introduction to the Jewish Interpretations of Scripture*. Cambridge, Cambridge University Press.

Boyarin, D. (1994). *A Radical Jew: Paul and the Politics of Identity*. Berkeley, University of California Press.

Bradshaw, P. F. (1981). *Daily Prayer in the Early Church*. London, SPCK.

(2002). *The Search for the Origins of Christian Worship: Sources and Methods for the Study of Early Liturgy*. London, SPCK, 2nd edn.

Bradshaw, P. B. and L. A. Hoffman (eds.) (1991). *The Making of Jewish and Christian Worship*. Notre Dame, University of Notre Dame.

Bregman, M. (1982). 'The Depiction of the Ram in the Aqedah Mosaic at Bet Alpha' [Hebrew]. *Tarbiz* 51: 306–9.

(1995). 'The Riddle of the Ram in Genesis Chapter 22: Jewish–Christian Contacts in Late Antiquity'. *The Sacrifice of Isaac in the Three Monotheisitic Religions*. F. Manns (ed.). Jerusalem, Franciscan Printing Press: 127–45.

(1997). 'Tanhuma'. *Oxford Dictionary of the Jewish Religion*. R. J. R. Werblowsky and G. Wigoder (eds.). Oxford, Oxford University Press: 673–4.

Brightman, F. E. (1896). *Liturgies: Eastern and Western*. Oxford, Clarendon Press.

Brock, S. P. (1974). 'Sarah and the Aqedah'. *Le Muséon* 87: 67–77.

(1981a). 'Genesis 22 in Syriac Tradition'. *Mélanges Dominique Barthelemy*. P. Casetti, O. Keel and A. Schenker (eds.). Freiburg, Editions Universitaires: 1–30.

(1981b). 'An Anonymous Syriac Homily on Abraham (Gen 22)'. *Orientalia Louvaniensia Periodica* 12: 61–129.

(1986). 'Two Syriac Verse Homilies on the Binding of Isaac'. *Le Muséon* 99: 61–129.

(1992). 'Jewish Traditions in Syriac Sources'. *Journal of Jewish Studies* 30: 212–32.

Brooks, R. (1988). 'Straw Dogs and Scholarly Ecumenism: The Appropriate Jewish Background for the Study of Origen'. *Origen of Alexandria*. C. Kannengiesser and W. L. Petersen (eds.). Notre Dame, Notre Dame University Press: 63–95.

Brown, M. (1982). 'Biblical Myth and Contemporary Experience: The Akedah in Modern Jewish Literature'. *Judaism* 31: 99–111.

Canevet, M. (1983). *Grégoire de Nysse et l'hermeneutique biblique*. Paris, Etudes augustiniennes.

Carleton Paget, J. (1994). *The Epistle of Barnabas: Outlook and Background*. Tübingen, Mohr.

(1996a). 'Jewish Proselytism at the Time of Christian Origins: Chimera or Reality?' *Journal for the Study of the New Testament* 62: 65–103.

(1996b). 'The Christian Exegesis of the Old Testament in the Alexandrian Tradition'. *History of the Interpretation of the Hebrew Bible/Old Testament*, I. M. Saebo (ed.). Göttingen, Vandenhoeck & Ruprecht: 478–542.

(1997). 'Anti-Judaism and Early Christian Identity'. *Zeitschrift für Antikes Christentum* 1: 195–225.

Chester, A. and R. P. Martin (1994). *The Theology of the Letters of James, Peter, and Jude*. Cambridge, Cambridge University Press.

Chilton, B. D. (1982). 'Irenaeus on Isaac'. *Studia Patristica*. E. A. Livingstone (ed.). Oxford, Pergamon: 643–7.

(1986a). 'Isaac and the Second Night: A Consideration'. *Biblica* 61: 78–88.

(1986b). 'Recent Discussion of the Aqedah'. *Targumic Approaches to the Gospels: Essays in the Mutual Definition of Judaism and Christianity*. B. D. Chilton (ed.). New York, University Press of America: 39–49.

Chilton, B. D. and P. R. Davies, (1978). 'The Aqedah: A Revised Tradition History'. *Catholic Biblical Quarterly* 40: 514–46.

Cohen, J. (1989). *Be Fertile and Increase, Fill the Earth and Master it: The Ancient and Medieval Career of a Biblical Text*. Ithaca, Cornell University Press.

Conybeare, F. C. (ed.) (1898). *The Dialogues of Athanasius and Zaccaeus and of Timothy and Aquila*. Anecdota Oxoniensia. Oxford, Clarendon Press.

Cosby, M. R. (1988). *The Rhetorical Composition and Function of Hebrews 11*. Macon, GA, Mercer University Press.

Dahl, N. A. (1969). 'The Atonement – An Adequate Reward for the Akedah? (Rom 8:32)'. *Neotestamentica et Semitica: Studies in Honour of Matthew Black*. E. E. Ellis and M. Wilcox (eds.). Edinburgh, T&T Clark.

Daly, R. J. (1977). 'The Soteriological Significance of the Sacrifice of Isaac'. *Catholic Biblical Quarterly* 39: 45–75.

(1978). *Christian Sacrifice: The Judeo-Christian Background before Origen*. Washington, DC, Catholic University of America Press.

Daniélou, J. (1950). *Sacramentum futuri: Etudes sur les origines de la typologie biblique*. Paris, Beauchesne.

(1967a). 'La typologie biblique de Grégoire de Nysse'. *Studi e materiali di storia delle religioni* 38: 185–96.

(1967b). 'Philon et Grégoire de Nysse'. *Philo d'Alexandrie*. Paris, Colloques Nationaux du Centre National de la Recherche Scientifique: 333–45.

Daube, D. (1960). 'Rabbinic Methods of Interpretation and Hellenistic Rhetoric'. *Hebrew Union College Annual* 22: 239–64.

Davids, P. H. (1982). *Epistle of James: A Commentary on the Greek Text*. Exeter, Paternoster Press.

Davidson, I., S. Assaf, *et al.* (eds.) (1970). *Siddur R. Sa'adia Gaon*. Jerusalem, n.p.

Davies, P. R. (1979). 'Passover and the Dating of the Akedah'. *Journal of Jewish Studies* 30: 59–67.

(1982). 'Martyrdom and Redemption'. *Studia Patristica*. E. A. Livingstone (ed.). Oxford, Pergamon: 652–8.

de Lange, N. R. M. (1976). *Origen and the Jews: Studies in Jewish–Christian Relations in Third Century Palestine*. Cambridge, Cambridge University Press.

(1992). 'Jews and Christians in the Byzantine Empire: Problems and Prospects'. *Christianity and Judaism*. D. Wood (ed.). Oxford, Oxford University Press: 15–32.

de Sola, D. A. (ed.) (1901). *The Festival Prayers According to the Ritual of the German and Polish Jews*. London, Vallentine.

Delaney, C. (1998). *Abraham on Trial: The Social Legacy of Biblical Myth*. Princeton, NJ, Princeton University Press.

Dequeker, L. (1986). 'Le zodiac de la synagogue de beth alpha et le midrash'. *Bijdragen Tijdscrift voor Filosofie en Theologie* 47: 2–30.

D'Espagne, J. (1655). *Shibboleth: or the Reformation of Severall places in the Translation of the French and English Bible*. London.

Dibelius, M. (1976). *James: A Commentary on the Epistle of James*. Philadelphia, Fortress Press.

Diehl, C. (1933). *La peinture byzantine*. Paris, E. van Oest.

Drobner, H. R. (1982). *Gregor von Nyssa: Die drei Tage zwischen Tod und Auferstehung unseres Herrn Jesus Christus*. Leiden, Brill.

Du Mesnil du Buisson, R. (1939). *Les peintures de la synagogue de Doura-Europos*. Rome, Biblical Institute Press.

Dugmore, C. W. (1964). *The Influence of the Synagogue upon the Divine Office*. London, Faith Press.

Dunhill, J. (1992). *Covenant and Sacrifice in the Letter to the Hebrews*. Cambridge, Cambridge University Press.

Dunn, J. D. G. (1988). *Romans*. Dallas, Word Books.

Ehrenstein, T. (1923). *Das Alte Testament im Bilde*. Vienna, Albert Kende.

Elbogen, I. (1993 [1913]). *Jewish Liturgy: A Comprehensive History*. R. P. Scheindlin (trans.). Philadelphia, Jewish Publication Society.

Eliade, M. (1960). *Myths, Dreams and Mysteries*. New York, Harper and Row.

Endres, J. C. (1987). *Biblical Interpretation in the Book of Jubilees*. Washington, DC, Catholic Biblical Association of America.

Evans, C. A. and J. A. Sanders (eds.) (1993). *Paul and the Scriptures of Israel*. Journal for the Study of the Old Testament Supplement Series. Sheffield, JSOT Press.

Fakhry, A. (1951). *The Necroplis of El Bagawat in Kharga Oasis*. Cairo, Services des Antiquités de l'Egypte.

Feldman, L. H. (1982). 'Josephus' Version of the Binding of Isaac'. *SBL Seminar Papers*. K. H. Richards (ed.). Chico, CA, Scholars Press: 113–28.

(1984). 'Josephus as Biblical Interpreter'. *Jewish Quarterly Review* 75: 212–52.

(1993). *Jew and Gentile in the Ancient World*. Princeton, Princeton University Press.

Feldman, L. H. (ed.) (1971). *The Biblical Antiquities of Philo: Now for the First Time Translated from the Old Latin Version by M. R. James (1917): Repr.: Prolegomenon by L. H. Feldman*. Library of Biblical Studies. New York, Ktav.

Feldman, L. H. and G. Hata (eds.) (1987). *Josephus, Judaism and Christianity.* Leiden, Brill.

Feldman, L. H. and G. Hata (eds.) (1989). *Josephus, the Bible and History.* Leiden, Brill.

Ferguson, E. (1993). 'Some Aspects of Gregory of Nyssa's Interpretation of Scripture Exemplified in his *Homilies on Ecclesiastes'. Studia Patristica 27.* E. A. Livingstone (ed.). Leuven, Peeters: 29–33.

Ferrua, A. (1960). *Le pitture della nuova catacomba di Via Latina.* Vatican City, Pontificia Commissione di Archeologia Sacra.

Finney, P. C. (1995). 'Abraham and Isaac Iconography on Late-Antique Amulets and Seals: The Western Evidence'. *Jahrbuch für Antike und Christentum* 38: 140–66.

Fishbane, M. (1985). *Biblical Interpretation in Ancient Israel.* Oxford, Clarendon Press.

Fitzmyer, J. A. (1993). *Romans: A New Translation with Introduction and Commentary.* London, Geoffrey Chapman.

(2002). 'The Sacrifice of Isaac in Qumran Literature'. *Biblica* 83: 211–29.

Fraade, S. D. (1985). *Enosh and his Generation: Pre-Israelite Hero in Post-Biblical Interpretation.* Chico, CA, Scholars Press.

Franxman, T. W. (1979). *Genesis and the Jewish Antiquities of Flavius Josephus.* Rome, Biblical Institute Press.

Gaboury, A. (1968). 'Deux fils uniques: Isaac et Jésus: Connexions vétéro-testamentaires de Mc 1,11 (et parallèles). *Studia Evangelica* 4: 198–204.

Geiger, A. (1872). 'Erbsünde und Versöhnungstod: Deren Versuch in das Judentum einzudringen'. *Jüdische Zeitscrift für Wissenschaft und Leben* 10: 166–71.

Gellman, J. I. (2003). *Abraham! Abraham! Kierkegaard and the Hasidim on the Binding of Isaac.* Aldershot, Ashgate.

Georgi, D. (1986). *The Opponents of Paul in Second Corinthians.* Philadelphia, Fortress Press.

Ginzberg, L. (1900). *Die Haggada bei den Kirchenvatern.* Berlin, Calvary.

(1909–55). *The Legends of the Jews.* Philadelphia, Jewish Publication Society.

Goldschmidt, E. D. (ed.) (1971). *Seder Rav Amram Gaon.* Jerusalem, Mosad ha-Rav Kuk.

Goodenough, E. R. (1953–68). *Jewish Symbols in the Greco-Roman Period.* Princeton, Princeton University Press.

Goodman, M. (1989). 'Proselytising in Rabbinic Judaism'. *Journal of Jewish Studies* 38: 175–85.

(1992). 'Jewish Proselytising in the First Century'. *The Jews among Pagan and Christians in the Roman Empire.* J. Lieu, J. North and T. Rajak (eds.). London, Routledge: 53–78.

(1994). *Mission and Conversion.* Oxford, Clarendon Press.

Grabar, A. (1968a). *L'art de la fin de l'antiquité et du Moyen Age II.* Paris, Collège du France.

(1968b). *Christian Iconography: A Study of its Origins.* London, Routledge.

Grelot, P. (1957). 'Une tosephta targoumique sur Genèse 22 dans un manuscript liturgique de la geniza du Caire'. *Revue des Etudes Juives* 116: 5–26.

Guttman, J. (1983). 'The Illustrated Midrash in the Dura Synagogue Paintings: A New Dimension for the Study of Judaism'. *Proceedings of the American Academy for Jewish Research* 50: 91–104.

(1984a). 'The Sacrifice of Isaac: Variation on a Theme in Early Jewish and Christian Art. *Thiasos ton Mouson*. D. Ahrens (ed.). Cologne, Bohlau: 115–22.

(1984b). 'Early Synagogue and Jewish Catacomb Art and its Relation to Christian Art'. *Aufstieg und Niedergang der römischen Welt* 2: 1313–41.

(1992). 'Revisiting the 'Binding of Isaac' Mosaic in the Beith Alpha Synagogue.' *Bulletin of the Asia Institute* 6: 79–85.

Haas, C. (1997). *Alexandria in Late Antiquity*. Baltimore, Johns Hopkins University Press.

Hachlili, R. (1988). *Ancient Jewish Art and Archaeology in the Land of Israel*. Leiden, Brill.

Hall, S. G. (1971). 'Melito in the Light of the Passover Haggadah'. *Journal of Theological Studies* 22: 29–46.

(1979). *Melito of Sardis: On Pascha and Fragments*. Oxford, Clarendon Press.

(1981). 'The Interpretation of the Old Testament in the Opening Section of Gregory of Nyssa, *De Tridui Spatio*'. *The Easter Sermons of Gregory of Nyssa: Translation and Commentary*. A. Spira and C. Klock (eds.). Philadelphia, Philadelphia Patristic Foundation: 139–52.

Harl, M. (1986). 'La "ligature" d'Isaac (Gen. 22:9) dans la Septante et chez lez pères grecs. *Hellenica et judaica: Homage à Valentin Nikiprowetzky*. A. Caquot, M. Hadas-Lebel and J. Riaud (eds.). Leuven, Peeters: 457–72.

Harnack, A. (1883). *Die Altercatio Simonis Iudaei et Theophili Christiani, nebst Untersuchungen über die antijüdische Polemik in der alten Kirche*. Leipzig, J. C. Hinrichs.

(1908 [1902]). *The Mission and Expansion of Christianity in the First Three Centuries*. J. Moffatt (trans.). London, Theological Translation Library.

Harrington, D., C. Perrot and P.–M. Bogaert (eds.) (1976). *Pseudo-Philon: Les Antiquités Bibliques*. SC 229, 230, Paris, Cerf.

Hartsoe, C. I. (1981). *Dear Daughter: Letters from Eve and Other Women of the Bible*. Wilton, CT, Morehouse Barlow.

Harvey, A. E. (1967). 'Melito and Jerusalem'. *Journal of Theological Studies* 17: 401–4.

Hays, R. B. (1989). *Echoes of Scripture in the Letters of Paul*. New Haven, Yale University Press.

Hayward, C. T. R. (1981). 'The Present State of Research into the Targumic Account of the Sacrifice of Isaac'. *Journal of Jewish Studies* 32: 127–50.

(1990). 'The Sacrifice of Isaac and Jewish Polemic Against Christianity'. *Catholic Biblical Quarterly* 52: 292–306.

(1995). *Saint Jerome's Hebrew Questions on Genesis – Translated with Introduction and Commentary*. Oxford, Oxford University Press.

Hedegard, D. (ed.) (1951). *Seder R. Amram Gaon*. Lund, Lindstedts Universitets Bokhandel.

Heinemann, J. (1977). *Prayer in the Talmud: Forms and Literary Patterns*. Berlin, De Gruyter.

Hengel, M. (1977). *Crucifixion in the Ancient World and the Folly of the Message of the Cross*. London, SCM Press.

(1981a). *The Atonement: A Study of the Origins of the Doctrine in the New Testament*. London, SCM Press.

(1981b). *Judaism and Hellenism: Studies in their Encounter in the Early Hellenistic Period*. London, SCM Press.

Herford, R. T. (1903). *Christianity in Talmud and Midrash*. London, Williams & Norgate.

Hilhorst, A. (2002). 'The Bodmer Poem on the Sacrifice of Abraham'. *The Sacrifice of Isaac: The Aqedah (Genesis 22) and its Interpretations*. E. Noort and E. Tigchelaar (eds.). Leiden, Brill.

Hirshman, M. (1988). 'The Greek Fathers and the Aggadah on Ecclesiastes: Formats of Exegesis in Late Antiquity'. *Hebrew Union College Annual* 59: 137–65.

(1996). *A Rivalry of Genius: Jewish and Christian Biblical Interpretation*. New York, State University of New York.

Hoffman, L. A. (1993). 'The Jewish Lectionary: The Great Sabbath, and their Lenten Calender: Liturgical Links between Christians and Jews in the First Three Christian Centuries'. *Time and Community: Essays in Honour of Thomas Julian Talley*. J. N. Alexander (ed.). Washington, DC, Pastoral Press.

Horbury, W. (1972). 'Tertullian on the Jews in the Light of *De Spectaculis* xxx. 5–6'. *Journal of Theological Studies* ns 23: 455–9.

(1988). 'Old Testament Interpretation in the Writings of the Church Fathers'. *Mikra: Text, Translation, Reading and Interpretation of the Hebrew Bible in Ancient Judaism and Early Christianity*. M. J. Mulder and H. Sysling (eds.). Assen/Maastricht, Van Gorcum: 727–89.

(1992). 'Jews and Christians on the Bible: Demarcation and Convergence [325–451]'. *Christliche Exegese zwischen Nicea und Chalcedon*. J. van Oort and U. Wickert (eds.). Kampen, Pharos: 72–103.

(1992). 'Jewish–Christian Relations in Barnabas and Justin Martyr'. *Jews and Christians: The Parting of the Ways: A. D. 70 to 135*. J. D. G. Dunn (ed.). Kampen, Kok Pharos: 315–345.

(1998). *Jews and Christians in Contact and Controversy*. Edinburgh, T&T Clark.

Horbury, W. and B. McNeil (eds.) (1981). *Suffering and Martyrdom in the New Testament: Studies Presented to G. M. Styler by the Cambridge New Testament Seminar*. Cambridge, Cambridge University Press.

Horton, F. L. (1976). *The Melchizedek Tradition*. Cambridge, Cambridge University Press.

Hurst, A. and J. Rudhardt (1999). *Papyri Bodmer XXX–XXXVII: Codex des visions*. Munich, Saur.

Jacobs, I. (1995). *The Midrashic Process: Tradition and Interpretation in Rabbinic Judaism*. Cambridge, Cambridge University Press.

Jacobson, H. (1996). *A Commentary on Pseudo-Philo's* Liber antiquitatum biblicarum. Leiden, Brill.

Jastrow, M. (1903). *A Dictionary of the Targumim, the Talmud Babli and Yerushalmi, and the Midrashic Literature.* London, Luzac.

Jensen, R. M. (1994). 'The Offering of Isaac in Jewish and Christian Tradition'. *Biblical Interpretation* 2: 85–110.

Jones, C., G. Wainwright *et al.* (eds.) (1992). *The Study of Liturgy.* London, SPCK.

Juster, J. (1914). *Les juifs dans l'empire romain.* Paris, Paul Geuthner.

Kalimi, I. (2002). *Early Jewish Exegesis and Theological Controversy.* Assen, Van Gorcum.

Kalmin, R. (1996). 'Patterns and Developments in Rabbinic Midrash of Late Antiquity'. *Hebrew Bible/Old Testament: The History of its Interpretation.* M. Saebo (ed.). Göttingen, Vandenhoeck & Ruprecht: 285–302.

Kamesar, A. (1993). *Jerome, Greek Scholarship, and the Hebrew Bible: A Study of the Quaestiones hebraicae in genesim.* Oxford, Oxford University Press.

—— (1994a). 'The Evaluation of the Narrative Aggada in Greek and Latin Patristic Literature'. *Journal of Theological Studies* 45: 37–71.

—— (1994b). 'The Narrative Aggada as Seen from the Graeco-Latin Perspective'. *Journal of Jewish Studies* 45: 52–70.

Kartun-Blum, R. (1988). 'Where Does this Wood in my Hand Come from?: The Binding of Isaac in Modern Hebrew Poetry'. *Prooftexts* 8(3): 293–310.

Kerrigan, A. (1952). *St. Cyril of Alexandria: Interpreter of the Old Testament.* Rome, Pontifical Biblical Institute.

Kierkegaard, S. (1985). *Fear and Trembling.* London, Penguin.

Kimmelman, R. (1980). 'Rabbi Yochanan and Origen on the Song of Songs'. *Harvard Theological Review* 73: 567–95.

Kinzig, W. (1991). '"Non-Separation': Closeness and Co-operation between Jews and Christians in the Fourth Century'. *Vigiliae Christianae* 45: 27–53.

Klein, M. L. (1986). *Genizah Manuscripts of the Palestinian Targums to the Pentateuch.* Cincinnati, Hebrew Union College.

Klijn, A. F. J. (1977). *Seth in Jewish, Christian and Gnostic Literature.* Leiden, Brill.

Kraeling, C. H. (1956). *The Synagogue: The Excavations of Dura-Europos Final Report VIII, Part I.* New Haven, Yale University Press.

—— (1967). *The Christian Building: The Excavations at Dura-Europos Final Report VIII Part II.* New Haven, Yale University Press.

Krauss, S. (1892–3). 'The Jews in the Works of the Church Fathers'. *Jewish Quarterly Review* 5, 6: 122–57; 82–9, 225–6.

Krauss S., ed. and rev. W. Horbury (1995). *The Jewish Christian Controversy from the Earliest Times to 1789.* Tübingen, Mohr.

Kretschmar, G. (1986). 'Early Christian Liturgy in the Light of Contemporary Historical Research'. *Studia Liturgica* 16: 31–53.

Kugel, J. L. (1997). *The Bible as it was.* Cambridge, MA, Harvard University Press.

—— (1998). *Traditions of the Bible: A Guide to the Bible as it Was at the Start of the Common Era.* Cambridge, MA, Harvard University Press.

Kugel, J. L. and R. A. Greer (1986). *Early Biblical Interpretation.* Philadelphia, Westminster Press.

Lahey, L. (2000). 'Jewish Biblical Interpretation and Genuine Jewish–Christian Debate in the Dialogue of Timothy and Aquila'. *Journal of Jewish Studies* 51: 281–97.

Lampe, G. W. H. and K. J. Woollcombe (1957). *Essays on Typology*. London, SCM Press.

Larsson, G. (1999). *Bound for Freedom: The Book of Exodus in Jewish and Christian Traditions*. Peabody, MA, Hendrickson.

Lauterbach, J. Z. (ed.) (1933–5). *Mekilta de Rabbi Ishmael*. Philadelphia, Jewish Publication Society.

Le Blant, E. (1878). *Étude sur les sarcophages chrétiens antiques de la ville d'Arles*. Paris, Imprimerie Nationale.

(1886). *Les sarcophages chrétiens de la Gaule*. Paris, Imprimerie Nationale.

Le Déaut, R. (1961). La présentation targumique du sacrifice d'Isaac et la sotériologie paulinienne. *Studiorum Paulinorum Congressus Internationalis Catholicus II*. Rome, Biblical Pontifical Institute. 18: 563–74.

(1963). *La nuit pascale: Essai sur la signification de la pâque juive à partir du targum d'Exode XII 42*. Rome, Biblical Institute Press.

Lerch, D. (1950). *Isaaks Opferung, christlich gedeutet*. Tübingen, Mohr.

Levenson, J. D. (1993). *The Death and Resurrection of the Beloved Son: The Transformation of Child Sacrifice in Judaism and Christianity*. New Haven, Yale University Press.

Lévi, I. (1912). 'Le sacrifice d'Isaac et la mort de Jésus'. *Revue des Études Juives* 64: 161–84.

Levine, A.-J. (1988). *The Social and Ethnic Dimensions of Matthean Salvation History: 'Go Nowhere among the Gentiles'*. Lampeter, Edwin Mellen.

Levine, L. I. (ed.) (1982). *Ancient Synagogues Revealed*. Jerusalem, Israel Exploration Society.

(1987). *The Synagogue in Late Antiquity*. Philadelphia, American Schools of Oriental Research.

Lewis, J. P. (1978). *A Study of the Interpretation of Noah and the Flood in Jewish and Christian Literature*. Leiden, Brill.

Lieberman, S. (1946). 'Palestine in the Third and Fourth Centuries'. *Jewish Quarterly Review* 36–37: 329–70; 31–54.

Lietzmann, H. (1950–56). *The Early Church*. London, Lutterworth.

(1979). *Mass and the Lord's Supper (with Introduction and Further Inquiry by R. D. Richardson)*. Leiden, Brill.

Lieu, J., J. North *et al.* (eds.) (1992). *The Jews among Pagans and Christians in the Roman Empire*. London, Routledge.

Lieu, J. M. (1996). *Image and Reality: The Jews in the World of the Christians in the Second Century*. Edinburgh, T&T Clark.

Limor, O. and G. G. Stroumsa (eds.) (1996). *Contra iudaeos: Ancient and Medieval Polemics between Christians and Jews*. Texts and Studies in Medieval and Modern Judaism. Tübingen, Mohr.

Loewe, R. (1957). 'The Jewish Midrashim and Patristic and Scholastic Exegesis of the Bible'. *Studia Patristica*, I. K. Aland and F. L. Cross (eds.). Berlin, Akademie Verlag: 492–514.

(1966). 'Apologetic Motifs in the Song of Songs'. *Biblical Motifs*. A. Altmann (ed.). Cambridge, MA, Harvard University Press: 159–96.

(1992). 'Midrashic Alchemy: Exegesis, Ethics, Aesthetics in Judaism'. *'Open Thou Mine Eyes . . .': Essays on Aggadah and Judaica Presented to Rabbi William G. Braude on his Eightieth Birthday*. H. J. Blumberg, B. Braude, B. H. Mehlman, J. S. Gurland and L. Y. Gutterman (eds.). Hoboken, NJ, Ktav: 109–38.

Lohse, E. (1955). *Märtyrer und Gottesknecht: Untersuchungen zur christlichen Verkündigung vom Sühntod Jesu Christi*. Göttingen, Vandenhoeck & Ruprecht.

Lucas, L. (1993 [1910]). *The Conflict between Christianity and Judaism: A Contribution to the History of the Jews in the Fourth Century*. F. D. Lucas (trans.). Berlin, Mayer & Mueller.

Maier, J. (1982). *Jüdische Auseinandersetzung mit dem Christentum in der Antike*. Darmstadt, Wissenschatliche Buchgesellschaft.

Malachi, Z. (1988). 'Jewish and Christian Liturgical Poetry: Mutual Influences in the First Four Centuries'. *Augustinianum* 28: 237–48.

Malbon, E. S. (1990). *The Iconography of the Sarcophagus of Junius Bassus*. Princeton, Princeton University Press.

Mann, J. (1940). *The Bible as Read and Preached in the Old Synagogue*. Cincinnati, Union of American Hebrew Congregations.

Manns, F. (ed.) (1995). *The Sacrifice of Isaac in the Three Monotheistic Religions*. Studium Biblicum Franciscanum. Jerusalem, Franciscan Printing Press.

Matons, G. de (1977). *Romanos de Mélode et les origines de la poésie à Byzance*. Paris, Beauchesne.

McGuckin, J. A. (1992). 'Origen on the Jews'. *Christianity and Judaism*. D. Wood (ed.). Oxford, Blackwell: 1–13.

McKnight, S. (1991). *A Light among the Gentiles: Jewish Missionary Activity in the Second Temple Period*. Minneapolis, Fortress Press.

Meeks, W. A. and R. L. Wilken (1978). *Jews and Christians in Antioch*. Missoula, MT, Society of Biblical Literature.

Meile, E. (1980). 'Isaaks Opferung, eine Note an Nils Alstrup Dahl'. *Studia Theologia* 34: 111–28.

Milgrom, J. (1988). *The Binding of Isaac: The Akedah, a Primary Symbol in Jewish Thought and Art*. Berkeley, CA, Bibal Press.

Milik, M. (ed.) (1994). *Qumran Cave 4*. Discoveries from the Judean Desert, 13. Oxford, Oxford University Press.

Milikowsky, C. (1988). 'The Status Quaestionis of Research in Rabbinic Literature'. *Journal of Jewish Studies* 39: 201–11.

Moberley, R. W. L. (1988). 'The Earliest Commentary on the Akedah'. *Vetus Testamentum* 38(3): 302–23.

(2000). *The Bible, Theology and Faith: A Study of Abraham and Jesus*. Cambridge, Cambridge University Press.

Murray, C. (1977). 'Art and the Early Church'. *Journal of Theological Studies* 28: 313–45.

Musurillo, H. (1972). *The Acts of the Christian Martyrs*. Oxford, Clarendon Press.

Neusner, J. (1987). *Judaism and Christianity in the Age of Constantine: History, Messiah, Israel, and the Initial Confrontation*. Chicago, Chicago University Press.

    (1991). *Jews and Christians: The Myth of a Common Tradition*. London, SCM Press.

Neusner, J., E. S. Frerichs *et al.* (eds.) (1985). *To See Ourselves as Others See Us: Christians, Jews, 'Others' in Late Antiquity*. Chicago, Chicago University Press.

Nikolasch, F. (1969). 'Zur Ikonographie des Widders von Genesis'. *Vigiliae Christianae* 23: 197–223.

Noort, E. *et al.* (eds.) (2002). *The Sacrifice of Isaac: The Aqedah (Genesis 22) and its Interpretations*. Themes in Biblical Narrative. Leiden, Brill.

O'Keefe, J. J. (1996). 'Christianizing Malachi: Fifth-Century Insights from Cyril of Alexandria'. *Vigiliae Christianae* 50: 136–58.

Orrieux, C. and E. Will (1992). *Proselytisme juif? Histoire d'une erreur*. Paris, Les Belles Lettres.

Ostriker, A. S. (1993). *Feminist Revision and the Bible*. Oxford, Blackwell.

Owen, W. (1963). *The Collected Poems of Wilfred Owen*. London, Chatto and Windus.

Parkes, J. (1934). *The Conflict of the Church and Synagogue: A Study in the Origins of Antisemitism*. London, Soncino Press.

Parmentier, M. F. G. (1996). *Isaak gebonden – Jezus gekruisigd: oudchristelijke teksten over Genesis 22*. Utrecht, Kampen.

Pelikan, J. (1964). *Luther's Works: Lectures on Genesis*. St Louis, MO, Concordia Publishing House.

Petit, F. (ed.) (1986). *Collectio Coisliniana*. Louvain, Peeters.

Petuchowski, J. J. (1957). 'The Controversial Figure of Melchizedek'. *Hebrew Union College Annual* 28: 127–36.

    (1975). *Theology and Poetry: Studies in the Medieval Piyyut*. London, Routledge & Kegan Paul.

Petuchowski, J. and M. Brocke (eds.) (1978). *The Lord's Prayer and Jewish Liturgy*. London, Burns and Oates.

    (1985). 'The Liturgy of the Synagogue: History, Structure, and Contents. *Approaches to Ancient Judaism, IV: Studies in Liturgy, Exegesis, and Talmudic Narrative*. W. S. Green (ed.). Atlanta, Scholars Press: 1–64.

Prigent, P. (1990). *Le judaïsme et l'image*. Tübingen, Mohr.

Rabel, G. (ed.) (1963). *Kant*. Oxford, Clarendon.

Reif, S. C. (1993). *Judaism and Hebrew Prayer: New Perspectives on Jewish Liturgical History*. Cambridge, Cambridge University Press.

Reinhartz, A. (2001). *Befriending the Beloved Disciple: A Jewish Reading of the Gospel of John*. London, Continuum.

Riesenfeld, H. (1947). *Jésus transfiguré: L'arrière plan du récit évangélique de la transfiguration de Notre-Seigneur*. Copenhagen, Ejnar Munksgaard.

Rives, J. B. (1995). *Religion and Authority in Rome and Carthage from Augustus to Constantine*. Oxford, Oxford University Press.

Rokeah, D. (1982). *Jews, Pagans and Christians in Conflict*. Leiden, Brill.

Rosenberg, R. A. (1965). 'Jesus, Isaac, and the 'Suffering Servant'. *Journal of Biblical Literature* 84: 381–8.

Rosenfeld, A. (ed.) (1956). *The Authorised Selichot for the Whole Year*. London, Labworth.

Rouiller, G. (1975). 'Le sacrifice d'Isaac (Genèse 22:1–19)'. *Exegesis: Problèmes de méthode et de lecture (Genèse 22 et Luc 15)*. G. Rouiller and F. Bovon (eds.). Paris, Bibliothèque Théologique.

Ruether, R. (1974). *Faith and Fratricide: The Theological Roots of Anti-Semitism*. New York, The Seabury Press.

Runia, D. (1993). *Philo in Early Christian Literature: A Survey*. Assen, Van Gorcum.

Rutgers, L. V. (1995). *The Jews in Late Ancient Rome*. Leiden, Brill.

Saldarini, A. J. (1982). 'Interpretation of the Akedah in Rabbinic Literature'. *The Biblical Mosaic: Changing Perspectives*. R. Polzin and E. Rothman (eds.). Philadelphia, Fortress Press: 149–165.

Salvesen, A. (1991). *Symmachus in the Pentateuch*. Manchester, University of Manchester.

Sandmel, S. (1961). 'Parallelomania'. *Journal of Biblical Literature* 80: 1–13.

(1971). *Philo's Place in Judaism: A Study of Conceptions of Abraham in Jewish Literature*. New York, Ktav.

Schäfer, P. (1986). 'Research into Rabbinic Literature: An Attempt to Define the Status Quaestionis'. *Journal of Jewish Studies* 37: 139–52.

(1989). 'Once Again the Status Quaestionis of Research in Rabbinic Literature: An Answer to Chaim Milikowsky'. *Journal of Jewish Studies* 40: 89–94.

Schirmann, J. (1953). 'Hebrew Liturgical Poetry and Christian Hymnology'. *Jewish Quarterly Review* 44: 123–61.

Schoeps, H. J. (1946). 'The Sacrifice of Isaac in Paul's Theology'. *Journal of Biblical Literature* 65: 385–92.

Schreckenberg, H. (1993). *Die christlichen Adversus-Judaeos-Texte und ihr literarisches und historisches Umfeld (1.–11.jh.)*. Frankfurt, Peter Lang.

Seeley, D. (1990). *The Noble Death: Greco-Roman Martyrology and Paul's Concept of Salvation*. Sheffield, JSOT Press.

Segal, A. F. (1984). ''He who Did not Spare his Only Son . . .' (Romans 8:32): Jesus, Paul and the Sacrifice of Isaac'. *From Jesus to Paul*. P. Richardson and J. C. Hurd (eds.). Ontario, Wilfrid Laurier University Press: 169–84.

(1990). *Paul the Convert: The Apostolate and Apostasy of Saul the Pharisee*. New Haven, Yale University Press.

(1996). 'The Akedah: Some Reconsiderations'. *Geschichte–Tradition–Reflexion: Festschrift für Martin Hengel zum 70. Geburtstag*. P. Schäffer (ed.). Tübingen, Mohr: 99–115.

Siker, J. S. (1991). *Disinheriting the Jews: Abraham in Early Christian Controversy*. Louisville, KY, Westminster/John Knox Press.

Simon, M. (1986). *Verus Israel: A Study of the Relationships between Christians and Jews in the Roman Empire AD135–425*. E.T. Oxford, Oxford University Press.

Simonetti, M. (1994). *Biblical Interpretation in the Early Church: An Historical Introduction to Patristic Exegesis*. Edinburgh, T&T Clark.

Singer, S. (ed.) (1962). *The Authorised Daily Prayer Book of the United Hebrew Congregations of the British Commonwealth of Nations*. London, Eyre and Spottiswoode.

Skarsaune, O. (1987). *The Proof from Prophecy: A Study in Justin Martyr's Proof-Text Tradition: Text-Type, Provenance, Theological Profile*. Leiden, Brill.

Sokoloff, M. and J. Yahalom (1999). *Jewish Palestinian Aramaic Poetry From Late Antiquity*. Jerusalem, Israel Academy of Sciences.

Sperber, D. (1984). *A Dictionary of Greek and Latin Legal Terms*. Bar-Ilan, Bar-Ilan University Press.

Spiegel, S. (1967). *The Last Trial: On the Legends and Lore of the Command to Abraham to Offer Isaac as a Sacrifice: The Akedah*. New York, Schocken.

Spilsbury, P. (1994). 'The Image of the Jew in Josephus' Biblical Paraphrase'. PhD thesis, Faculty of Divinity. Cambridge University.

Srawley, J. H. G. (ed.) (1903). *The Catechetical Orations of Gregory of Nyssa*. Cambridge Patristic Texts. Cambridge, Cambridge University Press.

Stemberger, G. (1974). 'Die Patriarchenbilder der Katakombe in der Via Latina im Lichte der jüdischen Tradition'. *Kairos* 16: 19–78.

(1996a). 'Exegetical Contacts between Christians and Jews in the Roman Empire'. *Hebrew Bible/Old Testament: The History of its Interpretation*, I. M. Saebo (ed.). Göttingen, Vandenhoeck & Ruprecht: 569–86.

(1996b). *Introduction to the Talmud and Midrash*. Edinburgh, T&T Clark.

Sukenik, E. L. (1932). *The Ancient Synagogue of Beith Alpha*. Jerusalem, Hebrew University.

Swainson, A. (1884). *The Greek Liturgies*. Cambridge, Cambridge University Press.

Swetnam, J. (1981). *Jesus and Isaac: A Study of the Epistle to the Hebrews in the Light of the Aqedah*. Rome, Biblical Institute Press.

Talley, T. J. (1986). *The Origins of the Liturgical Year*. Collegeville, MN, Liturgical Press.

Taylor, M. S. (1995). *Anti-Judaism and Early Christian Identity: A Critique of the Scholarly Consensus*. Leiden, Brill.

Ter Haar Romeny, R. B. (1997). *A Syrian in Greek Dress: The Use of Greek, Hebrew and Syriac Biblical Texts in Eusebius of Emesa's Commentary on Genesis*. Louvain, Peeters.

Trebilco, P. R. (1991). *Jewish Communities in Asia Minor*. Cambridge, Cambridge University Press.

Trible, P. (1991). 'Genesis 22: The Sacrifice of Sarah. *Not in Heaven: Coherence and Complexity in Biblical Narrative*. J. P. Rosenblatt and J.C. Sitterson (eds.). Indiana, Indiana University Press.

Urbach, E. E. (1975). *The Sages: The World and Wisdom of the Rabbis of the Talmud*. Cambridge, MA, Harvard University Press.

Van Bekkum, W. G. (1988). *The Qedushta'ot of Yehudah According to Genizah Manuscripts*. Groningen, Rijksuniversiteit.

Van Buren, P. (1998). *According to the Scriptures: The Origins of the Gospel and of the Church's Old Testament.* Grand Rapids, MI, Eerdmans.

Van den Hoek, A. (1988). *Clement of Alexandria and his use of Philo in the Stomateis: An Early Christian Reshaping of a Jewish Model.* Leiden, Brill.

Van Henten, J. (1986). 'Datierung und Herkunft des vierten Makkabäerbuches'. *Tradition and Reinterpretation in Jewish and Early Christian Literature: Festschrift für J. Lebram.* J. Van Henten *et al.* (eds.). Leiden, Brill: 136–49.

(1997). *The Maccabean Martyrs as Saviours of the Jewish People.* Leiden, Brill.

Van Rompay, L. (1993). 'Romanos le mélode: Un poète syrien à Constantinople'. *Early Christian Poetry: A Collection of Essays.* J. Den Boeft and A. Hilhorst (eds.). Leiden, Brill: 283–96.

Van Woerden, I. (1961). 'The Iconography of the Sacrifice of Abraham'. *Vigiliae Christianae* 15: 214–55.

Vermes, G. (1961). 'Redemption and Genesis XXII: The Binding of Isaac and the Sacrifice of Jesus'. *Scripture and Tradition in Judaism.* Leiden, Brill: 193–227.

(1996). 'New Light on the Sacrifice of Isaac from 4Q225'. *Journal of Jewish Studies* 47: 140–6.

Visotzky, B. L. (1995). *Fathers of the World: Essays in Rabbinic and Patristic literatures.* Tübingen, Mohr.

Waegeman, M. (1986). 'Les traités adversus judaeos: Aspects des relations judéo-chrétiennes dans le monde grec'. *Byzantion* 56: 296–313.

Weinberger, L. J. (1998). *Jewish Hymnography: A Literary History.* London, Vallentine Mitchell.

Weiss, Z. and E. Netzer (1996). *Promise and Redemption: A Synagogue Mosaic from Sephhoris.* Jerusalem, The Israel Museum.

Weitzmann, K. and H. L. Kessler (1990). *The Frescoes of the Dura Synagogue and Christian Art.* Washington, DC, Dumbarton Oaks Research Library.

Werblowsky, R. J. Z. and G. Wigoder (eds.) (1997). *The Oxford Dictionary of the Jewish Religion.* Oxford, Oxford University Press.

Werner, E. (1966). 'Melito of Sardis: the First Poet of Deicide'. *Hebrew Union College Annual* 37: 191–210.

Wevers, J. W. (1993). *Notes on the Greek Text of Genesis.* Atlanta, Scholars Press.

(1996). 'The Interpretative Character and Significance of the Septuagint Version'. *Hebrew Bible/Old Testament: The History of its Interpretation,* I. M. Saebo (ed.). Göttingen, Vandenhoeck & Ruprecht: 84–107.

Wiesel, E. (1976). *Messengers of God: Biblical Portraits and Legends.* New York, Random House.

Wilken, R. L. (1971). *Judaism and the Early Christian Mind: A Study of Cyril of Alexandria's Exegesis and Theology.* New Haven, Yale University Press.

(1976). 'Melito, the Jewish Community at Sardis and the Sacrifice of Isaac'. *Theological Studies* 37: 53–69.

(1983). *John Chrysostom and the Jews: Rhetoric and Reality in the Late Fourth Century.* Berkeley, University of California Press.

Wilkinson, J. (1971). *Egeria's Travels: Newly Translated (from the Latin) with Supporting Documents and Notes.* London, SPCK.

Williams, A. L. (1935). *Adversus judaeos*. Cambridge, Cambridge University Press.

Wilpert, G. (1929). *I sarcofagi cristiani antichi*. Rome, Pontifica Inst. Archeol. di Cristiana.

Wilson, S. G. (1995). *Related Strangers: Jews and Christians: 70–170 C.E.* Minneapolis, Fortress Press.

Wischnitzer, R. (1948). *The Messianic Theme in the Paintings of the Dura Synagogue*. Chicago, Chicago University Press.

Wollaston, I. (1995). 'Traditions of Remembrance: Post-Holocaust Intepretations of Genesis 22'. *Words Remembered, Texts Renewed: Essays in Honour of J. A. Sawyer*. J. Davies, G. Harvey and W. G. E. Watson (eds.). Sheffield, Sheffield Academic Press: 41–51.

(1996). *A War against Memory? The Future of Holocaust Remembrance*. London, SPCK.

Wood, J. E. (1968). 'Isaac Typology in the New Testament'. *New Testament Studies* 14: 583–9.

Wright, B. G. (1995). 'Doulos and Pais as Translation of Eved: Lexical Equivalences of Conceptual Transformations. *IX Congress of the International Organisation for Septuagint and Cognate Studies*. B. A. Taylor (ed.). Atlanta, Scholars Press: 263–77.

Yuval, I, J. (1999). Easter and Passover as Early Jewish–Christian Dialogue. *Passover and Easter: Origin and History to Modern Times*. P. F. Bradshaw and A. Hoffman (eds.). Notre Dame, Notre Dame University Press.

Index

Lightning Source UK Ltd.
Milton Keynes UK
UKOW041231240412

191370UK00002B/13/A